Queerying Families of Origin

This book provides an original insight into how families of origin of Gay, Lesbian, Bisexual and Transgender (GLBT) people are involved in negotiating meanings and experiences of sexuality and intimacy, an underexplored dimension of queer family life. Delving into the perspectives of families of origin and showing the complexity and heterogeneity of the ways people with their different gender and sexual identities "do" families across generations, it contributes to queerying the very distinction between families of origin and families of choice, and questions the (hetero)normative assumptions about forms and boundaries of family this distinction rests upon. A focus on marginal contexts, such as Southern Europe, and on marginal subjects, like bisexuals or black lesbians, is proposed as a way to challenge the universality of privileged narratives within heteronormativity, homonormativity and anglocentrism, and to reveal unexpected resources families of origin mobilise to make sense of GLBT identities and lived experiences. The book poses a crucial question: how can alliances along family ties develop on the basis of shared stories of family diversity and marginalised identities, rather than of loving (and normative) support to GLBT people in need and an advocacy in their name from a position of heterosexual privilege?

This book was originally published in *Journal of GLBT Family Studies*.

Chiara Bertone, Ph.D., Sociologist, is Assistant Professor at the University of East Piedmont, Italy. Her main interests lie in sexuality and family change. She is author of *Le omosessualità* (Rome 2009) and has recently co-edited the special issue *The politics of sexuality in contemporary Italy* for *Modern Italy*.

Maria Pallotta-Chiarolli, Ph.D, is Senior Lecturer in the School of Health and Social Development, Deakin University, Australia and author of ten books. Her research is concerned with social diversity (genders, cultures, families and sexualities), and she is a founding committee member of AGMC Inc. (Australian GLBTIQ Multicultural Council).

Queerying Families of Origin

Edited by
Chiara Bertone and
Maria Pallotta-Chiarolli

LONDON AND NEW YORK

First published 2015 by Routledge

2 Park Square, Milton Park, Abingdon, Oxfordshire OX14 4RN
711 Third Avenue, New York, NY 10017

Routledge is an imprint of the Taylor & Francis Group, an informa business

First issued in paperback 2018

Copyright © 2015 Taylor & Francis

All rights reserved. No part of this book may be reprinted or reproduced or utilised in any form or by any electronic, mechanical, or other means, now known or hereafter invented, including photocopying and recording, or in any information storage or retrieval system, without permission in writing from the publishers.

Notice:
Product or corporate names may be trademarks or registered trademarks, and are used only for identification and explanation without intent to infringe.

British Library Cataloguing in Publication Data
A catalogue record for this book is available from the British Library

ISBN 13: 978-1-138-82910-7 (hbk)
ISBN 13: 978-1-138-38390-6 (pbk)

Typeset in ITC Garamond
by RefineCatch Limited, Bungay, Suffolk

Publisher's Note
The publisher accepts responsibility for any inconsistencies that may have arisen during the conversion of this book from journal articles to book chapters, namely the possible inclusion of journal terminology.

Disclaimer
Every effort has been made to contact copyright holders for their permission to reprint material in this book. The publishers would be grateful to hear from any copyright holder who is not here acknowledged and will undertake to rectify any errors or omissions in future editions of this book.

Contents

Citation Information — vii
Notes on Contributors — ix
Dedications and Acknowledgments — x

1. Introduction: Putting Families of Origin into the Queer Picture — 1
   Chiara Bertone and Maria Pallotta-Chiarolli

2. The Transparent and Family Closets: Gay Men and Lesbians and Their Families of Origin — 15
   Alenka Švab and Roman Kuhar

3. Becoming the Parent of a GLB Son or Daughter — 36
   Erika L. Grafsky

4. Suffering As the Path to Acceptance: Parents of Gay and Lesbian Young People Negotiating Catholicism in Italy — 58
   Chiara Bertone and Marina Franchi

5. "We Are with Family": Black Lesbian Couples Negotiate Rituals with Extended Families — 79
   Valerie Q. Glass

6. Bisexuality and Family: Narratives of Silence, Solace, and Strength — 101
   Janet B. Watson

7. "It's Always the Mother's Fault": Secondary Stigma of Mothering a Transgender Child — 124
   Susan L. Johnson and Kristen E. Benson

8. The Influence of Psychiatric and Legal Discourses on Parents of Gender-Nonconforming Children and Trans Youths in Spain — 145
   Raquel (Lucas) Platero

9. Familiarising the Gay, Queering the Family: Coming Out and Resilience in *Mambo italiano* — 168
   Michela Baldo

10. Queer TV Moments and Family Viewing in Italy — 188
    Luca Malici

CONTENTS

11. Sexual Citizenship in Private and Public Space: Parents of Gay Men and Lesbians Discuss Their Experiences of Pride Parades — 211
    Valeria Cappellato and Tiziana Mangarella

12. Mars to Venus or Earth to Earth? How Do Families of Origin Fit into GLBTQ Lives? — 231
    Esther D. Rothblum

    Index — 243

Citation Information

The chapters in this book were originally published in *Journal of GLBT Family Studies*, Volume 10, Issues 1-2, (February 2014). When citing this material, please use original page numbering for each article, as follows:

Chapter 1
Introduction: Putting Families of Origin into the Queer Picture: Introducing This Special Issue
Chiara Bertone and Maria Pallotta-Chiarolli
Journal of GLBT Family Studies, Volume 10, Issues 1-2, (February 2014) pp. 1-14

Chapter 2
The Transparent and Family Closets: Gay Men and Lesbians and Their Families of Origin
Alenka Švab and Roman Kuhar
Journal of GLBT Family Studies, Volume 10, Issues 1-2, (February 2014) pp. 15-35

Chapter 3
Becoming the Parent of a GLB Son or Daughter
Erika L. Grafsky
Journal of GLBT Family Studies, Volume 10, Issues 1-2, (February 2014) pp. 36-57

Chapter 4
Suffering As the Path to Acceptance: Parents of Gay and Lesbian Young People Negotiating Catholicism in Italy
Chiara Bertone and Marina Franchi
Journal of GLBT Family Studies, Volume 10, Issues 1-2, (February 2014) pp. 58-78

Chapter 5
"We Are with Family": Black Lesbian Couples Negotiate Rituals with Extended Families
Valerie Q. Glass
Journal of GLBT Family Studies, Volume 10, Issues 1-2, (February 2014) pp. 79-100

Chapter 6
Bisexuality and Family: Narratives of Silence, Solace, and Strength
Janet B. Watson
Journal of GLBT Family Studies, Volume 10, Issues 1-2, (February 2014) pp. 101-123

CITATION INFORMATION

Chapter 7
"It's Always the Mother's Fault": Secondary Stigma of Mothering a Transgender Child
Susan L. Johnson and Kristen E. Benson
Journal of GLBT Family Studies, Volume 10, Issues 1-2, (February 2014) pp. 124-144

Chapter 8
The Influence of Psychiatric and Legal Discourses on Parents of Gender-Nonconforming Children and Trans Youths in Spain
Raquel (Lucas) Platero
Journal of GLBT Family Studies, Volume 10, Issues 1-2, (February 2014) pp. 145-167

Chapter 9
Familiarising the Gay, Queering the Family: Coming Out and Resilience in Mambo italiano
Michela Baldo
Journal of GLBT Family Studies, Volume 10, Issues 1-2, (February 2014) pp. 168-187

Chapter 10
Queer TV Moments and Family Viewing in Italy
Luca Malici
Journal of GLBT Family Studies, Volume 10, Issues 1-2, (February 2014) pp. 188-210

Chapter 11
Sexual Citizenship in Private and Public Space: Parents of Gay Men and Lesbians Discuss Their Experiences of Pride Parades
Valeria Cappellato and Tiziana Mangarella
Journal of GLBT Family Studies, Volume 10, Issues 1-2, (February 2014) pp. 211-230

Chapter 12
Mars to Venus or Earth to Earth? How Do Families of Origin Fit into GLBTQ Lives?
Esther D. Rothblum
Journal of GLBT Family Studies, Volume 10, Issues 1-2, (February 2014) pp. 231-241

Please direct any queries you may have about the citations to
clsuk.permissions@cengage.com

Notes on Contributors

Michela Baldo, University of London, London, England

Kristen E. Benson, North Dakota State University, Fargo, North Dakota, USA

Valeria Cappellato, University of Turin, Turin, Italy

Marina Franchi, London School of Economics, London, England

Valerie Q. Glass, Virginia Tech, Blacksburg, Virginia, USA

Erika L. Grafsky, Virginia Tech, Blacksburg, Virginia, USA

Susan L. Johnson, Bright Horizons Family Solutions, Cary, North Carolina, USA

Roman Kuhar, University of Ljubljana, Ljubljana, Slovenia

Luca Malici, University of Birmingham, Birmingham, England

Tiziana Mangarella, Meters Studi E Ricerche, Bari, Italy

Raquel (Lucas) Platero, Universidad Complutense de Madrid, Madrid, Spain; Universidad Nacional de Educacíon a Distancia, Madrid, Spain

Esther D. Rothblum, San Diego State University, San Diego, California, USA

Alenka Švab, University of Ljubljana, Ljubljana, Slovenia

Janet B. Watson, Deakin University, Melbourne, Australia

Dedications and Acknowledgments

Chiara wishes to thank all the people who worked with enthusiasm and vision at the Family Matters project, and especially the parents and siblings within and outside Agedo who generously shared their stories. She would also like to thank Chiara Saraceno, Anna Rosa Favretto, Sasha Roseneil and her colleagues at Birkbeck, and Tone Hellesund for the enlightening discussions along the way of this long-term project.

This book would not be here without a life-changing encounter with Lucia Bonuccelli: Chiara dedicates it to her. Her overwhelming passion for life and big-heartedness, and her extraordinary insight will always be missed.

Maria would like to dedicate this book to all the PFLAG groups in Australia, especially pioneer mothers Nan McGregor and Shelley Argent who found themselves publicly vilified for their passionate and unshakeable support of GLBTIQ young people.

Maria would like to acknowledge the pioneering work of AGMC Inc (Australian GLBTIQ Multicultural Council) which for ten years has been providing support, education and social networks for families of diverse cultures and faiths whose children are GLBTIQ.

Maria would also like to acknowledge what a gift it has been working with someone as insightful, generous, good-humoured and collaborative as Chiara. And Chiara reciprocates full heartedly, being very grateful that Maria agreed to join this project with her great competence and passion. That meeting at the conference in Prato was certainly a pivotal moment!

Finally, we wish to acknowledge our deepest respect, appreciation and sheer pleasure working with this wonderful team of researchers, activists and writers who have shown such collegiality and joy in contributing to this book. This includes Paz De Galupo, the editor of the *Journal of GLBT Family Studies*, whose enthusiastic and insightful editing was much appreciated.

INTRODUCTION

Putting Families of Origin into the Queer Picture

CHIARA BERTONE
University of East Piedmont, Alessandria, Italy

MARIA PALLOTTA-CHIAROLLI
Deakin University, Melbourne, Australia

INTRODUCTION

Gay, lesbian, bisexual, and transgender (GLBT) individuals have been socially constructed as "family outlaws" (Calhoun, 2000, p. 132), but in relation to partnership and parenting, far-reaching changes have taken place in the past few decades, and research has kept an attentive eye on these changes. We proposed this special issue to the *Journal of GLBT Family Studies* because since its first issue, it has also kept an attentive eye on research on families of origin and shifting discourses and constructions of family. Thus, it seemed to us a very conducive site within which to further develop these reflections, by getting a sense of what we know, and where and how to move further.

In undertaking our own separate research projects and in our cross-continental comparative analyses of those projects, we became aware of the gaps between the richness of research on GLBT lives, including experiences of intimacy and parenthood, and the paucity of research on their relations with their families of origin. Still marginal is, in particular, research on the perspectives of the families of origin themselves: parents, but also siblings, grandparents, and other members of extended families. For the purposes of this special issue, we are deploying the term *families of origin* to mean heterosexual-identifying family members (at least as they publicly perform and display their sexualities), living within a heteronormative socio-politico-cultural system. As we will argue in this introduction, however, there is a need to document and research, and thereby historically situate, family diversity, including the increasing shifting discourses and lived experiences of same-sex and other queer families of origin.

QUEERYING FAMILIES OF ORIGIN

The limited research into heteronormative families of origin is a striking absence, especially if viewed with Southern European eyes, where intergenerational closeness and dependence mark people's lives. In a country like Italy, where GLBT people develop their identities and form their personal communities under "the Southern European shadow of the parental household" (Therborn, 2004, p. 221), the need to take a closer look into how families of origin are involved in negotiating meanings and experiences of sexuality and intimacy appear fairly obvious, and the research outcomes prove highly valuable (see Bertone & Franchi and Cappellato & Mangarella in this issue). In fact, one of the purposes of this issue that arose in our discussions as Italian and Italian-Australian researchers, with our shared and differing experiences of family and, we believe, one of its strengths, is to make visible research being conducted in Southern and Eastern Europe. These research locations are marginal in relation to the international visibility of research being conducted in Anglophone Western countries (United States, United Kingdom, Canada, Australia), but their research findings have much to say on intergenerational relations. Thus, in providing a location for dialogue between various countries and their internally culturally diverse communities, this special issue offers insights into the importance of contextualization, of connecting variations in family experiences with local family cultures, sexual minority configurations, and the political, economic, religious, health, and educational conditions that define configurations of citizenship and human rights.

These concerns are best addressed, we believe, through an interdisciplinary dialogue, which is another main goal of this issue. There is a need to build a bridge between research aiming at providing tools to promote family acceptance and prevent GLBT youths from experiencing distress, and research focusing upon how family practices are related to social constructions of gender, sexuality, and intimate life. Going beyond the goal of putting the families of origin into the queer picture, this dialogue can help us develop a more comprehensive attention to the complexity and heterogeneity of the ways people with their different gender and sexual identities "do" families. Indeed, its main result can be a queerying of the very distinction between the families GLBT people come from (families of origin), and the ones they create (families of choice), by questioning the (hetero)normative assumptions about forms and boundaries of family this distinction rests upon. These issues will be discussed in more detail later in this introduction.

QUEERYING THE FAMILIES OF ORIGIN

The importance of the relations of GLBT people with their families of origin for well-being, living conditions, identity, and lifestyle choices is generally recognised. The negative effects of physical, emotional, and sexual violence, or familial reactions of refusal, rejection, and denial to disclosure, are well researched and acknowledged (D'Augelli, Grossman, & Starks, 2005; Pallotta-Chiarolli, 2005b). Studies exploring how families negotiate a member's GLBT identity have noted that acceptance of that member's chosen partner and/or friends is key to supportive family relationships. Evidence in this respect comes mainly from the United States (Herdt & Koff, 2000; Oswald, 2002), but also from other contexts. Respondents in Mayock, Bryan, Carr, and Kitching's (2008) study on the mental health and well-being of young people coming out in Ireland who felt supported within an affirmative family environment appeared to benefit greatly from this experience. Family support certainly enhanced self-confidence and self-esteem and also appeared to facilitate respondents' ability to negotiate broader societal challenges. Mayock and colleagues (2008) also found that because of the complex interconnections of lives in the family, critical events create "countertransitions" (Boxer, Cook, & Herdt, 1991, p. 64). In other words, events that occur in the life of one family member also affect others in the family. Thus, "the coming out process in a child may potentially initiate a parallel process for the parent" (p. 64). This was also evident in Pallotta-Chiarolli's (2005b, 2005c) research with Australian parents of young people coming out. While there were parents who had never considered their children's coming out as "a problem" and indeed "felt blessed to have a gay child," many parents discussed three initial reactions: "their coming out means I'm going into a closet about my child's sexuality and life"; "their coming to shore has set tidal waves off in my life," where issues within the family, such as conflicts between siblings and between husbands and wives, which have been submerged or lain dormant, suddenly come to the fore; and "they have made me have bad feelings about myself," wherein parents experience self-blame, shame, guilt, disappointment, and despair, and sometimes doubly so as they may also feel guilty for being disappointed or ashamed of their own child (2005c, pp. 20–24).

Studies on family acceptance often assign a centrality to coming out as an act of revelation triggering family change. However, the idea that a supportive family environment is conditional upon mutual disclosure and open communication, which self-help literature powerfully conveys, has also come under empirical research scrutiny. In fact, one of the most complex countertransitions for families of origin is what Petronio (2002, 2010) calls Communication Privacy Management (CPM), the complex process of privacy regulation in personal relationships. For example, Lannutti (2013) used CPM as a theoretical framework to describe how married or engaged same-sex couples regulate their private information during interactions with family members about legally recognized same-sex marriage (SSM). Couples described how SSM triggered a privacy rule change among family members. Couples and family members experienced either privacy boundary rule coordination and/or privacy turbulence surrounding sharing news about the couples' SSM and about the couples' relationship details. The articles by Švab and Kuhar, and Glass, in this issue address family silences and CPM in relation to children coming out, and to children in same-sex relationships participating in families-of-origin rituals and events. Questioning the imperative of disclosure, Poulos also argues that there may be "occasions—perhaps even daily, in many people's lives—where it is best to withhold, edit, or avoid revealing so-called secret knowledge, thoughts or fantasies" (2009, p. 32). Poulos (2009) refers to this as a "strategy of silence" whereby withholding information prevents disclosures that "can unleash all sorts of grief" and "gives off at least the illusion of control.(...) And thus secret-keeping can become a central form of family communicative practice" (p. 38). Bertone (2013) discusses the class specificity of stories of family change framed as narratives of disclosure, and shows how an emphasis on open communication and negotiation works at making children accountable to their parents for their lifestyle choices as well as for the very definition of their identity.

Given the clear potential fruitfulness of such insights into families, closets, and disclosures, why then has there not been greater interest in understanding the family dynamics within which the reactions and "countertransitions" mentioned occur? What makes some family members go into their own closets while others proudly and confidently air their children's and their own realities "on the clothesline" and undertake strategies such as getting informed, creating and joining social and support networks, and assisting in their children's ongoing coming-out processes with other family members, in schools and in the wider societal spaces (Pallotta-Chiarolli, 2005c, p. 25)? To what extent and how do families of origin and their GLBT children's later families of choice develop and/or maintain interwoven ties?

Weston (1991) provides some insights into the place assigned to families of origin in GLBT studies. In her work on gay and lesbian communities in San Francisco, she shows how the "ideological construction of gay families" established an opposition between "straight" and gay and lesbian families—the families gay and lesbian people came from, and those they created—based on a fundamental difference in the definition of family ties: "love, choice, and creation" against biology and blood (p. 27). Weston relates this opposition to the experience of lesbian and gay people with their families of origin. When coming out to relatives became a normative step in the construction of their identity, gay and lesbian people had to face the possibility of being rejected by one's family. Kinship ties, based on blood and on unconditional love, could not be taken for granted anymore. Notwithstanding its actual diffusion as an experience, the very possibility of rejection introduced a dimension of choice in the notion of kinship, which became central in the construction of what Weston's interviewees defined as their present families. Through the construction of the image of gay and lesbian families as creative, innovative experiences, freed from the constraints of traditional family models, a categorical distinction between straight and gay and lesbian families was established. By associating straight families to "the fixedness often attributed to biology in this culture," this distinction "echoes old dichotomies such as nature versus nurture and real versus ideal" (p. 38). To what extent has the construction of this dichotomous opposition influenced the goals and perspectives of research on the families of origin? And if this construction is linked to and based on GLBT experiences in the United States and United Kingdom (mainly white middle-class) metropolitan communities, what happens in other geographical and cultural contexts?

Research looking at the families of origin of GLBT people has mainly developed in the field of psychology, and in the U.S. context, and has mostly been concerned with their reactions to disclosure and with the conditions fostering a development of their attitudes towards full acceptance. In her review published in the first issue of this journal, Connolly (2005) remarked that "The literature is geared toward family nonacceptance or acceptance of a GLBT member; it is often implied that families remain somewhat static or move in a linear progression toward the more positive end of the change continuum" (p. 14). In this picture, the families of origin seem to take a rather passive role, as objects of a pressure to change.

A smaller body of research in the fields of sociology or anthropology has explored the connections between family responses and social change, moving the focus from what fosters acceptance to what is accepted, how the boundaries of what is socially acceptable are redefined. In these studies, a tension can be grasped between interpretations of families of origin as forces of normalization of GLBT lives, of pressure towards making them conform to heteronormative models such as being monogamous, getting married where legally possible, and raising children (Fields, 2001; Marsh, 2011), and those emphasizing a non-heteronormative model of influence, pointing to the fact that more and more people have to deal with family members who do not conform to the heteronormative model of family, and arguing that, as a consequence, its hegemony as the ideal of the good life is losing ground (Stacey, 1996).

Discussions in both these directions of interpretation of current changes often bear a common risk: to assume straight and gay and lesbian families as two distinct and polarized objects of inquiry and theorization. Such a distinction carries, in turn, the risk of losing sight of complexity and heterogeneity, both in GLBT and heterosexual experiences, which are actually highly differentiated, primarily on the basis of gender, but also of class and other structural and cultural dimensions (Hicks, 2005). The upsurge of critical research on heterosexuality in everyday life has revealed, in fact, how multidimensional, variable, contradictory it can be as an institution, and as an experience (Jackson & Scott, 2010). Questioning the opposition between the straight family, representing the guardian of tradition or the rather passive receiver of innovation, and the gay and lesbian "new" families, we can look at how people "do family" (Morgan, 1996) in their everyday lives, at the same time reproducing and challenging hierarchies of gender and sexuality, as well as other social hierarchies. This is the direction undertaken by recent scholarship on queer relationships and family configurations such as polyamorous families (Pallotta-Chiarolli, 2010a,b; Pallotta-Chiarolli, Haydon, & Hunter, 2013) and mixed-orientation families (Pallotta-Chiarolli, 2014, in press). From this perspective we can also trace an increasing attention paid to bisexual and transgender young people coming out, as we have presented in this issue in several articles, who are often the marginalized or silenced B and T in GLBT research (Costello, 1997; Heath, 2010; Norwood, 2013; see also Goldberg & Allen, 2013); as well as to migrant, ethnic, and racial minority families of origin, also evident in this issue (see also Pallotta-Chiarolli, 2005a,c; Beckett, Mohummadally, & Pallotta-Chiarolli, 2014).

What emerges from research developments in these past decades is thus a more nuanced, diverse, and contextualized picture of the relations between GLBT people and their families of origin, which we have also sketched out in this introduction. On the one hand, a closer look at the practices of intimacy, care, solidarity, and parenting among GLBT people has shown the importance of the ties with members of the families of origin and of the extended family in their everyday lives (Shipman & Smart, 2007). On the other hand, a closer look at the families of origin has questioned homogenized representations and linear views of their changes. Studies are moving beyond parents, to explore the experiences of siblings (Rothblum, 2010), grandparents (Scherrer, 2010), and extended families. Family diversity along social hierarchies has also been explored, albeit more in relation to race or ethnicity (Merighi & Grimes, 2000) than to class. Although Horne, Rostosky, Riggle, and Martens (2010) have argued that there is still little research modeling "the experience of family members within the contemporary sociopolitical context," contextual specificity has been addressed, for instance, in studies discussing the impact of antigay movements and policies (Arm, Horne, & Levitt, 2009).

We see this issue as contributing to further movement in this same direction, mainly by proposing visions from the margins: a focus on marginal contexts and marginal subjects as a way to challenge the universality of privileged narratives within heteronormativity, homonormativity, and Anglocentrism. From the articles in this issue, visions from the margins reveal crucial resources parents mobilize to make sense of their children's GLBT identities and lived experiences. What is still lacking, however, is a more attentive eye throughout most of the articles on gendered differences between mothers' and fathers' responses and reactions, and a broader picture of family relations extending beyond parenting, an issue addressed in Rothblum's final commentary.

AN OVERVIEW OF THE ISSUE

The first two articles explore the identity construction of both sexual minority youths and their parents as relational processes, addressing issues of contextualization and temporality. Undertaking this exploration from the perspective of gay and lesbian Slovenians, Švab and Kuhar question a view of coming out in the family as a step towards a visible gay and lesbian identity, showing how family silences shape new closets. Coming out, they argue, is an ongoing struggle on the conditions of acceptance, conditions that are informed not only by family relations but by the wider social and cultural context.

Investigating parents' perspectives in the United States, Grafsky also describes the redefinition of their identities as parents of a queer son or daughter after disclosure as a long-term relational process. The perception of how welcoming or hostile the social world outside the family can be for their children, and the possibility of imagining a happy life for them, emerge as important contextual conditions. In line with recent studies focusing upon the positive aspects of parents' experiences after disclosure (Gonzalez, Rostosky, Odom, & Riggle, 2013), Grafsky discusses how these positive narratives depart from the grieving processes through which parents' reaction to the coming out of a sexual minority child has often been interpreted.

Parents' accounts—this time in Italy—are explored again in Bertone and Franchi's contribution, which focuses on a more specific aspect, namely the ways parents of gay men and lesbians deal with Catholicism. They argue that a narrative of suffering plays an important role, providing a bridge between Christian notions of mercy and therapeutic narratives of authentic love, while preserving parents' privileged position as heterosexuals. The authors also call for an attention to the uneven social distribution of the cultural tools enabling parents to develop socially legitimate narratives.

In the next four articles, new subjects, which have been largely overlooked in research on the families of origin of sexual minority youths, come to the fore. An intersectional perspective is developed by Glass, who provides an original insight into black lesbian couples dealing with the invisibility of their multiply marginalized identities through the lens of rituals. The article shows how the possibility of rejection upon which, according to Weston (1991), lies the opposition between straight families and gay and lesbian families of choice, does not hold for these black families, where severing the ties is never considered a real possibility. Rather, negotiations concern how to be a participant in different types of family rituals, which identities can find a place, and which ones get silenced.

Watson also deals with processes of becoming and with negotiations of the closet, by exploring experiences of bisexuality in Australia. The diversity and fluidity of bisexual experiences challenge a singular view of change in the families of origin as triggered by the disruptive event of coming out. Her research shows, in fact, how people are involved in ongoing negotiations of family secrets regarding different ways of crossing the boundaries of gender and sexual norms, and how complete or selective silence on non-normative choices works as a viable option. Costello (1997) speculated that the experiences of bisexual people coming out to their families of origin may be influenced by the extent to which they conform to socially constructed notions of family (being married to a different-sex partner, with children). This is also discussed in Watson's article.

Two articles, coming from Spain and the United States, deal with parents of gender non-conforming children and youths. These address Norwood's (2013) concern regarding how disclosure of trans identities has been shown to bring about change in family relationships, yet little is known about how trans identities function as family stressors. The meanings families assigned to trans identity, the complex processes by which they arrived at those meanings, and how meanings fostered or hindered support for their trans family members require much more examination. The first article to address trans identities and meanings is based on Platero's interviews with parents and professionals. It shows how the medical framework is taken up by parents as a resource for challenging stigmatization and blaming, and for voicing their need for help from professionals, although they are seldom satisfied with what they receive. At the same time, pointing to the essentializing and oppressive implications of this framework for gender-nonconforming subjects, she poses the question of how to develop forms of support outside a medicalized perspective of pathologization.

In their case study on the single mother of a transgender child in the United States, Johnson and Benson draw our attention to the need to explore families of origin beyond the "straight" couple-family image of the heterosexual household. The article describes how this mother faced multiple layers of stigmatization, and how she responded with a narrative on the positive aspects of experiencing difference, and with engaging in advocacy for both her child and herself. Drawing on the mixed assessment of this mother's encounters with mental health professionals, the authors provide suggestions for improving therapeutic work.

Another significant perspective provided in this issue is the relationship between media representations of families and families of origin as media consumers. Two theories which endeavor to analyze and understand this relationship are pertinent to the next two articles. First, Cultivation Theory (Gerbner, Gross, Morgan, & Signorielli, 2002) states that the effects of media messages involve a *passive* process: exposure over a prolonged period of time to portrayals of reality as defined by the media will lead to perceptions of reality that are consistent with these portrayals. Thus, the increasing representations of GLBT children in families of origin will mainstream these families and allow for greater family and community acceptance and affirmation. Second, Social Cognitive Theory (Bandura, 2002) states that individuals may *actively* observe media portrayals for insight into how they themselves could behave, especially if they are performed by individuals perceived as attractive, powerful, and popular and if the outcomes are viewed as appealing. So if an observed behavior, such as accepting and affirming a GLBT child, results in a desired outcome in the film, television program, or festival event, individuals will engage in similar behavior, believing that in doing so they will gain the same benefits. In this issue, Baldo provides a case in which a vision from the margins via film turns out to be a resource for families of origin. In her reading of the representations of Italian-Canadian families in the film *Mambo italiano*, she shows how parents in this film creatively draw upon their experiences of migration and of belonging to an ethnic minority to "familiarise" their offspring's sexual minority identity. Family rituals emerge in the film, again, as crucial moments in this process.

One of these moments is the object of Malici's original research on practices of media consumption, namely the everyday ritual of watching television together, which in Italy remains a common aspect of family life. Exploring the impact of the increasing GLBT televisibility in Italy, Malici points to the disruptive potential of "queer moments," when GLBT experiences break into family silence, and open space for discussion after the TV viewing is over. On the other hand, he shows how hard it is to break up the persistent privileging of a heterosexual gaze. Malici's work also reminds us of the need to consider localities, cultural and ethnic specificities in assessing the significance of media representations (Dines & Rigoletto, 2012).

Given the discussion on the significance of ritual, celebrations, and social occasions for families of origin, Cappellato and Mangarella provide a very original insight into families of origin participating in queer rituals and festivals through their study of Pride parades and how they are experienced by Italian parents of gay men and lesbians with different levels of involvement, from watching the parades on the TV or on the streets, to organizing the participation of the national parents' association, AGEDO (Associazione di Genitori di Omosessuale). A pioneering work on this issue, their analysis shows the importance of moving out of the family context in exploring the role of families of origin in shaping life conditions for GLBT people: in this case, parents' role in the process of familization of gay and lesbian citizenship rights.

FURTHER QUESTIONS AND DIRECTIONS

A question seems to be lingering throughout this special issue: under which conditions can the encounter with sexual minority experiences open up possibilities for queer coalitions (Phelan, 1994) between parents and gender-nonconforming and nonheterosexual children? In other words, and extending the scope of the question, how can alliances along family ties develop on the basis of shared stories of family diversity and marginalized identities, rather than of loving (and normative) support to GLBT people in need, and an advocacy in their name from a position of heterosexual privilege?

In the stories told in this issue's contributions both possibilities are depicted, but certainly more research exploring the diversity of experiences within families and between families is needed to address this question. The families of origin of GLBT people have been a hard-to-reach population, and this has certainly limited and oriented this kind of research. The samples of existing studies, including those hosted in this issue, are often mainly recruited through organizations like PFLAG (Parents, Families, and Friends of Lesbians and Gays) in the United States, or similar ones in other countries (like AGEDO in Italy). A thorough discussion on the implications of this recruitment requires that these organizations become themselves objects of inquiry, about how they shape meanings, identities, and motives for action (Broad, Crawley, & Foley, 2004; Broad, 2011; Johnson & Best, 2012), and about how they may reproduce hierarchies of gender and sexuality, but also of race and class (Broad, Alden, Berkowitz, & Ryan, 2008). Qualitative studies, based on small samples, have been recently joined by online surveys (Horne et al.,2010; Conley, 2011; Gonzalez et al., 2013), which might also contribute to exploring differences between more active parents (and other family members) and those developing their coping strategies without contact with these organizations. What shapes parents' narratives is, however, a complex question to address. The pervasiveness of self-help material (Martin, Hutson, Kazyak, & Scherrer, 2010), which is produced or influenced by these same organizations' frames, must be taken into account.

Finally, in the light of our goal and discussion of the need to engage with the complexity and heterogeneity of families of origin, such as class and cultural differences, we are cognizant that another limitation is that our endeavors to provide a site for marginal voices have not led to a greater diversity of cultural representations. There is a need for greater international visibility of contributions and explorations of families of origin in Asia, Africa, the Middle East, and South America, within which nations have experienced the impacts of religious fundamentalism (e.g., Christianity or Islam) and/or colonialism and therefore colonial legal, political, and social constructions of gender, sexuality, and family. The ongoing processes of decolonization and post-colonial multiplicities and their significance in the everyday worlds of families of origin and their nonheterosexual and gender-nonconforming children, in both non-Western worlds and in the First Peoples of Western worlds, requires much more research and international recognition.

REFERENCES

Arm, J. R., Horne, S. G., & Levitt, H. M. (2009). Negotiating connection to GLBT experience: Family members' experience of anti-GLBT movements and policies. *Journal of Counseling Psychology, 56*(1), 82–96. doi: 10.1037/a0012813

Baldo, M. (2014). Familiarising the gay, queering the family. Coming out and resilience in *Mambo italiano*. *Journal of GLBT Family Studies, 10*(1–2), 168–187.

Bandura, A. (2002). Social cognitive theory of mass communication. In B. Jennings & D. Zillmann (Eds.), *Media effects: Advances in theory and research* (pp. 121–153). Hillsdale, NJ: Lawrence Erlbaum Associates.

Beckett, S., Mohummadally, A., & Pallotta-Chiarolli, M. (2014). Queerying Muslim identities. In A. Ata (Ed.), *Education integration challenges: The case of Australian Muslims* (pp. 96–106). Melbourne, Australia: David Lovell Publishing.

Bertone, C. (2013). Citizenship across generations: Struggles around heteronormativities. *Citizenship Studies, 17*(8), 985–999. doi: 10.1080/13621025.2013.851147

Bertone, C., & Franchi, M. (2014). Suffering as the path to acceptance: Parents of gay and lesbian young people dealing with Catholicism in Italy. *Journal of GLBT Family Studies, 10*(1–2), 58–78.

Boxer, A. M., Cook, J. A., & Herdt, G. (1991). Double jeopardy: Identity transitions and parent-child relations among gay and lesbian youth. In K. A. Pillemer & K. McCartney (Eds.), *Parent-child relations throughout life* (pp. 59–92). Hillsdale, NJ: Lawrence Erlbaum Associates.

Broad, K. (2011). Coming out for Parents, Families and Friends of Lesbians and Gays: From support group grieving to love advocacy. *Sexualities, 14*(4), 399–415. doi: 10.1177/1363460711406792

Broad, K. L., Alden, H., Berkowitz, D., & Ryan, M. (2008). Activist parenting and GLBTQ families. *Journal of GLBT Family Studies, 4*(4), 499–520. doi: 10.1080/15504280802191749

Broad, K. L., Crawley, S. L., & Foley, L. (2004). Doing "real family values": The interpretive practice of families in the GLBT movement. *The Sociological Quarterly, 45*(3), 509–527. doi: 10.2307/4120861

Calhoun, C. (2000). *Feminism, the family, and the politics of the closet. Lesbian and gay displacements*. Oxford, England: Oxford University Press.

Cappellato, V., & Mangarella, T. (2014). Sexual citizenship in private and public space: Parents of gay men and lesbians discuss their experiences of Pride parades. *Journal of GLBT Family Studies, 10*(1–2), 211–230.

Conley, C. L. (2011). Learning about a child's gay or lesbian sexual orientation: Parental concerns about societal rejection, loss of loved ones, and child well being. *Journal of Homosexuality, 58*, 1022–1040. doi: 10.1080/00918369.2011.598409

Connolly, C. M. (2005). A process of change. *Journal of GLBT Family Studies, 1*(1), 5–20. doi: 10.1300/J461v01n01_02

Costello, C. Y. (1997). Conceiving identity: Bisexual, lesbian and gay parents consider their children's sexual orientations. *Journal of Sociology and Social Welfare, 24*(3), 63–89.

D'Augelli, A. R., Grossman, A. H., & Starks, M. T. (2005). Parents' awareness of lesbian, gay and bisexual youths' sexual orientation. *Journal of Marriage and Family, 67*, 474–482. doi: 10.1111/j.0022-2445.2005.00129

Dines, M., & Rigoletto, S. (2012). Country cousins: Europeanness, sexuality and locality in contemporary Italian television. *Modern Italy, 17*(4), 479–491. doi: 10.1080/13532944.2012.706999

Fields, J. (2001). Normal queers: Straight parents respond to their children's "coming out." *Symbolic Interaction, 24*(2), 165–187. doi: 10.1525/si.2001.24.2.165

Gerbner, G., Gross, L., Morgan, M., & Signorielli, N. (2002). Growing up with television: The cultivation perspective. In M. Morgan (Ed.), *Against the mainstream: The selected works of George Gerbner* (pp. 193–213). New York, NY: Peter Lang.

Glass, V. Q. (2014). "We are with family": Black lesbian couples negotiate rituals with extended families. *Journal of GLBT Family Studies, 10*(1–2), 79–100.

Goldberg, A., & Allen, K. (Eds.). (2013). *LGBT-parent families: Innovations in research and implications for practice*. New York, NY: Springer.

Gonzalez, K. A., Rostosky, S. S., Odom, R. D., & Riggle, E. D. (2013). The positive aspects of being the parent of an LGBTQ child. *Family Process, 52*, 325–337. doi: 10.1111/famp.12009

Grafsky, E. (2014). Becoming the parent of a GLB son or daughter. *Journal of GLBT Family Studies, 10*(1–2), 36–57.

Heath, M. A. (2010). Who's afraid of bisexuality. *Gay and Lesbian Issues and Psychology Review, 6*(3), 118–121.

Herdt, G., & Koff, B. (2000). *Something to tell you: The road families travel when a child is gay*. New York, NY: Columbia University Press.

Hicks, S. (2005). Is gay parenting bad for kids? Responding to the "very idea of difference" in research on lesbian and gay parenting. *Sexualities, 8*(2), 153–168.

Horne, S. G., Rostosky, S. S., Riggle, E. D., & Martens, M. P. (2010). What was Stonewall? The role of GLB knowledge in marriage amendment-related affect and activism among family members of GLB individuals. *Journal of GLBT Family Studies, 6*, 349–364. doi: 10.1080/1550428X.2010.511066

Jackson, S., & Scott, S. (2010). *Theorizing sexuality*. Milton Keynes, England: McGraw-Hill.

Johnson, J. L., & Best, A. L. (2012). Radical normals: The moral career of straight parents as public advocates for their gay children. *Symbolic Interaction, 35*(5), 321–339. doi: 10.1002/symb.23

Johnson, S. L., & Benson, K. E. (2014). "It's always the mother's fault": Secondary stigma of mothering a transgender child. *Journal of GLBT Family Studies, 10*(1–2), 124–144.

Lannutti, P. J. (2013). Same-sex marriage and privacy management: Examining couples' communication with family members. *Journal of Family Communication, 13*(1), 60–75. doi: 10.1080/15267431.2012.742088

Malici, L. (2014). Queer TV moments and family viewing in Italy. *Journal of GLBT Family Studies, 10*(1–2), 188–210.

Marsh, V. (Ed.). (2011). *Speak now: Australian perspectives on same-sex marriage*. Melbourne, Australia: Clouds of Magellan.

Martin, K. A., Hutson, D. J., Kazyak, E., & Scherrer, K. S. (2010). Advice when children come out: The cultural "tool kits" of parents. *Journal of Family Issues, 31*(7), 960–991. doi: 10.1177/0192513x09354454

Mayock, P., Bryan, A., Carr, N., & Kitching, K. (2008). *Supporting LGBT lives: A study of mental health and well-being*. Dublin, Ireland: Glen and BelongTo.

Merighi, J. R., & Grimes, M. D. (2000). Coming out to families in a multicultural context. *Families in Society, 81*(1), 32–41. doi: 10.1037/a0012813

Morgan, D. H. J. (1996). *Family connections. An introduction to family studies.* Cambridge, England: Polity Press.

Norwood, K. (2013). Meaning matters: Framing trans identity in the context of family relationships. *Journal of GLBT Family Studies, 9*(2), 152–178. doi: 10.1080/1550428X.2013.765262

Oswald, R. (2002). Resilience within the family networks of lesbians and gay men: Intentionality and redefinition. *Journal of Marriage and Family, 64*(2), 374–383. doi: 10.1111/j.1741-3737.2002.00374.x

Pallotta-Chiarolli, M. (2005a). Ethnic identity. In J. T. Sears (Ed.), *Youth, education, and sexualities: An international encyclopedia* (pp. 303–306). Westport, CT: Greenwood Publishing Group.

Pallotta-Chiarolli, M. (2005b). Parents' responses to homosexuality. In J. T. Sears (Ed.), *Youth, education, and sexualities: An international encyclopedia* (pp. 605–608). Westport, CT: Greenwood Publishing Group.

Pallotta-Chiarolli, M. (2005c). *When our children come out: How to support gay, lesbian, bisexual and transgendered young people.* Sydney, Australia: Finch Publishing.

Pallotta-Chiarolli, M. (2010a). *Border sexualities, border families in schools.* New York, NY: Rowman & Littlefield.

Pallotta-Chiarolli, M. (2010b). "To pass, border or pollute": Polyfamilies go to school. In M. Barker & D. Langridge (Eds.), *Understanding non-monogamies* (pp. 182–187). London, England: Routledge.

Pallotta-Chiarolli, M. (2014). "New rules, no rules, old rules or our rules": Women designing mixed-orientation marriages with bisexual men. In M. Pallotta-Chiarolli & B. Pease (Eds.), *The politics of recognition and social justice: Transforming subjectivities and new forms of resistance* (pp. 91–108). London, England: Routledge.

Pallotta-Chiarolli, M. (in press). *"Outside belonging": Women in relationships with bisexual men.* New York, NY: Lexington Books.

Pallotta-Chiarolli, M., Haydon, P., & Hunter, A. (2013). "These are *our* children": Polyamorous parenting. In A. Goldberg & K. Allen (Eds.), *LGBT-parent families: Innovations in research and implications for practice* (pp. 117–131). New York, NY: Springer.

Petronio, S. (2002). *Boundaries of privacy: Dialectics of disclosure.* Albany, NY: SUNY Press.

Petronio, S. (2010). Communication privacy management theory: What do we know about family privacy regulation? *Journal of Family Theory & Review, 2,* 175–196. doi: 10.1111/j.1756-2589.2010.00052.x

Phelan, S. (1994). *Getting specific: Postmodern lesbian politics.* Minneapolis, MN: University of Minnesota Press.

Platero, R. L. (2014). The influence of psychiatric and legal discourses on parents of gender-nonconforming children and trans youths in Spain. *Journal of GLBT Family Studies, 10*(1–2), 145–167.

Poulos, C. N. (2009). *Accidental ethnography: An inquiry into family secrecy.* Walnut Creek, CA: Left Coast Press.

Rothblum, E. D. (2010). Lesbian, gay, bisexual and transgender siblings. In J. Caspi (Ed.), *Sibling development: Implications for mental health practitioners* (pp. 123–145). New York, NY: Springer Publishing Company.

Scherrer, K. S. (2010). The intergenerational family relationships of grandparents and GLBQ grandchildren. *Journal of GLBT Family Studies, 6*, 229–264. doi: 10.1080/1550428X.2010.490898

Shipman, B., & Smart, C. (2007). "It's made a huge difference": Recognition, rights and the personal significance of civil partnership. *Sociological Research Online, 12*(1). doi: 10.5153/sro.1340

Stacey, J. (1996). *In the name of the family*. Boston, MA: Beacon Press.

Švab, A., & Kuhar, R. (2014). The transparent and family closets: Gay men and lesbians and their families of origin. *Journal of GLBT Family Studies, 10*(1–2), 15–35.

Therborn, G. (2004). *Between sex and power. Family in the world, 1900–2000*. London, England: Routledge.

Watson, J.B. (2014). Bisexuality and family: Narratives of silence, solace, and strength. *Journal of GLBT Family Studies, 10*(1–2), 101–123.

Weston, K. (1991). *Families we choose*. New York, NY: Columbia University Press.

The Transparent and Family Closets: Gay Men and Lesbians and Their Families of Origin

ALENKA ŠVAB and ROMAN KUHAR
University of Ljubljana, Ljubljana, Slovenia

This article builds on data collected in research on the everyday lives of gay men and lesbians in Slovenia, focusing on the families of origin and family relations. It pays special attention to the process of coming out and its consequences for further relationships among family members. It concentrates on the process of negotiating new family relations after coming out. The authors introduce the concepts of "transparent closet" and "family closet" to describe a situation in which family members are informed about a child's homosexuality but refuse to accept the consequences of their child's coming out. All of this holds important consequences for gay men and lesbians and their family members.

INTRODUCTION

During the past few decades, the possibility of living openly as a lesbian or gay man has increased thanks to the constitution of new spaces of everyday life (Bell & Valentine, 1995). It is especially the young generations of gay men and lesbians that are believed to increasingly organize their lives beyond the closet (Seidman, 2002). This has all had important political consequences. According to Plummer (1995, p. 144), the stories we tell about ourselves are closely connected with the morality and politics of a specific society. New intimate narratives imply moral and political changes and are a form of empowerment for anyone who has a similar story. Nevertheless, these aspects

---

The research project was supported by the Slovenian Ministry of Labour, Family and Social Affairs, and the Open Society Institute, New York. The authors would like to thank the anonymous reviewers for their helpful comments on an earlier draft of this article.

of late-modern social change should be understood as being embedded in specific social, political, and cultural contexts. Among others, the everyday lives of gay men and lesbians are still strongly determined by heteronormativity (Švab & Kuhar, 2005). Consequently, the late-modern narratives told by gay men and lesbians are at the same time (still) often determined by counter-stories: those of rejection, homophobia, and homophobic violence.

Scherrer (2012, p. 4) points out that "this increasingly out population has important implications for relationships with family members." Coming out to the immediate family is a central event for the majority of gay men and lesbians in the process of their sexual identity formation, but, as Markowe (1996) notes, it can also be destructive because it endangers conventional expectations about gender roles that underpin all family relations. In other words, the family of origin is a social milieu where both types of narratives—of acceptance and of rejection—are being experienced by gay men and lesbians. Although young gay men and lesbians are being increasingly more accepted by family members, there are also stories of negative reactions and rejection (Švab & Kuhar, 2005). In fact, individual narratives of coming out to one's family of origin are usually permeated by a mixture of negative and positive reactions pointing to the complexities of family relationships. Therefore, "even good case scenarios sometimes negatively impact immediate and extended family relationships" (Scherrer, 2012, p. 4).

Based on the data from our research, this article focuses on *gay men and lesbians' narratives of coming out* within the family of origin and points to the relational character of the coming-out process.[1] Although the study focused on gay men's and lesbians' narratives and therefore does not present original voices of parents, but rather their children's interpretation of parental voices, the data nevertheless reveal some information regarding parental views and reactions to coming out which are valuable for explaining the interpersonal relations and social contexts in which coming out within the family occurs.

We see acts of coming out within the family of origin not only as a turning point in the life course of a gay man or a lesbian, but also as a process that importantly shapes family reality and relationships between family members. Furthermore, re-creating family relationships after coming out is not only a matter of interpersonal aspects of family reality, but also or even primarily about the embeddedness of family relationships in the social and cultural contexts of heteronormativity and homophobia.

The structure of this article is as follows. First, we present the key characteristics of the social and political context of the everyday life of gay men and lesbians in Slovenia. Then we outline the conceptual framework and describe the research. This is followed by a presentation of the research results focusing first on the period prior to coming out to parents and, second, the characteristics of the first coming out to parents. We consider these two aspects an important starting point and contextual information for further discussing the relational character of coming out. In the main part of the article we focus on two distinct social situations created within the family of origin after coming out that seem to be crucial for (re)building family relationships and gay/lesbian identity, namely the "transparent closet" and the "family closet." In the last section of the article, we present patterns of building new relationships between gay men/lesbians and their parents after coming out, and the coping strategies gay men and lesbians adopt when rebuilding family relationships after coming out. The implications of the findings for understanding the complexities of family realities are further elaborated in the discussion and conclusion.

SOCIAL AND POLITICAL CONTEXT

Slovenia is a former Yugoslav republic, which gained its political independence in 1991. It was only marginally affected by the Balkan wars in the 1990s and its path to European Union (EU) membership was steady. In 2004, Slovenia joined the EU and in 2007 it became part of the Eurozone, introducing the euro as its national currency.

The gay, lesbian, bisexual, and transgender (GLBT) movement in Slovenia emerged in the early 1980s as part of the feminist, peace, ecological, and other social movements which then formed a "tolerated opposition" to the one-party socialist political system (Lešnik, 2005). Unlike in the West, the movement emerged only after homosexuality had been decriminalized in 1977.[2] It played a crucial role in relocating the issue of homosexuality from the psychiatric and medical context of the 1970s to the cultural and political contexts of the 1980s. Their political interventions contributed to the media and the general public paying greater attention to the GLBT community.

The EU accession process intensified the adoption of antidiscrimination legislation, although the prohibition on discrimination on the basis of sexual orientation had been included in Slovenian legislation since the early 1990s. Registered same-sex partnership legislation was adopted in 2005. In 2009, the Slovenian government proposed a new Family Code which put heterosexual and homosexual partnerships on an equal legal footing, but the law was rejected in a public referendum in March 2012.

The social distance towards minorities in Slovenia (Toš et al., 1999) has been measured since the early 1990s, when around 60% of Slovenian citizens claimed they "would not like a homosexual to be their neighbor," while a poll from 2011 showed that this number is now about 35%.

CONCEPTUAL FRAMEWORK

Coming-out narratives and the construction of gay/lesbian identity have been studied since the early 1970s. Scholars have proposed various ideal-type stage models of the formation of homosexual identity in order to explain the trajectories of individuals dealing with the stigma attached to homosexuality (Cass, 1979; Dank, 1971; Troiden, 1988).

In the context of these models, coming out of the closet is understood as the ultimate stage when internal conflicts are resolved by external declarations. The majority of these models presuppose a linear transition from one stage to the next, creating an impression that the formation and acceptance of gay/lesbian identity progresses in simple steps from the initial stage to the final, fixed and stable identity. Yet some authors acknowledge that the linear progression can be disturbed, stopped, or even reversed (see Troiden, 1988). Furthermore, critics of the developmental models point out the problematic implicit suggestion that the endpoint of each stage is the only and the best outcome of identity formation. In addition, other aspects of identity, such as ethnicity, gender, class, religion, and culture, which might influence identity formation, are often neglected. It is important to take into account that sexual identity is constructed within the system of power relations based on race, gender, class, etc. The fluid and dynamic nature of sexuality should also be taken into consideration.

When analyzing the changed relations that emerge between an out gay person and his/her *parents*, scholars have suggested—in accordance with the developmental models—several stages that parents pass through after they learn about their child's homosexuality (see Savin-Williams & Dubé, 1998). Parents have to do identity work to construct their new identity in relation to their children (Broad, 2011; Fields, 2001). In this process, they reconstruct their perceptions of their child's identity and their expectations about his or her future.

One of the criticisms of the stage models suggests that "individuals may have been conscripted into stages rather than the stages being produced to correspond to reality" (La Placa, 2000, p. 22). In order to avoid this, we will employ a more fluid interpretation of the narratives about coming out to parents and frame these reactions in the context of a *relational* understanding of coming out.

RELATIONAL COMING OUT: THE TRANSPARENT AND FAMILY CLOSETS

Despite the fact that today coming out is mostly understood as a process rather than an act, the process of coming out is implicitly analyzed as a series or a chain of (unrelated) coming-out *acts*. The *process* therefore refers to the fact that one has to come out continuously, that is, each time he or she enters new social settings where heterosexual identity is unconditionally assumed. While the emphasis on coming out as a continual "never-ending" practice is an important step forward in understanding coming out as such, it also has a weakness in that it treats each act of coming out as independent or at least unrelated to other acts of coming out.

One aim of this article is to point to the *relational* understanding of coming out. This means that, first, the closet may exist only *in relation* to other individuals or society as such and, second, the process of coming out cannot be understood solely as continuous sequences of numerous coming outs, but also as acts that are in certain social setting(s) inevitably *interrelated* and have concrete implications not only for the subsequent coming outs but also for the relationships between the individuals involved. In other words, coming out is relational, as the sexual identity of an individual who comes out no longer affects just him or her, but also the people to whom he or she came out, and their relationships. To borrow an expression from Eve Kosofsky Sedgwick (1993), coming out becomes a contagion which thrusts those to whom one has come out into the closet dictated by the heteronormative society. As a result, a child's coming out also compels the parents to confront the same homophobic society with which their child has been coping.

In the context of the family of origin we propose two concepts by which the relational nature of coming out can be analyzed and understood: the *transparent closet* and the *family closet* (see Kuhar, 2011; Švab & Kuhar, 2005). The transparent closet refers to those social situations where a child's homosexual orientation is acknowledged within the family but is not further discussed. Parents (or other family members) refuse to accept and deal with the consequences and meanings of the new information.

Usually there are two moments that describe the coming-out narratives within the family of origin: after the first shock (often accompanied by psychological violence, such as emotional blackmailing), the consolidation phase follows when the disturbance caused by coming out is resolved through cloaking the child's homosexuality in a transparent closet. The fact of one's homosexuality is recognized, but as a rule it is not discussed within the family any further or it is discussed with great discomfort. In this way, a person who has just come out of the closet is pushed back into the closet—*a transparent closet*. The transparent closet is therefore a form of rejection by parents and/or other family members after a child has come out. The transparent closet is not only a social situation that can develop within the family context, but is also applicable to other social contexts (for this aspect see Kuhar, 2011). As such, it has important implications not only for displaying but also for the very definition of a gay/lesbian identity. Troiden (1988) clearly showed that a person developing his or her homosexual identity starts to question it if it is rejected by their "significant others." Ending up in a transparent closet is namely a clear signal on the side of the parents that only a heterosexual identity is acceptable to them.

After the child comes out, the family is often also pushed into a broader *family closet*, a situation within the family of origin where family members are put into the closet in relation to the broader kinship network, neighbors, friends and acquaintances, colleagues from work, and other social and community contexts. Information about the child's sexual orientation is now shared among (some or all) family members and this affects not only family relations but also the actions of family members in relation to the outside world. The family closet can be seen as a direct result of the social environment being permeated by homophobia and heteronormative expectations.

METHODS AND SAMPLE

This article is based on data from the research on the everyday lives of gay men and lesbians in Slovenia, conducted in 2003–2004 (Švab & Kuhar, 2005). In developing the concept of the research project, we aimed to build a model that would enable us to explain how (stigmatized) social identity intertwines with individual identity in a heteronormative context. The study consisted of a quantitative (survey) and qualitative parts (focus groups).

Survey

First, we conducted a quantitative questionnaire-based survey in order to obtain basic statistical data on the sample of 443 self-identified gay men and lesbians. Sixty-six percent of the sample was male, 34% female. Sixty-two percent of the respondents lived in an urban center at the time of the survey. Their educational level was above the Slovenian average. Ninety-five percent of the respondents had never been married. The majority of respondents were between ages 21 and 40 years. The majority (45%) shared a household with their parents; 26% lived with their partner, and nearly 19% lived alone. Although not asked specifically, it is very likely that the majority of our respondents lived with their parents at the time they came out to them.

Focus Groups

Seven focus groups (4 male and 3 female) were carried out with 36 participants in total, 53% male and 47% female. Their average age was 27; the youngest one was 19 years old, and the oldest 40. At the time of conducting the focus group interviews, the majority of participants had an intimate partner.

In the following sections we present the research results focusing on coming out to parents and family relationships after coming out. We also endeavor to point to the relational aspects of the process of coming out created within the social setting of the family of origin.

RESULTS AND DISCUSSION

Prior to Coming Out to Parents

Seventy-seven percent of our respondents came out first to their friends in comparison to 7% of respondents who first came out to their mother, 5% to their brother/sister, and 3% to their father. Seventy-four percent of the surveyed gay men and lesbians reported experiencing a positive and supportive reaction to their first coming out, 18% reported neutral, and 4% negative reactions. However, some respondents interpreted silence and non-reaction as a form of a positive or at least a neutral reaction because they had expected a much worse response.

Our respondents were on average age 19.5 years when they first came out. While there are no differences between genders in this respect (significance = 0.946), statistically significant differences were observed between age groups (significance = 0.000) as younger generations came out at an earlier age than their older counterparts. The latter had to confront greater stigmatization and some even lived through the time when homosexuality was a crime. It seems that the older generation had no choice: an apparent heterosexual life and a hidden homosexual life constituted their only option, one that exacted a large degree of mimicry. For younger generations, however, the closet is only a transitional phase during which they destigmatize their gay/lesbian identity.

Although the first coming out to friends is an important experience, one of the most important milestones is coming out to parents. Some focus group participants thought that coming out to parents was the only real coming out since no other instance of coming out is as demanding in terms of the emotional strain involved.

> *I can't say that coming out to my best friend was my real coming out. My first real coming out was to my parents because that is when all the barriers were broken; from that point on I didn't care much (about the reactions to my coming out) .... This is the coming out which gives you self-confidence.* (Igor, gay man, 27)

Coming out to the immediate family was a central event for the majority of our respondents. It was usually a well-thought-out endeavor, planned in advance, although such events cannot be totally controlled.

Fear As a Guiding Feeling in Coming Out to the Family

One common feeling that most gay men and lesbians have reported prior to their coming out to family members, especially parents, is a feeling of fear. They feared rejection, negative reactions and consequences such as parents withdrawing financial support, the possibility of being thrown out of the family home and similar situations (see also D'Augelli, Grossman, & Starks, 2005).

> *I expected that they were going to show me the door. Because when my dad watched some such movie he'd say "these people are sick."* (Vivika, lesbian, 27)

While feelings of fear might guide gay men's and lesbians' decisions and preparations for coming out, the family members' reactions were often not in line with the anticipated negative reactions. Our respondents often reported being positively surprised by the acceptance they had received from their family members.

> *Now I get along with my parents very well ... they accepted my girlfriend very well and we are now like a family, so I think that my fear back then was unnecessary.* (Vivika, lesbian, 27)

Those gay men and lesbians who reported having good relationships with their parents less often talked about strong feelings of fear. They found it easier to talk to their parents; they tend to come out earlier and are more likely to do so at all than those who do not live in such a supportive family context.

Nevertheless, one should not overlook the fact that the fear of negative reactions operates as a mechanism which in many ways limits the everyday lives of gay men and lesbians prior to coming out. It functions as a panopticon (Foucault, 1984) in its heteronormative form (Kuhar, 2011; Švab & Kuhar, 2005), producing internalized silencing and imposing self-surveillance, self-policing, and self-regulation in response to real or imagined threats. The heteronormative panopticon is an all-pervasive and powerful technology of control by the heteronormative society (in public and private spheres), which forces gay men and lesbians into becoming self-controlling objects of the heteronormative society (see Kuhar, 2011). Similar mechanisms of control are also at work with other family members once a child comes out of the closet.

First Coming Out to Parents

The narratives about coming out to one's parents are diverse and in many ways depend on the respondents' previous relations with family members. Our survey showed that gay men and lesbians have the most reservations about coming out to their fathers (see also D'Augelli et al., 2005). While 67% of our respondents came out to their mothers, significantly fewer, 46%, came out to their fathers, and 40% came out to both parents.

Qualms about the disclosure of a gay/lesbian identity to the father can be attributed to weak, in some cases even nonexistent, communication between the child and the alienated father. Although a growing shift away from the patriarchal family model can be observed in Slovenia, characterized by the erosion of the father's authority (Švab, 2001), it seems that the patriarchal order of the family, if only at the symbolic level, is still in place to a certain degree and can manifest itself in the form of a fear of the father as an authority.

There were no statistically significant differences between the genders with respect to coming out to fathers. The focus group participants who did not come out to their fathers most frequently claimed that they did not do so because they did not have a good enough relationship with them. Furthermore, no communication pattern had been established with their fathers that would allow intimate issues to be discussed.

I didn't explain it to my father because I have no relationship with him, and because I never talked to him about myself. In fact, he doesn't know a thing about me. (Tara, lesbian, 30)

Out of these constellations, mothers are often assigned the role of a mediator both in terms of sharing this information with the father or other family members (usually upon the request of a child who fears coming out to them) and as a mitigator of reactions between the child and other family members.

Actually I let my mother deal with this (telling my father), because she knows better than me how to deal with him. (Timotej, gay man, 22)
I told my mother that I cannot talk about it with my father, but if she wanted she could do it. And then she actually told him about it. (Vida, lesbian, 25)

The fear of fathers and the consequent strategies employed by family members (in most cases mothers) to prevent the information from leaking to the father clearly point to the social construction of normative hegemonic masculinity (Connell & Messerschmidt, 2005). It positions a man/father not only as a patriarchal leader of the family who possesses power over other family members, but also as being constructed through its opposition, that is, the subordinated masculinities. In our case, a particular kind of subordinated masculinity, non-heterosexual masculinity (or even non-heterosexuality as such), is seen to undermine hetero-patriarchal power. The fear of the father's reaction to coming out might be driven precisely by the expectation that non-heterosexuality in the family would undermine his normative role as a successful and powerful leader of that family.

Nevertheless, it is possible to expect that the fear of the father would also be reduced in connection with coming out due to the growing shift away from the patriarchal family model. To some degree, these changes can already be traced in the responses from the younger participants in the research; they not only come out at an earlier age, but, as a rule, they also come out to both parents.

First Parental Reactions to Coming Out

The survey showed that 67% of our respondents who came out to their mother described her first reaction as negative or neutral. Similarly, 66% of those who came out to their father experienced his reaction as negative or neutral. However, the majority of them believed that in the long run their coming out did not dramatically affect or change their relationship with parents: 12% of the respondents reported their relationship with their mother had become alienated after coming out, while 11% of them claimed that their relationship with their father had worsened after coming out.

Barbara and Tara talked about negative reactions of their mothers:

The first reaction was . . . hysterical. She was upset, she was crying, screaming, not to mention everything that she said to me! (Barbara, lesbian, 26)
She screamed at me uncontrollably for half an hour and started to talk nasty, vulgarities I was not aware she could think of. . . . If I hadn't come out I'd still be convinced that my mother is a more or less sensible person. (Tara, lesbian, 30)

Those parents who reacted positively as a rule rationalized their child's coming out in terms of love being more important than one's sexual orientation.

When I came out to my mother, we both cried. I asked her: "Do you still love me?" She said yes and that she would always love me and support me. She said she cannot understand this but, if it is okay for me, it is okay for her, too. (Ana, lesbian, 28)

Another form of rationalization reported by our respondents was found in those parents' reactions where a homosexual orientation was judged to be a lesser evil compared to some other forms of behavior the parents found problematic.

When I came out to my mother, she said: "Well, it's better to see you with a girlfriend holding hands than with a cigarette." Later she told my father. He said that if I'm good at school, there's no problem. (Amalija, lesbian, 26)

> *When I came out to my parents ... my father said: "Well, it is better to be this way than to be an alcoholic!"* (Maruša, lesbian, 27)

According to the focus group data (and being aware that these are not the direct voices of parents but their children's), one can define various social models of homosexuality that parents draw upon in their first reactions. All these models rest on a perception that homosexuality is a deviant opposition to heterosexuality, something that is neither "normal" nor "natural" and falls outside of the heterosexual matrix. The most common are variations of an idea that homosexuality is a disease. It can be perceived either as a mental disorder or as sexual perversion, and in both cases as something that calls for psychiatric treatment. Medicalized images of homosexuality can also be traced in the idea that homosexuality equals HIV/AIDS. Those parents who drew on this model mainly expressed a fear that their son could become infected and they feared the worst outcomes. Some parents did not perceive homosexuality in medicalized terms, but their reactions were framed within a fear of the potential negative consequences their child might experience due to being gay/lesbian (for example, social stigma, social exclusion, violence, etc). These perceptions seem to be difficult to change, but the relational character of the coming-out process, which not only includes revealing the information on the part of a gay man or a lesbian, but also the consequent reaction of a parent, forces parents to reflect upon the new situation and also change their views regarding homosexuality. In the long run, this might contribute to accepting their child as a gay/lesbian.

Some parents try to "change" things.   Parents are confronted with several salient issues and questions after their child comes out. "Why is my child gay?" is the most common initial question parents ask.

According to our respondents, parents often blame themselves, which leads them to attempt to "correct the mistake." In this context, sexual orientation is understood as changeable and correctable, for which professional psychiatric, psychological, or medical help is needed. Such interpretations are characteristic of those first reactions of parents where they proposed or even demanded the curing of the homosexual orientation.

> *My father had this kind of ideas .... He said there are some clinics in America where they can heal homosexuality successfully.* (Patrick, gay man, 20)
>
> *When I came home on a Sunday evening, my mother said: "We haven't given up yet. There are these therapies!" I told her it was her who needed treatment, not me.* (Oskar, gay man, 24)

Nevertheless, blaming themselves for a child's sexual orientation might not be the only reason that parents propose such treatments. In some cases, such proposals are a consequence of a lack of relevant information on homosexuality and also the shock they face when their child comes out. Initial reactions of parents and other family members usually rest on the stereotypical images and perceptions about gay men and lesbians they had prior to the coming out, including ideas that homosexuality is a mental disease and therefore "curable."

There might also be other factors affecting parents' reactions, such as religiosity and age. Although some respondents mentioned their parents as being very religious in order to "rationalize" their negative reactions, the biggest difference seems to be related to the time period involved: the stories about coming out told by younger generations differed substantially from those of older generations, with the former experiencing much more positive reactions. Quite often the older generations never really came out in terms of revealing this information to their parents. The fact about their sexual orientation became a logical conclusion on the basis of some other signs, such as living together with a same-sex partner ("a friend") in the same apartment.

Parents facing a gap between their expectations and the "new" reality. After their child comes out, parents have to deal with several issues related to their unconsciously existent heteronormative scenarios: coming out threatens their perceptions of the "normalcy" of their family, which is based on binary sexual matrix and related heterosexual rituals such as marriage or having grandchildren. These implicit heteronormative expectations are dashed when their child comes out.

> *My mother had a feeling that I destroyed all her life plans.* (Tara, lesbian, 30)
> *My father talked about grandchildren twenty-four/seven.... I told them I won't have children just because they wanted me to have them.* (Gabrijel, gay man, 40)

Parental attempts to control their child's life are often related to broader social contexts. In Slovenia, the so-called phenomenon of protective childhood is widespread (Švab, 2001). This means that parents try to impose their expectations on their children out of a protective attitude they have towards them. However, reasons for such parental acts might not be solely altruistic. The manifested care might also be motivated by social imperatives regarding "successful" and "responsible" parenting, imposing a great burden on parents as they strive to be socially acknowledged as successful parents. In our case, the outcomes of their efforts are additionally endangered by the sexual orientation of their child. Consequently, parents' acts might be driven by more egoistic reasons, that is, to present themselves as good parents according to the normative model of parenthood. This might also be the reason that many parents try to keep the information about their child's sexual orientation within the family closet (as discussed later). While some participants tried to understand their parents' position by interpreting their reactions as a sign of powerlessness and distress, others reported feeling sorry for them as they felt responsible for pushing them into the new situation. In this way, gay men and lesbians take responsibility into their own hands.

> *I knew that I had created a burden for her (my mother) and that she needed somebody to talk to. I told her many times that if she needed to talk about it, I was here to talk about it ... However, I did tell her that I cannot change the facts.* (Sebastjan, gay man, 31)

Transparent and Family Closet

The tensions which emerge after coming out in the family are most often dealt with by conditional acceptance: the parents consolidate, but demand that the child's sexual orientation is swept under the carpet. In this way a transparent closet is established: one comes out of the closet, but is then pushed back into it as hiding/not discussing his or her sexual orientation is still expected of him or her. Coming out as a *relational process* is thus not only about the acceptance of a new piece of information, but is "a constant struggle against those who, on the one hand, accept the disclosure and then, on the other, refuse to accept its implications" (Davies, 1992, p. 80).

> *We haven't talked about it for a long time ... about how I live. Later when I heard from others about their coming outs, I realized that after the first shock parents never ask about anything, no matter if the reaction was positive or negative.... This is a sign of certain uneasiness.* (Maruša, lesbian, 27)
>
> *In our house my being gay is a "pro forma," but nothing more than that. We do not talk about it. It's better if I don't mention it.... I tried several times, but then there were emotions, tears, arguments, punishments.* (Igor, gay man, 27)

Silence is the main characteristic of a transparent closet and might be understood as a form of parental reaction to the situation in which they find themselves. This situation is characterized by *three dimensions that coincide*: (1) they do not know how to react; (2) they lack information on homosexuality; and (3) they find themselves in the social vacuum of a family closet as a result of the homophobic society.

After a child comes out family members find themselves in a new situation, which demands a redefinition of interpersonal relationships within the family along with a reflection of the new situation in relation to the broader environment. In this respect, coming out initially positions family members in a closet—the family closet—and compels them to confront the homophobic society.

Keeping the Information to Oneself

The family closet can be seen as a form of social vacuum in which family members usually do not know how to react and how to proceed. There are several strategies family members try to adopt after finding themselves in this situation.

Keeping the Information to Oneself

The survey showed that most parents were only partially able to cope with heteronormative expectations. Fifty-seven percent of the respondents reported they know or presume that their parents did not talk about their homosexuality with any of their closest friends or relatives or anyone else. One reason for that is the stigma: parents refuse to talk about their child's sexual orientation as they find it shameful. They are also not equipped to discuss such an intimate topic with other people. Furthermore, the child's homosexuality also threatens the representation of themselves in their social networks.

> *After all these years I've noticed that my mother has not come out to anyone.... I've also noticed that she can hardly bring herself to utter that word.* (Ksenja, lesbian, 30)
>
> *I'm not sure if she has discussed this with anybody. I don't think so. She sees these things very negatively and, as far as I know her, she doesn't want to promote such things outside of the family. She wants to present herself in a good light in front of her friends.* (Martin, gay man, 25)

Gatekeeping

Some parents try to keep the information to themselves by using various strategies to prevent the information from leaking out of the family. In this case, they frequently require from their child that the information is not disseminated outside the family. According to our study, one of the most common situations is that the mother assumes the role of a gatekeeper in order for the information to be kept within the family or hidden from some family members, most often the father. Sometimes the parents assume the role of gatekeeper for protective reasons. For example, Vida's father was afraid she would have troubles because of her sexual orientation.

> *There were no special reactions on his part except that he said that he's not against it. However, he would like this information to stay within the family, so that I wouldn't be exposed. And then when I had my first girlfriend, he totally freaked out when he saw me kissing her in front of the building where we live. He said that I should be careful so that the neighbors don't see it.* (Vida, lesbian, 25)

While parents might keep the information hidden from other family members so as to protect their child, there is also an element of control in the attempt to prevent the information spreading. However, there are also other reasons for control. For example, as shown in Ksenja's case, mothers are afraid they will be blamed for their child's sexual orientation. In order to protect themselves, they keep the information hidden.

> *My mother said that it wouldn't be wise to tell my father as he is not that kind of a person and ... he wouldn't know how to react. He would calculate why this had happened to his child, probably blaming my mother for this. She would carry the entire burden.* (Ksenja, lesbian, 30)

Some mothers took opposing controlling strategies. They demanded their child also come out to other family members. In some cases, such a strategy was used as some kind of punishment, as part of psychological violence, as was the case with Barbara's mother.

> *Her first reaction was negative. We never talked about it, but then she demanded I talk about it with my father as she didn't want to carry this burden alone. But I didn't want to tell my father.* (Barbara, lesbian, 26)

Attempts to Go Beyond the Family Closet

Parents hidden in the family closet eventually encounter similar problems related to the heteronormative expectations of society experienced by their child while they were in the closet. It seems that parents also react in a similar way, trying to find support within their own circles of close friends. As a result, the steps out of the family closet are similar to those of their own child who came out.

> *A few years later I found out that all my parents' friends know that I am a lesbian. This means that she had talked about it with them, which I found okay. I found it positive that she didn't have this locked inside of her and that she talked about it. She told all of their friends and my grandmother.* (Maruša, lesbian, 27)

Building New Relationships after Coming Out

Narratives of Acceptance

Although narratives of acceptance, whereby coming out did not negatively affect family relations, are not told by the majority of our respondents, we can argue that it is especially the parents of those respondents from younger generations who were more likely to react positively and reconcile with the fact that their child is a gay man or a lesbian.

The reactions depend on various factors but interpersonal relationships seem to be the most significant. The previous quality of family relationships is the basis for the continuation of a good relationship after coming out.

> *My mother was excellent when I was destroyed and vulnerable. She said: "It's okay You'll just have a girlfriend instead of a boyfriend!" Then we started talking, and I brought her a lot of literature (about homosexuality).* (Vida, lesbian, 25)

Age differences regarding parental reactions can be explained by the changes in intergenerational relations within the family that have characterized Slovenia in the past few decades. If the older generations were more likely to experience intergenerational conflict, the younger generations are now more likely to experience so-called generational peace (Rener, 1996), characterized by good relationships and an absence of conflict between parents and children. Parents have changed their attitude toward children; the values of parents and children are moving closer together and the relationships between parents and children are becoming more harmonious and protective. Furthermore, the coming out (as a sign of deep trust between the child and the parents) can sometimes function as a channel for a further improvement of the existing relationships.

> *Our relationships became more honest. We now discuss things more concretely. My father once told me that it was very courageous of me to tell them (about my homosexuality) and that it is important in life to challenge lies, otherwise lies can suffocate you.* (Gašper, gay man, 27)

We did not record any narrative of a proactive affirmation or celebration of a child's homosexual orientation. In most cases of positive narratives in our study, the sexual orientation of a child did not negatively influence the existing family relationships. As a rule, these positive narratives were provided by gay men and lesbians who already had satisfying relationships with parents prior to them coming out and the coming out did not lead to a transparent or family closet. In the majority of cases, the narratives of acceptance rest on the idea "you are still my child," which implies that homosexuality is nevertheless something negative. This is why we cannot call this "unconditional acceptance." Parents are prepared to accept the new situation and they actually adapt to it. One could argue that these narratives are based on the protective attitudes parents have toward their child rather than a celebration of the new situation. Consequently, these narratives do not contribute to changing attitudes to homosexuality, but perpetuate the existing negative attitudes. In this sense, narratives of acceptance are not transgressive as a proactive affirmation or celebration as they are based on a negative understanding of homosexuality. Similarly, Fields (2001) points out that those parents who respond to a child's homosexual orientation by de-stigmatizing the identity nevertheless rely on a conventional understanding of gender, sexuality, and parenting and thereby paradoxically help perpetuate heteronormative conceptions of normalcy.

Narratives of Rejection and Coping Strategies

According to the focus group participants, sometimes the initial negative reactions of parents are prolonged and become a long-term non-acceptance of the child's sexual orientation. In this case, family relationships are characterized by negative emotions and different forms of psychological violence.

> *My mum reacted like all other mums. Perhaps she was even worse, because she is cunning and manipulative enough to gamble with certain emotions. She staged a nervous breakdown which I later witnessed three more times. Exactly like before. It was so bad that at first I thought, gosh, I hope she's not going to do something to herself. And then you promise many things, that you'll change, that you'll think about it, that you'll do I don't know what.* (Martin, gay man, 25)

From the data gathered, it could be argued that mothers feel more responsible for their child's upbringing as the patriarchal culture constitutes her as the primary parent. They are thus more likely to blame themselves and be blamed for their child's sexual orientation. Mothers feel greater responsibility and might see their child's sexual orientation as a mistake or inadequacy in her mothering and child rearing capabilities. Moreover, being primary caretakers, mothers usually develop more emotionally intense relationships with their children than fathers who—according to our respondents—react more "rationally," while in the case of negative reactions it is mothers who often carry out emotional violence.

The initial impulses of the parents to try to change their child's sexual orientation can also give rise to the interpretation of homosexuality as being "just a phase" or a transitory identity, flippant and experimental, and therefore unacceptable. According to Kosofsky Sedgwick (1993), these types of reactions indicate the problematic character of the concept of homosexual identity and the intensity with which society resists it. Some parents therefore do not give up hoping that their child will change and even cherish the hope that their child's homosexuality is only transitory:

> *My mother was really happy each time I broke up with a girlfriend. She thought I'm straight now and normal again. We got along much better*

during those periods ... However, when I got a new girlfriend she was sad again. (Eva, lesbian, 26)

When gay men and lesbians are faced with parental negative reactions, especially long-lasting ones, they employ different strategies in order to protect themselves and to find some kind of rationalization of the situation confronting them. Some gay men and lesbians develop a sort of *denial strategy* by which they downplay the importance of the relationship with their parents.

I don't need to have a close relationship with my parents .... At one point I realized that I don't feel like dealing with my family anymore. I really don't care. (Barbara, lesbian, 26)

Another coping approach is a *defense strategy*. Gay men and lesbians reestablish their own space within the family by demanding that their parents do not interfere in their own private matters. In other words, they pull back by drawing a line and creating a gap between themselves and their parents.

I told my mother that if she didn't want to know the truth, she shouldn't ask (about it). Now they don't interfere with these things. (Martin, gay man, 25)

The last typical coping strategy the focus group respondents mentioned is the *not-giving-up* strategy. This means that they put much effort into continuous communication with their parents. They initiate conversations about homosexuality and offer their parents additional information concerning it.

I just brought him some materials and demanded that he read them .... After he read it, we started a conversation. He realized that I function completely normally, that I don't have any problems with people around me and that a lot of people know about (me being a gay man) and that they are cool about it. (Patrick, gay man, 20)

CONCLUSION

Through the example of coming-out narratives within the family of origin this article strived to point to the relational character of the coming-out process. Both the concept of the transparent and the family closet have been used in order to highlight the *relational* nature of coming out. The process of coming out is relational as much as the non-heteronormative sexual identity of an individual no longer affects just him or her, but also the people who he or she came out to, and their relationships. While the transparent closet and the family closet are most often simultaneously established within the family—and the existence of one conditions the existence of the other—situations where only one of these closets exists are possible. One respondent from our study reported her parents discussing her homosexuality with their friends, but at the same time they refused to talk about it with her. However, such situations are exceptional.

When a child comes out, parents seem to be stretched between two situations: on one hand, they have stereotypical perceptions of homosexuality as promoted and reinforced by the heteronormative society. This creates the identity of their child as socially deviant and as such stigmatized, shameful, and unacceptable. On the other hand, there are feelings of affection and parental love. Placed between these opposing situations, they are confronted with a conflict which they often (at least temporarily) resolve by entering into a family closet. In this sense, the outcomes of coming out depend on the relationships among the family members. In other words, the family closet is relationally and contextually conditioned.

Various factors influence the outcome of this situation and they can be placed on a continuum of behavioral patterns, which are created after a child comes out. On one side of the continuum there are extremely negative reactions which might result in the breaking off of all relations with the child or in the non-acceptance of the child's sexual orientation. On the other side of the continuum there are behavioral patterns of positive reactions. This allows open relationships to be created where all family members accept a child's sexual orientation. Based on our research, the majority of gay men and lesbians find themselves together with their family members somewhere in between the two extremes, in the transparent closet, with the potential to move towards long-term positive outcomes—the latter being typical of younger generations of gay men and lesbians. Which patterns will be employed after a child comes out depends on various *relational contexts and factors*, ranging from wider societal and cultural contexts to close social networks, from interpersonal to intrapersonal factors. How each of these factors influences the selection of the patterns warrants further research.

Although the data from our research offer a rich source of narratives of coming out in family settings, some limitations of our research have to be mentioned. First, although we combined quantitative and qualitative methods in order to collect high-quality data, our study is limited due to the non-representative sample. Second, the study focused only on gay men and lesbians and did not include interviews with their parents. In this respect, the results presented in this article are "secondhand" interpretations of parental voices. Third, the study was conducted nearly 10 years ago. This should be taken into account when interpreting the data and applying them to the current situation. We assume that family relations have changed somewhat in the past 10 years, probably in the direction of the pluralization of family relations and consequently towards the greater acceptance of non-heteronormative family patterns. The decreasing social distance and increasingly more positive media representations of gay men and lesbians support this speculation.

NOTES

1. The sample consists only of those who self-identified as gay men or lesbians. Bisexual and transgender persons were excluded in order not to frame their specific experiences into the context of gay/lesbian narratives.

2. Throughout the text *homosexuality* and *heterosexuality* will be used either to point to binary understanding of sexual orientation or when explicitly used by the authors we refer to. It will also be used when referring to the language and terminology used by the respondents in focus groups.

REFERENCES

Bell, D., & Valentine, G. (1995). The sexed self: Strategies of performance, sites of resistance. In S. Pile & N. Thrift (Eds.), *Mapping the subject: Geographies of cultural transformation* (pp. 143–157). London, England; New York, NY: Routledge.

Broad, K. L. (2011). Coming out for parents, families and friends of lesbians and gays: From support group grieving to love advocacy. *Sexualities, 14*(4), 399–415. doi: 10.1177/1363460711406792

Cass, V. (1979). Homosexual identity formation: A theoretical model. *Journal of Homosexuality, 4*(3), 219–235. doi: 10.1300/J082v04n03_01

Connell, R. W., & Messerschmidt, J. W. (2005). Hegemonic masculinity: Rethinking the concept. *Gender & Society, 19*(6), 829–859. doi: 10.1177/0891243205277504

Dank, B. M. (1971). Coming out in the gay world. *Psychiatry, 34*, 60–77.

D'Augelli, A. R., Grossman, A. H., & Starks, M. T. (2005). Parents' awareness of lesbian, gay and bisexual youths' sexual orientation. *Journal of Marriage and Family, 67*, 474–482. doi: 10.1111/j.0022-2445.2005.00129.x

Davies, P. (1992). The role of disclosure in coming out among gay men. In K. Plummer (Ed.), *Modern homosexualities: Fragments of lesbian and gay experience* (pp. 75–83). London, England; New York, NY: Routledge.

Fields, J. (2001). Normal queers: Straight parents respond to their children's coming out. *Symbolic Interaction, 24*(2), 165–187. doi: 10.1525/si.2001.24.2.165

Foucault, M. (1984). *Nadzorovanje in kaznovanje*. Ljubljana, Slovenia: Delavska Enotnost.

La Placa, V. (2000). *Homosexuality and the family*. Unpublished doctoral dissertation, Nottingham Trent University, United Kingdom.

Kosofsky Sedgwick, E. (1993). Epistemology of the closet. In H. Abelove, M. A. Barale, & D. M. Halperin (Eds.), *The lesbian and gay studies reader* (pp. 45–61). London, England; New York, NY: Routledge.

Kuhar, R. (2011). The heteronormative panopticon and the transparent closet of the public space in Slovenia. In R. Kulpa & J. Mizielińska (Eds.), *De-centering Western sexualities: Central and Eastern European perspectives* (pp. 149–165). Farnham, UK; Burlington, VT: Ashgate.

Lešnik, B. (2005). Melting the iron curtain: The beginning of the LGBT movement in Slovenia. In M. Chateauvert (Ed.), *New social movements and sexuality* (pp. 86–96). Sophia, Bulgaria: Bilitis Resource Center.

Markowe, A. L. (1996). *Redefining the self (coming out as a lesbian)*. Cambridge, England: Polity Press.

Plummer, K. (1995). *Telling sexual stories: Power, change and social worlds*. London, England; New York, NY: Routledge.

Rener, T. (1996). Mladina in družina [Young people and the family]. In M. Ule (Ed.), *Predah za študentsko mladino [A respite for studying youths]* (pp. 119–152). Ljubljana, Slovenia: Juventa.

Savin-Williams, R. C., & Dubé, E. M. (1998). Parental reactions to their child's disclosure of a gay/lesbian identity. *Family Relations, 47*(1), 7–13.

Scherrer, K. S. (2012). The intergenerational family relationships of grandparents and GLBQ grandchildren. *Journal of GLBT Family Studies, 6*(3), 229–264. doi: 10.1080/1550428X.2010.490898

Seidman, S. (2002). *Beyond the closet: The transformation of gay and lesbian life*. New York, NY: Routledge.

Švab, A. (2001). *Družina: Od modernost k postmodernosti [Family: from modernity to postmodernity]*. Ljubljana, Slovenia: ZPS.

Švab, A., & Kuhar, R. (2005). *The unbearable comfort of privacy: Everyday life of gays and lesbians*. Ljubljana, Slovenia: The Peace Institute.

Toš, N., Klinar, P., Roter, Z., Markič, B., Mlinar, Z., Trampuž, C., ... Uhan, S. (1999). *Vrednote v prehodu II: Slovensko javno mnenje 1990–1998 [Values in transition II: Slovenian public opinion 1990–1998]*. Ljubljana, Slovenia: Fakulteta za družbene vede, IDV – CJMMK.

Troiden, R. (1988). A model of homosexual identity formation. In P. Nardi & B. E. Schneider (Eds.), *Social perspectives in lesbian and gay studies* (pp. 261–278). London, England: Routledge.

Becoming the Parent of a GLB Son or Daughter

ERIKA L. GRAFSKY
Virginia Tech, Blacksburg, Virginia, USA

Recent research has documented the importance of parental reactions to disclosure for sexual minority youths (SMY) (e.g., Ryan, Huebner, Diaz, & Sanchez, 2009). The purpose of this study was to develop a deeper understanding of the parent perspective of the disclosure to family experience of SMY ages 14 to 21. In-depth interviews were conducted with eight parents in the United States who had experienced a child disclose their gay, lesbian, or bisexual (GLB) orientation to them. Constructivist grounded theory and symbolic interaction theory informed the methodology and data analysis for the project. Analysis revealed that the process of becoming the parent of a GLB son or daughter is an appropriate narrative to conceptualize the parental experience of the disclosure-to-family process. The findings highlight how disclosure introduces new roles into the existing family system, which affects the consideration and interpretation of the salience of particular identities, such as being the parent of a GLB son or daughter. Understanding how parents experience the disclosure-to-family process—particularly, how they understand and re-envision the meaning of being a parent—is crucial for research and intervention to help families become supportive of SMY. Limitations and suggestions for future research are presented.

Author note: This project was supported by Award Number R36DA026958 from the National Institute on Drug Abuse. The content is solely the responsibility of the author and does not necessarily represent the views of the National Institute on Drug Abuse or the National Institute of Health. The author would like to thank the participants who shared their experiences and Katherine Hickey and Dana Riger for their assistance on the preparation of the manuscript for publication.

INTRODUCTION

Recent research has documented the importance of the family context, and parental reactions in particular, for the health outcomes for SMY (Bouris et al., 2010; Ryan, Huebner, Diaz, & Sanchez, 2009; Ryan, Russell, Huebner, Diaz, & Sanchez, 2010; Saewyc, 2011). In order to address the documented health disparities, numerous researchers have called for the development of effective interventions for SMY (e.g., Bouris et al., 2010; Ryan et al., 2010; Saewyc, 2011). However, in order to most effectively intervene with SMY, including the family may be integral to the process (e.g., Bouris et al., 2010; Ryan et al., 2009; Ryan et al., 2010; Saewyc, 2011). Furthermore, it is important to have a breadth of empirical scholarship on the psychosocial development and context of SMY and their families in order to develop components of effective interventions. This study seeks to add to the body of literature of the disclosure-to-family experience of SMY by exploring the parent perspective.

Youth Disclosure of Sexual Orientation to Family

The prevailing literature on disclosing to family suggests that sharing sexual orientation information with family can provoke feelings of anxiety and threats to personal well-being (D'Augelli & Hershberger, 1993; D'Augelli, Hershberger, & Pilkington, 1998). Despite these feelings, disclosing one's gay, lesbian, bisexual, or queer (GLBQ) orientation to family is a common and important step of the larger sexual identity development and integration process that is commonly referred to as *coming out*. According to Rosario, Hunter, Maguen, Gwadz, and Smith (2001), sexual identity development "consists of exploring the emerging sexual identity and reducing the cognitive dissonance attributed to internalized negative evaluations of gays, lesbians, and bisexuals" (p. 135). Furthermore, "Identity integration includes acceptance of one's gay, lesbian, bisexual identity and sharing that aspect of the self with other individuals" (Rosario et al., 2001, p. 135). D'Augelli (1994, 2006) has proposed a human development model of GLB youth development within the family and larger ecological context which conceptualizes that disclosure to family or *becoming a GLB offspring* is an integral part of the sexual identity development and integration process. A recent report of a study of 10,000 GLBT-identified youths ages 13 to 17 found that 56% were out to their immediate family (Human Rights Campaign, 2012).

Most of the research on the experience of disclosing one's GLBQ orientation to family centers on initial parental reactions and subsequent outcomes of the SMY. Savin-Williams and Ream (2003) found that the most common reactions of parents were reported as supportive or very supportive or slightly negative, including feelings of disbelief that their child was GLB (e.g., the parent thought it was a phase) or concern that their child would face a difficult life. Initial parental reactions of rejection, physical attack, or screaming have been reported at rates of 4% to 18% (D'Augelli & Hershberger, 1993; Savin-Williams & Ream, 2003). Differences between mothers' and fathers' reactions has been mixed; some research has indicated no differences between males and females on their mothers' or fathers' reactions to their sexual orientation (D'Augelli, Grossman, & Starks, 2005; Kuhar, 2007; Savin-Williams & Ream, 2003) while others consistently report that fathers respond more negatively than mothers (D'Augelli, 2002; D'Augelli, Hershberger, & Pilkington, 2001; Sullivan & Wodarski, 2002).

Despite the prevailing negative rhetoric around disclosing to family, many parent-child relationships either stay the same or improve after disclosure (Kuhar, 2007; Savin-Williams & Ream, 2003). Recent research indicates that there may be both short- and long-term gains for SMY to disclose their sexual orientation to family, particularly within a family environment of openness and connectedness. In addition, current literature has documented clear health benefits, such as higher self-esteem and less substance abuse, for adolescents who experience accepting reactions from their parents as a result of disclosure (Ryan et al, 2010). The research further suggests that adolescents who have disclosed experience greater comfort with their sexuality, less internalized homophobia, and fewer problems disclosing their sexual orientation to friends (D'Augelli, 2002; D'Augelli et al., 1998; Hershberger & D'Augelli, 1995).

It is likely that youths who choose not to disclose to parents have their reasons, such as protecting themselves from disclosure-related violence, verbal harassment, or other negative consequences (Bontempo & D'Augelli, 2002; D'Augelli & Hershberger, 1993; D'Augelli et al., 1998; Safren & Heimberg, 1999; Savin-Williams, 1994). Ryan and colleagues (2009) found that GLB youths and young adults who reported higher levels of family rejection during adolescence were 8.4 times more likely to have attempted suicide, 5.9 times more likely to report high levels of depression, and 3.4 times more likely to report illegal drug use and to have engaged in unprotected sexual intercourse compared with peers from families that reported no or low levels of family rejection.

The Parent Perspective

Relatively little research explores why parents react the way they do. Parental reactions can be negatively affected by misinformation, religious beliefs, and homophobia (Sullivan & Wodarski, 2002; Newman & Muzzonigro, 1993). Positive family dynamics such as cohesion, adaptability, and authoritative parenting have been found to be related to positive familial reactions and fewer negative outcomes to a child's disclosure of a sexual minority orientation (Beaty, 1999; Willoughby, Malik, & Lindahl, 2006).

It is important to note that much of the research on parental reactions relies on the GLB youths' recollection of parents' responses (D'Augelli, 2006).

However, some studies have described parental responses as reported by the parents. Studies have found that it is not uncommon for parents to report experiencing sadness, denial, regret, depression, guilt/shame, and concern for their child's well-being (Herdt & Koff, 2000; Robinson, Walters, & Skeen, 1989). Boxer, Cook, and Herdt (1991) described parents experiencing a period of family disruption following learning of their child's sexual minority orientation. However, Ben-Ari (1995) noted that both GLB youths and their parents saw honesty as the greatest benefit of disclosure.

Several recent qualitative studies have attended to the parent experience of disclosure beyond initial reactions. Using an anthropological approach with participants of a GLB parent support group, Fields (2001) identified several themes that reflected what these parents were struggling with: lack of social scripts to assist them in learning their child was GLB, dealing with a sense of loss, wanting to encourage heterosexual norms with their children, and confronting the concept of normalcy. Saltzburg (2004) elicited five themes from her in-depth interviews:

1. awareness that their child was different,
2. feelings of distress associated with knowing with certainty after coming out,
3. a period of emotional detachment between parents and children,
4. fear of estrangement as a parent and role model due to an inability to relate to the GLB subculture, and
5. a time of adjustment and education by seeking community resources and social support.

In the past few years, several studies have departed from the prevailing deficit approach to studying SMY and their families, and instead focused on positive themes such as development, success, and positive experiences. Phillips and Ancis (2008) and Goodrich (2009) explored a new process of identity development as the parent of a sexual minority child. Phillips and Ancis (2008) took a narrative approach and described three periods of adjustment that contained cognitive-behavioral elements with "turning points" (p. 132) as transition periods. Goodrich (2009) focused on parents who had successfully integrated their experience since their child disclosed to them, describing an emergent model characterized by emotional, cognitive, and behavioral responses that led to a successful integration of their identity. A recent qualitative survey study by Gonzalez, Rostosky, Odom, and Riggle (2013) found that many parents experienced and associated positive emotions, improved closeness, and personal growth with parenting a gay, lesbian, bisexual, transgender, or queer (GLBTQ) child.

STATEMENT OF PURPOSE

This study seeks to extend the research on the parent perspective of the experience of disclosure to family of SMY. While there has been some movement across the literature base to examine the disclosure experience from the perspective of youths or parents, move beyond initial reactions, and away from a deficit approach, the literature is largely focused on an individual, rather than an interpersonal or family systems, perspective. The author approached the study from a constructionist grounded theory perspective (Charmaz, 2006), rooted in the interpretive constructionist paradigm and informed by symbolic interaction theory.

METHODOLOGY

The data from this study come from a larger project of youths and parents conducted to understand SMY's experience with disclosure of sexual orientation information to family of origin.

Participants

Institutional Review Board (IRB) procedures for the protection of human subjects were employed for this study. Convenience sampling was the primary purposeful sampling strategy (Patton, 1990). Participants were primarily recruited through advertising efforts with local GLBQ and GLBQ-serving organizations (e.g., local Parents, Families and Friends of Lesbians and Gays [PFLAG] chapters) in a Midwestern state in the United States. Recruitment sites/venues were provided with flyers and cards with information about the project for posting and distribution. In addition, project advertisements were placed in local shops and stores and a letter about the project and a flyer was sent to several area churches that are known for being open and affirming to the GLBQ community in the surrounding metropolitan area. Participants who responded to recruitment efforts were screened to determine if they met the eligibility criteria for participation. Parents were eligible if they had a child who was between the ages of 14 and 21 when the child disclosed their sexual orientation to them. This disclosure had to have occurred within the past five years. The five-year time frame is appropriate because a child's disclosure of a same-sex orientation is a significant autobiographical event for parents. Literature on memory indicates that events resulting in emotional arousal are remembered more accurately and consistently (Smith, Bibi, & Sheard, 2003). Interview strategies were employed in order to prompt successful recall of the disclosure event itself and the autobiographical detail associated with it. This includes contextualizing the event to time, environment, and person.

Exclusion criteria included the ability to speak and understand English. This was imperative given the verbal nature of the project. Of those formally screened, only one parent did not meet eligibility criteria to participate. In addition, after screening and during the time of the interview, it was revealed that one participant's child had first disclosed at age 13. This participant's experience is included in the sample.

Data Collection

Two methods of qualitative data collection were employed: questionnaires and individual interviews. The purpose of the pre-interview questionnaire was to gather demographic and biographical information in an unobtrusive and time-efficient way so that the interview and data analysis could be informed by this information. Participants were encouraged to elaborate on answers in the margins or space provided at the end of the questionnaire to encourage more contextualized information rather than forced responses. The questionnaire gathered basic demographic information (age, gender, ethnicity/race) as well as information about their sexual minority child's sexual identity development and integration milestones. Parent-child closeness was assessed using the Parent Child Closeness inventory (PCC; Buchanan, Maccoby, & Dornbusch, 1991). The original instrument was modified to obtain the parent's perspective of closeness with their child. Sum scores for the 9 items range from 9 to 45. In this sample, internal consistency was high ($\alpha = .84$). The insights garnered from the questionnaires were used to further contextualize the participant's psychosocial context.

Individual, semistructured, in-depth interviews were employed to elicit parental perceptions of the disclosure process and experience, and to gain insight into how substance use may affect the family context within which disclosure to family occurs. The interviews were conducted using a semistructured constructivist grounded theory format (Charmaz, 2006). In addition, the tone of the interview followed a responsive interviewing style (Rubin & Rubin, 2005). This style of qualitative research interview enables interview questions, probes, and follow-up questions and the tenor of the interview to be tailored to each participant. Questions and probes in four main areas guided the interviews:

1. description of family context and dynamics,
2. relationship with child prior to disclosure,
3. detailed information about the disclosure experience, and
4. current relationship with child.

The average length of the interviews was 84 minutes long with a range of 66 minutes to 123 minutes. Interviews were transcribed and then double-checked for accuracy and to verify identifying information was removed.

Data Analysis

Constructivist grounded theory methods for data analysis were employed (Charmaz, 2000, 2002) for this study. Preliminary analysis of transcripts and pre-interview questionnaires began as soon as transcription for each interview was complete, resulting in interviews and data analysis occurring simultaneously. Deeper analysis occurred once the majority of data were collected. Analysis of the questionnaires involved synthesizing the information and was used to describe, situate, and contextualize the experiences of the participants to provide a richer description of participants' experiences by further contextualizing their experiences and aid in the reporting of the findings. The heterogeneity of participants' demographic and biographical characteristics and other lived experiences provides a generative source for different categories of analysis.

Constructivist grounded theory (Charmaz, 2000, 2002) data analysis employs "constructivist induction" (p. 48). Understanding emerges from the data that are created through the researcher and participant interaction (Daly, 2007). A three-part coding scheme was developed through the use of initial line-by-line, open coding to identify concepts or "meaning units" (Charmaz, 2000) within each interview. Selective coding involves using recurrent concepts to begin to create categories and sorting through data. Through the use of open and selective coding, themes began to emerge. The constant comparative method was used to sort and make sense of emerging concepts, categories, and themes within and across interviews. Concepts, categories, and themes were all coded. Charmaz (2000) describes that the constant comparative method means (1) comparing interviews, (2) comparing data within the same interview, (3) comparing situations and concepts within and across interviews, (4) comparing data with the emerging category, and (5) comparing categories to one another. As concepts, categories, and themes emerge from the data analysis, interview probes and follow-up questions were used to allow for emerging concepts to be explored with new participants in an effort to move towards saturation and to achieve "thick description" (Geertz, 1973). The software NVivo 9.0 was utilized in this study to aid data analysis. Several steps were taken to increase the rigor of the study (e.g., the use of knowledgeable insiders, peer debriefing, negative case analysis, analytical triangulation, and an audit trail).

FINDINGS

Quotes and excerpts from the interviews are presented to both describe and enrich the findings. Following the quotes, participant pseudonym and age of parent will be identified in parentheses (e.g., Eve, age 47). As this is a primarily qualitative study, statistical results are used only to provide a richer understanding of the findings. First, demographic and descriptive information related to sexual identity are presented followed by a brief discussion of the family dynamics of the participants. Second, findings related to the disclosure event will be presented. Finally, the emerging theoretical narrative of the process of *becoming the parent of a GLB son or daughter* will be presented and enriched by the parent perspective of the ongoing disclosure experience. The use of this phrasing is an elaboration upon the process of "becoming an LGB offspring" referenced in D'Augelli's (1994; 2006) human development model of LGB sexual identity development.

Demographic and Descriptive Characteristics of Participants

Eight parents participated in the study. The sample included 6 mothers and 2 fathers, ages 34 to 57 ($M = 47.3$, $SD = 8.14$). All parents identified their ethnicity/race as white with one exception, where one participant identified himself as black. Four of the parents identified their religious and/or spiritual identity as Protestant or nondenominational Christianity, two parents described having no religious or spiritual identity, one parent identified as Catholic, and one as spiritual. Educational background and socioeconomic status information was not collected. Table 1 presents the demographic characteristics of the parents who participated in this study.

Six of the parents had a son and two had a daughter who they reported identified as a sexual minority. Parents reported that their child first disclosed their sexual minority orientation to them between the ages of 13 and 21 ($M = 16.62$, $SD = 3.15$). Two parents stated they were "very comfortable" when their child first disclosed their sexual orientation to them, two parents stated they were "somewhat comfortable," three parents stated they were "somewhat uncomfortable," and one parent stated they were "very uncomfortable." Regarding comfort with their child's sexual orientation at the time of the interview, three parents reported they were "very comfortable" and five reported they were "somewhat comfortable." None of the parents reported they were currently uncomfortable with their child's sexual orientation. Further analysis indicated younger parents experienced increased comfort, suggesting a salient interplay between age of parents and their reaction to their child's disclosure. In addition, nearly all participants reported that their religious or spiritual identity was unrelated to their comfort with their child's sexual orientation. For example, only one parent reported that his religion/spirituality or moral values "very much" affected his comfort with his son's sexual identity and this parent's spiritual identity was centered on acceptance for all. Five parents reported that their comfort with their child's sexual orientation was "not at all" affected by their religion/spirituality or moral values.

TABLE 1 Demographic Characteristics of Participants and Disclosure Events

Pseudonym	Relationship to Youth	Parent Age	Parent Race/Ethnicity[a]	Religious or Spiritual Identity	Youth Identity	Age of Youth (at Disclosure)	Method of Disclosure
Alice	Mother	42	White	None	Gay	20	In person, private
Bette	Mother	56	White	Nondenominational Christian	Gay[b]	15	In person, private
Clay	Father	46	White	Spiritual	Gay[b]	15	Secondhand, from mother
Dara	Mother	57	White	Nondenominational Christian	Lesbian	21	Phone
Eve	Mother	47	White	Christian	Gay	14	In person, private
Faith	Mother	34	White	None	Lesbian	13	In person, private
Greg	Father	42	Black	Methodist	Bisexual Male	20	In person, public
Hannah	Mother	55	White	Catholic	Gay	15	In person, private

[a]White = not of Hispanic origin, [b]same child

Family Dynamics

The interviews revealed that parents in the sample typically described their families as high-functioning, healthy families (i.e., exhibiting a high degree of closeness, open communication, and having flexible, but firm, boundaries). "I would describe our family dynamic as close... I think of us as, in many ways, very solid, middle-of-the-road" (Dara, age 57). Another parent said, " I always thought we were kind of a *Leave it to Beaver* family... dinner at the table every night" (Bette, age 56).[1] Many of the participants made statements such as, "the kids and I are so close" (Alice, age 42), "we are very loving" (Eve, age 47), and "we talk about just about everything" (Faith, age 34). The interviews evidenced some variance in the description of the discipline or parenting styles. Where some parents said, "I'm not very strict" (Hannah, age 55) others said, "I always felt we were stricter than most parents" (Bette, age 56). Participants' descriptions of their parenting typically reflected an authoritative parenting style—"They would have to sit on the couch and tell me why they chose that course of action" (Alice, age 42)—but ranged from slightly authoritarian to slightly permissive parenting styles. The majority of mothers described their relationship with their child as very close, while the fathers reported a lower degree of closeness. The two fathers reported scores on the Parent-Child Closeness Inventory (PCC; Buchanan et al., 1991) of 20 (Clay, age 46) and 35 (Greg, age 42), whereas the mothers all reported scores of 39 or above ($M = 37$, $SD = 7.30$; maximum sum score of 45). Furthermore, Greg's son lived out of state with his mother during a period of his adolescence and this affected the degree of closeness experienced. Despite reporting lower levels of closeness with their children, neither father in this sample reported feeling uncomfortable with their child's sexual orientation at the time of disclosure. Given the overall lack of variability in the way parents in this sample described their family dynamics, the data did not suggest any significant findings that could be attributed to specific family dynamics described in the interviews.

The Disclosure Event

Three of the eight parents reported that they had suspected their child was non-heterosexual prior to the disclosure event. For example, one father said, "We were kind of talking about it because, you know, the whole prom thing. There were some weird things going on. And we were like, huh" (Greg, age 42). One parent reported that she did not have suspicions prior to her daughter disclosing, but during the disclosure event, she knew instinctively when her daughter asked if she had time to talk.

Table 1 also illustrates the disclosure events of the parents and their child. The interviews with parents revealed varied perceptions of the circumstances that preceded the disclosure event. The parents described disclosure experiences with their child that indicated five planned disclosures and three unplanned disclosures. In six of the instances, the interviews suggested that the youth experienced some degree of readiness related to his or her personal sexual identity development process. For example, when asked why she felt her son chose to come out when he did, one parent said, "I think he thought, why go years and years and years trying to deny who I am?" (Hannah, age 55). Two parents described a perception of readiness and relationship circumstances: "I think he might've met someone online. I think he wanted to finally open up, say here it is, I need to start dating" (Alice, age 42). Relationship difficulties could also precede disclosure to parents. In one case, the disclosure was unplanned and prompted because the mother noticed a change in the youth participant's mood—that something had shifted. The mother said, "We were in the TV room on the sofa and I said, 'I've had it. What is going on? You're not yourself. What happened'?" (Bette, age 56) Secondhand disclosure occurred for one of the unplanned disclosure events. In this instance, Clay (age 46) found out about his son's nonheterosexual orientation from the mother, who called him immediately after.

Emotional Context and Initial Reactions

Parents described the disclosure event in ways that indicated a high degree of stress and/or emotionality. It was not uncommon for the child and/or parent to cry during the disclosure event. One parent shared her experience very viscerally:

He's like, "uh, why don't we pull over somewhere. I need to talk to you."... At this point, I'm getting a little nervous... I undo my [seat] belt and I look at him... his eyes start to get misty and I'm like, Oh God, he's got a girl pregnant.... And then he just looks at me and out of his mouth comes, I'm gay. When I get taken by surprise I start to turn red from my chest up and I could feel heat and redness just rising; I can't tell if he's joking, I can't tell if he's serious. And I look at him and then I see the tears in his eyes. He starts crying and I start crying and I'm just like, "That's all you had to tell me?" (Alice, age 42)

Other parents described the disclosure event as having a more composed level of emotionality that still indicated a significant degree of tension felt by the parent and/or child:

He came downstairs and said he had to talk to me. I'm like, okay, and popped off the TV. He just sat down and said that he had something to tell me and he didn't want me to worry about him. Then he told me he was bisexual. And I said, "Okay. What does that mean?" So then we talked a lot of that kind of stuff over.... I asked him pretty personal questions. (Hannah, age 55)

Hannah's son later disclosed that he was gay and not bisexual.

A few parents described feeling surprised: "Shock. I didn't see it coming" (Bette, age 56). Some parents said that one of the first reactions they experienced when their child disclosed to them was feeling as if the picture they had envisioned of their child's life was shattered:

Everything that I had envisioned, you know parents have this like little ball of fantasy in their head for their children, the white picket fence, the dog, the kids, the wife. [Gay son]'s popped [snaps fingers] and it was like this void.... And it's really scary 'cause you don't know how to fill it.... I've spent twenty-some years with this whole reality for him and now there's this empty void and I don't know how to fill it. (Alice, age 42)

It was also common for parent participants to describe becoming increasingly worried for their child's well-being once they disclosed. For example, when asked how she would describe her reaction when her son first disclosed, Eve (age 47) stated,

I was afraid. Fear, fear was my biggest thing. I was petrified. I thought somebody would hurt him, I mean, all the horrors of um, people not accepting him. Is life gonna be hard? Afraid of him being harassed at school. How do I tell people? How are people going to treat him?

Becoming the Parent of a GLB Son or Daughter

As the data analysis progressed, the grounded theoretical category of *becoming the parent of a GLB son or daughter* emerged as a salient representation of how the disclosure experience changes family roles. Parents had to create new identities for themselves as the parents of GLB sons or daughters.

Parents described becoming more comfortable with their child's orientation over time. One parent who reacted by becoming overprotective and hypervigilant of her son's safety and well-being said, "Once I finally realized that my son was gonna be safe, I got that out of my system. Then we just went back to normal life" (Alice, age 42). Only one parent described grieving; you "have to bury your expectation of your child's life" (Dara, age 57).

All of the parents were able to reflect on what they felt went well regarding the disclosure-to-family experience. Some parents described that their children experienced relief once they disclosed to them: "It just seemed like the universe came off his shoulders" (Alice, age 42). One father described how he believed his relationship with his son has improved since he had a favorable reaction to his son's disclosure: "I think our relationship has opened up quite a bit; it's loosened up a little bit. Because he was always a bit worried that I wouldn't care about him if he wasn't what I wanted him to be" (Greg, age 42).

It was common for parents to describe their fears and vulnerabilities with understanding what it means for them to be the parent of a GLB son or daughter. Dara (age 57) expressed her fear that she would make mistakes in relating with her daughter now that she knew that her daughter identified as a lesbian. She said, "You're like an ocean liner trying to turn around in the middle of the Pacific; and you're bound to have some missteps along the way." When asked how accepting she considers herself of her son's identification as a gay male, Hannah (age 55) stated,

> *Well, right now, I can sit here and tell you "oh, I'm really accepting," but he's not brought a man home yet, so that'll be a different thing that I'll have to, I mean that will actually be, when he's in a relationship, that will tell the tale of how accepting I really am inside.*

Disclosing to others that their child is not heterosexual and dealing with others' reactions to this knowledge are significant experiences of the process of becoming the parent of a GLB son or daughter. Eve (age 47) shared the following:

> *Now I gotta start dealing with it. If he wants to bring [her son's boyfriend] around family events and things like that, well then, we're gonna have to tell the family, because I'm not gonna exclude him. And then I got to the point where, if people weren't gonna accept him, then they were not gonna be in my life. I made a decision, if anybody gives me any type of negative feedback or you know, says bad things or don't want him around or don't wanna accept him, then I'm done with them. I drew a line.*

DISCUSSION

The purpose of this study was to develop a deeper understanding of the parent perspective of the disclosure to family experience of SMY, while conceptualizing disclosure not as an event but as a process impacting the entirety of the family system. The current literature has largely focused on the child or the parent, without considering the interpersonal dynamics at work during and after disclosure. The findings of the study suggest that *becoming the parent of a GLB son or daughter* is an appropriate narrative to conceptualize the parental experience of the process of disclosure to family. Relevant literature and family theory are used throughout the discussion to contextualize the findings from this study. Limitations of the study are discussed and areas for future research and implications for families and professionals are provided.

Becoming the parent of a GLB son or daughter is a complex process that emphasizes the relational nature of the experience of disclosure to family. Parents of SMY describe how the disclosure experience can be challenging and results in new understandings of what it means to be a parent of a child who identifies as a sexual minority. The narrative of *becoming* emphasizes that it is an active, ongoing process. The disclosure experience is shaped by a dynamic process that involves a dyadic, reciprocal, simultaneous exchange between SMY and their parent(s). Symbolic interaction describes the process through which individuals enact shared symbols and create meaning of self, others, and situations (LaRossa & Reitzes, 1993). The disclosure experience changes the parent-child relationship in that a parent's perceptions and interactions with their child are necessarily affected. Parental appraisals of self (and a SMY's perception of parental appraisals of self) shape how a SMY experiences disclosure to family.

Disclosing to parent(s) introduces new roles into the family. Interactions among family members that occur throughout the disclosure process affect the consideration and interpretation of the salience of particular identities. SMY must consider what it will mean to become a GLB son or daughter. The traditional, linear view of sexual orientation identity development is concentrated on the individual experience of "coming out" to oneself (e.g., Carrion & Lock, 1997; Cass, 1979, 1984; Coleman, 1982; Rosario et al., 2001; Troiden, 1988, 1989). D'Augelli's (1994, 2006) human development model of GLB youth sexual identity development considers the role of the family and larger ecological context within the sexual identity development and integration process of sexual minority individuals. The findings from this project support D'Augelli's assertion of the importance of disclosing to family as an integral component of the sexual identity development and integration process. SMY do not "become" GLB sons or daughters upon disclosing to their parents; rather, the process is continual, if not cyclical, a dynamic interplay between their sexual identity and their role as sons or daughters (e.g., Grafsky, 2011). Few studies emphasize the relational nature of the disclosure experience. This project provides further evidence that the sexual identity development and integration process may not be adequately understood from an individual perspective.

Parent-child relationships that were perceived by the youth participant to have a high degree of emotional closeness prior to disclosure were less likely to evidence a decrease in closeness after disclosure. While this is not a causal relationship, it does support research that suggests that positive disclosure experiences are related to existing positive family dynamics (Savin-Williams & Ream, 2003). Most of the participants in the study also said that parents became more accepting over time, which is consistent with previous research (e.g., Beeler & DiProva, 1999; Goodrich, 2009; Lee & Lee,

2006; Phillips & Ancis, 2008; Potoczniak, Crosbie-Burnett, & Saltzburg, 2009; Savin-Williams & Ream, 2003).

The multiple levels of self-reflexivity that occur within a family become emphasized when viewing the process of disclosure through the lens of symbolic interaction theory. Individuals are cognizant of the fact that other family members attach various meanings and interpretations to their interactions. This theoretical notion is evidenced in the data, as some of the parents described experiencing shattered expectations, while attempting to conceal that internal dialogue from their child. As noted by Fields (2001), the quality of one's parenting is often assumed to be directly reflected in children's outcomes. Being the parent of a GLB child might be perceived as a moral failure. Parents struggle to reconcile their inability to have a "normal" child with external perceptions and judgments of parental inadequacy.

The theme of parental concern and worry for the safety and well-being of their sexual minority child was evidenced across the youths and parents in the study as an initial reaction and an actual cost and reward. For example, concern and worry were interpreted as costs when the parent was perceived as being overprotective and interpreted as a reward when the youth expressed feeling supported by their parent. Johnson and Colucci (1999) suggest that adjustment of family rules, expectations, and boundaries necessary in adolescence and emerging adulthood may be difficult when a family is dealing with fear of social persecution. Some parents may have difficulty balancing the desire to protect their child and keep them safe and believing their child can be safe and happy in a social environment where homophobia is still prevalent. The parents in this sample described struggling with these issues and often sought the support of friends, other family members, various forms of social media, and groups such as Parents, Families and Friends of Lesbians and Gays (PFLAG). Other researchers have found that parents who are supportive of their sexual minority children also have benefited from these forms of support (Goodrich, 2009; Phillips & Ancis, 2008).

Younger parents in this sample reported feeling increased comfort at the time of the initial disclosure. It is unclear whether this finding is due to the age of the parent at the time of the child's disclosure or the age of the child, but it does suggest that further research should consider age of parents and children as an important variable in the disclosure to family experience. A 2011 United States public opinion poll found that more than 6 in 10 respondents younger than age 50 agreed that same-sex orientations should be accepted (Pew Research Center, 2011). Furthermore, a recent international opinion poll found that younger respondents were far more likely to report that society should be accepting of homosexuality (Pew Research Center, 2013). This is consistent with a global societal trend of increasingly greater acceptance of diverse sexual orientations (Pew Research Center, 2011, 2013) and a transformation of North American disclosure experiences occurring in the past decade (see Murray, 2010).

Anticipated reactions to disclosure seem to be influenced considerably by social norms and perceptions; media reports on youth-parent relations often contribute to stereotypes of negative consequence as a normal parental response (Savin-Williams & Ream, 2003). The findings related to age and the overall positive nature of the disclosure experiences described by the parents in this sample suggest that the dominant discourse of *coming out* to family may be changing. A recent study examining the positive aspects associated with being the parent of a GLBTQ child support this finding (Gonzalez et al., 2013). Furthermore, parents who experienced feelings of shock, sadness, or lost expectations experienced these emotions during the initial disclosure event and not as part of their ongoing adjustment. While certainly not conclusive, these findings suggest the body of literature on parental reactions might not be reflective of contemporary North American family experiences. Given the movement towards greater acceptance of same-sex orientation and relationships (Pew Research Center, 2011, 2013), scholars should be cognizant of the fast pace in which these changes are taking place.

The parents in the sample typically described their families as high-functioning, healthy families (i.e., exhibiting a high degree of closeness, open communication, and having flexible, but firm, boundaries). Given that the existing literature on SMY and their families has been criticized for overestimating negative experiences and worst-case scenarios (Bouris et al., 2010; Savin-Williams, 2001), this study provides a pertinent contribution to the literature. While there is a dearth of research exploring the family dynamics of SMY, Darby-Mullins and Murdock (2007) found that family environment (i.e., conflict, cohesion, and expressiveness) was found to predict significant variance in the GLB youth's emotional adjustment (i.e., symptoms of depression and anxiety) and parental attitudes towards homosexuality were found to contribute to additional variance explained above and beyond that predicted by family environment alone.

Limitations

There are a number of limitations in this study. First, the findings of this study cannot be generalized to all SMY and parents of SMY. The participants in the study resided in one Midwestern U.S. state. The sample for this study was not ethnically or racially diverse. Previous research has documented that there may be unique factors that affect the disclosure to family experience for ethnic and racial minorities (e.g., Bouris et al., 2010; Merighi & Grimes, 2000). The small number of non-white participants in the project does not allow for comparisons to be made by race and ethnicity. In addition, educational background and socioeconomic status data were not collected; thus no comparisons can be made by class differences. Finally, this sample of parents is small and only included two fathers. Theoretical sampling, a hallmark of grounded theory methodology, was not exhaustive. In constructivist grounded theory, theoretical sampling involves seeking pertinent data to continue to develop the emerging theory (Charmaz, 2006). Constructivist grounded theory methodology adopts a critical view of saturation that goes beyond repetition and finding the same patterns. Rather, saturation is dependent upon theoretical sampling (Charmaz, 2006). As such, saturation was not achieved for this project. Data from additional parents, from diverse locales, would likely provide a richer understanding of the disclosure experience from the perspective of parents that could enrich the description of the process emerging from the findings of this study.

Future Research

The findings from this study suggest several areas for future research that would deepen and strengthen the literature base on the disclosure-to-family experience. For example, the findings suggest that family dynamics may play an important role in the disclosure experience. Future research should include standardized measures of family dynamics such as the Family Adaptability and Cohesion Evaluation Scale (FACES- IV; Olson, 2011), which assesses adaptability, cohesion, communication, and satisfaction. In addition, research has already documented that parental responses to disclosure and emotional aspects of the parent-child relationship are related to health outcomes for SMY (see Bouris et al., 2010, for a review). Given the extent of scholarly support for the development of interventions for SMY (e.g., Bouris et al., 2010; Ryan et al., 2010; Saewyc, 2011), a detailed understanding of the family context of the youth and the parental perspective on the experience is warranted in order to effectively intervene.

Implications for Families and Helping Professionals

Beyond assisting with the disclosure decision process, helping professionals might be tasked with preparing SMY with disclosing to a particular family member. In general, more research is needed before specific suggestions can be made that would direct how elements of the disclosure event will affect subsequent disclosure outcomes. However, the findings from this study suggest that the disclosure event is likely to be highly emotional for the parent. Furthermore, this study, as well as literature on disclosure decisions in general, suggests that intimate disclosures (such as those that occur within the parent-child relationship) which contain a higher degree of emotion may be viewed more positively as compared to more fact-based disclosures that may contain little emotional content (Chaudoir & Fisher, 2010). Youths should be prepared to expect a high degree of emotion and helping professionals could work with them to increase their capacity and self-efficacy for handling the emotional climate of the disclosure event. In addition, it is likely that parents and other family members will ask questions such as "Are you sure?," "How long have you known?," "Why didn't you tell me earlier?," "Do you have a boyfriend/girlfriend?," and "Have you been sexually active with someone of the same sex?" It would be helpful for youths to consider what kinds of questions they may be asked and how much information they are willing to share with their parents. Furthermore, helping professionals working with parents should be intentional about communicating to them that their child's sexual orientation does not necessarily impose a victim-centered narrative or pejorative label upon their family. Instead, in the spirit of symbolic interaction, parents and children are free to negotiate, co-create, and redefine their roles and family themes as they see fit, and adjust them as they become more comfortable with having a child with a non-heterosexual identity.

CONCLUSION

This study provides a unique contribution to the literature that places the emergent findings of the disclosure to family experience within the existing theoretical framework of symbolic interaction theory. Understanding how parents experience the disclosure to family process—particularly, how they understand and re-envision the meaning of being a parent—is crucial for research, intervention, and professionals to help families become supportive of SMY. The *process of becoming the parent of a GLB son or daughter* may be an appropriate narrative that may help parents become more supportive of their SMY. Assisting youths in disclosing their sexual orientation to their families and coping with parental reactions is an important challenge (Ryan et al., 2010). Such focus can help these youths become integrated into their families, decrease future risk, and enhance family support and closeness (D'Augelli et al., 2005). Despite the encouraging findings of this study, positive parent-child relationships are still strained for many SMY given the presence of social stigma, fear of discrimination, and anticipation of a negative disclosure experience, contributing to the isolation of these youths from their families (Russell, Driscoll, & Truong, 2002). Although disclosing one's GLBQ orientation to family is only one aspect of the sexual identity development and integration process of a sexual minority individual, it is a lifelong component due to the primacy of families in most people's lives (Laird, 1993).

NOTE

1. *Leave It to Beaver* is a sitcom from the 1950s starring an all-white and heterosexual family representing the quintessential "American family" structured around the father, the family patriarch, and his relationship with his wife and children.

REFERENCES

Beaty, L. A. (1999). Identity development of homosexual youth and parental and familial influences on the coming out process. *Adolescence, 34*, 597–601.

Beeler, J., & DiProva, V. (1999). Family adjustment following disclosure of homosexuality by a member: Themes discerned in narrative accounts. *Journal of Marital and Family Therapy, 25*, 443–459.

Ben-Ari, A. (1995). The discovery that an offspring is gay: Parents', gay men's and lesbians' perspectives. *Journal of Homosexuality, 30*, 89–112.

Bontempo, D. E., & D'Augelli, A. R. (2002). Effects of at-school victimization and sexual orientation on lesbian, gay, or bisexual youths' health risk behavior. *Journal of Adolescent Health, 30*, 364–374.

Bouris, A., Guilamo-Ramos, V., Pickard, A., Shiu, C., Loosier, P. S., Dittus, P., & Waldmiller, J. M. (2010). A systematic review of parental influences on the health and well-being of lesbian, gay, and bisexual youth: Time for a new public health research and practice agenda. *The Journal of Primary Prevention, 31*, 273–309.

Boxer, A. M., Cook, J. A., & Herdt, G. (1991). Double jeopardy: Identity transitions and parent-child relations among gay and lesbian youth. In K. A. Pillemer & K. McCartney (Eds.), *Parent-child relations throughout life* (pp. 59–92). Hillsdale, NJ: Erlbaum.

Buchanan, C. M., Maccoby, E. E., & Dornbusch, S. M. (1991). Caught between parents: Adolescents' experience in divorced homes. *Child Development, 62*, 1008–1029.

Carrion, V., & Lock, J. (1997). The coming out process: Developmental stages for sexual minority youth. *Clinical Child Psychology and Psychiatry, 2*, 369–377.

Cass, V. C. (1979). Homosexual identity formation: A theoretical model. *Journal of Homosexuality, 4*, 219–235.

Cass, V. C. (1984). Homosexual identity formation: Testing a theoretical model. *Journal of Sex Research, 20*, 143–167.

Charmaz, K. (2000). Grounded theory: Objectivist and constructivist methods. In N. Denzin & Y. Lincoln (Eds.), *Handbook of qualitative research* (2nd ed.) (pp. 509–535). London, England: Sage.

Charmaz, K. (2002). Qualitative interviewing and grounded theory analysis. In J. Gubrium & J. Holstein (Eds.), *Handbook of interview research: Context and method* (pp. 675–694). Thousand Oaks, CA: Sage.

Charmaz, K. (2006). *Constructing grounded theory: A practical guide through qualitative analysis.* Thousand Oaks, CA: Sage.

Chaudoir, S. R., & Fisher, J. D. (2010). The disclosure processes model. *Psychological Bulletin, 136*, 236–256.

Coleman, E. (1982). Developmental stages of the coming-out process. In W. Paul, J. D. Weinrich, J. C. Gonsiorek, & M. E. Hotvedt (Eds.), *Homosexuality: Social, psychological and biological issues* (pp. 150–158). Beverly Hills, CA: Sage.

Daly, K. J. (2007). *Qualitative methodology for family studies and human development.* Thousand Oaks, CA: Sage.

Darby-Mullins, P., & Murdock, T. B. (2007). The influence of family environment factors on self-acceptance and emotional adjustment among gay, lesbian, and bisexual adolescents. *Journal of GLBT Family Studies, 3*, 75–91.

D'Augelli, A. R. (1994). Identity development and sexual orientation: Toward a model of lesbian, gay, and bisexual development. In E. J. Trickett, R. J. Watts, & D. Birman (Eds.), *Human diversity: Perspectives on people in context* (pp. 312–333). San Francisco, CA: Jossey-Bass.

D'Augelli, A. R. (2002). Mental health problems among lesbian, gay, and bisexual youths ages 14 to 21. *Clinical Child Psychology and Psychiatry, 7*, 433–456.

D'Augelli, A. R. (2006). Stress and adaptation among families of lesbian, gay, and bisexual youth: Research challenges. In J. J. Bigner (Ed.), *An introduction to LGBT family studies* (pp. 135–157). Binghamton, NY: The Haworth Press, Inc.

D'Augelli, A. R., Grossman, A. H., & Starks, M. T. (2005). Parents' awareness of lesbian, gay, and bisexual youths' sexual orientation. *Journal of Marriage and Family, 67*, 474–482.

D'Augelli, A. R., & Hershberger, S. L. (1993). Lesbian, gay and bisexual youth in community settings: Personal challenges and mental health. *American Journal of Community Psychology, 21*, 421–450.

D'Augelli, A. R., Hershberger, S. L., & Pilkington, N. W. (1998). Lesbian, gay, and bisexual youth and their families: Disclosure of sexual orientation and its consequences. *American Journal of Orthopsychiatry, 68*, 361–371.

D'Augelli, A. R., Hershberger, S. L., & Pilkington, N. W. (2001). Suicidality patterns and sexual orientation-related factors among lesbian, gay, and bisexual youths. *Suicide & Life-Threatening Behavior, 31*, 250–264.

Fields, J. (2001). Normal queers: Straight parents respond to their children's "coming out." *Symbolic Interaction, 24*, 165–187.

Geertz, C. (1973). *The interpretation of cultures*. New York, NY: Basic.

Gonzalez, K., Rostosky, S., Odom, R., & Riggle, E. (2013). The positive aspects of being the parent of an LGBTQ child. *Family Process, 52*, 325–337.

Goodrich, K. M. (2009). Mom and dad come out: The process of identifying as a heterosexual parent with a lesbian, gay, or bisexual child. *Journal of LGBT Issues in Counseling, 3*, 37–61.

Grafsky, E. L. (2011). *Qualitative research on family disclosure and substance use among SMY*. Unpublished doctoral dissertation, The Ohio State University, Columbus, OH.

Herdt, G., & Koff, B. (2000). *Something to tell you: The road families travel when a child is gay*. New York, NY: Columbia University Press.

Hershberger, S. L., & D'Augelli, A. R. (1995). The impact of victimization on the mental health and suicidality of lesbian, gay, and bisexual youths. *Developmental Psychology, 31*, 65–74.

Human Rights Campaign. (2012). *Growing up LGBT in America*. Retrieved from http://www.hrc.org/files/assets/resources/Growing-Up-LGBT-in-America_Report.pdf

Johnson, T. W., & Colucci, P. (1999). Lesbians, gay men, and the family life cycle. In B. Carter & M. McGoldrick (Eds.), *The expanded family life cycle: Individual, family, and social perspectives* (3rd ed., pp. 346–361). Needham Heights, MA: Allyn & Bacon.

Kuhar, R. (2007). The family secret: Parents of homosexual sons and daughters. In R. Kuhar, & J. Takács (Eds.), *Beyond the pink curtain. Everyday life of GLBT people in Eastern Europe* (pp. 35–48). Slovenia: The Peace Institute.

Laird, J. (1993). Lesbian and gay families. In F. Walsh (Ed.), *Normal family processes* *(2nd ed.*, pp. 282–328). New York, NY: Guilford.

LaRossa, R., & Reitzes, D. C. (1993). Symbolic interactionism and family studies. In P. Boss, W. Doherty, R. LaRossa, W. Schumm, & S. Steinmetz (Eds.), *Sourcebook of family theories and methods: A contextual approach* (pp. 135–163). New York, NY: Plenum Press.

Lee, M. M., & Lee, R. E. (2006). The voices of accepting and supportive parents of gay sons: Towards an ecosystemic strengths model. *Journal of GLBT Family Studies, 2,* 1–27.

Lincoln, Y., & Guba, E. (1985). *Naturalistic inquiry.* Newbury Park, CA: Sage.

Merighi, J. R., & Grimes, M. D. (2000). Coming out to families in a multicultural context. *Families in Society, 81,* 32–41.

Murray, H. (2010). *Not in this family: Gays and the meaning of kinship in postwar North America.* Philadelphia, PA: University of Pennsylvania Press.

Newman, B. S., & Muzzonigro, P. G. (1993). The effects of traditional values on the coming out process of gay male adolescents. *Adolescence, 28,* 213–226.

Olson, D. (2011). FACES IV and the circumplex model: Validation study. *Journal of Marital and Family Therapy, 37,* 64–80.

Patton, M. (1990). Purposeful sampling. In M. Patton (Ed.), *Qualitative evaluation and research methods* (2nd ed., (pp.169–186). Newbury Park, CA: Sage.

Pew Research Center. (2011). *Beyond red vs. blue: Political typology.* Retrieved from http://www.people-press.org/files/legacy-pdf/Beyond-Red-vs-Blue-The-Political-Typology.pdf

Pew Research Center. (2013). *The global divide on homosexuality; Greater acceptance in more secular and affluent countries.* Retrieved from http://www.pewglobal.org/2013/06/04/the-global-divide-on-homosexuality/

Phillips, M. J., & Ancis, J. R. (2008). The process of identity development as the parent of a lesbian or gay male. *Journal of LGBT Issues in Counseling, 2,* 126–158.

Potoczniak, D., Crosbie-Burnett, M., & Saltzburg, N. (2009). Experiences regarding coming out to parents among African American, Hispanic, and white gay, lesbian, bisexual, transgender, and questioning adolescents. *Journal of Gay & Lesbian Social Services, 21,* 189–205.

Robinson, B. E., Walters, L. H., & Skeen, P. (1989). Response of parents to learning that their child is homosexual and concern over AIDS: A national study. *Journal of Homosexuality, 18*(1–2), 59–80.

Rosario, M., Hunter, J., Maguen, S., Gwadz, M., & Smith, R. (2001). The coming-out process and its adaptational and health-related associations among gay, lesbian, and bisexual youths: Stipulation and exploration of a model. *American Journal of Community Psychology, 29,* 133–160.

Rubin, H. J., & Rubin, I. S. (2005). *Qualitative interviewing: The art of hearing data (2nd ed.).* Thousand Oaks, CA: Sage Publications.

Russell, S. T., Driscoll, A. K., & Truong, N. (2002). Adolescent same-sex romantic attractions and relationships: Implications for substance use and abuse. *American Journal of Public Health, 92,* 198–202.

Ryan, C., Huebner, D., Diaz, R. M., & Sanchez, J. (2009). Family rejection as a predictor of negative health outcomes in white and Latino lesbian, gay, and bisexual young adults. *Pediatrics, 123,* 346–352.

Ryan, C., Russell, S. T., Huebner, D., Diaz, R., & Sanchez, J. (2010). Family acceptance in adolescence and the health of LGBT young adults. *Journal of Child and Adolescent Psychiatric Nursing, 23*, 205–213.

Saewyc, E. M. (2011). Research on adolescent sexual orientation: Development, health disparities, stigma, and resilience. *Journal of Research on Adolescence, 21*, 256–272.

Safren, S. A., & Heimberg, R. G. (1999). Depression, hopelessness, suicidality, and related factors in sexual minority and heterosexual adolescents. *Journal of Consulting and Clinical Psychology, 67*, 859–866.

Saltzburg, S. (2004). Learning that an adolescent child is gay or lesbian: The parent experience. *Social Work, 49*, 109–118.

Savin-Williams, R. C. (1994). Verbal and physical abuse as stressors in the lives of lesbian, gay male, and bisexual youths: Associations with school problems, running away, substance abuse, prostitution, and suicide. *Journal of Consulting and Clinical Psychology, 62*, 261–269.

Savin-Williams, R. C. (2001). A critique of the research on sexual-minority youths. *Journal of Adolescence, 24*, 5–13.

Savin-Williams, R. C., & Ream, G. L. (2003). Sex variations in the disclosure to parents of same-sex attractions. *Journal of Family Psychology, 17*, 429–438.

Smith, M. C., Bibi, U., & Sheard, D. E. (2003). Evidence for the differential impact of time and emotion on personal and event memories for September 11, 2001. *Applied Cognitive Psychology, 17*, 1047–1055.

Sullivan, M., & Wodarski, J. S. (2002). Social alienation in gay youth. *Journal of Human Behavior in the Social Environment, 5*, 1–17.

Troiden, R. R. (1988). Homosexual identity development. *Journal of Adolescent Health Care, 9*, 105–113.

Troiden, R. R. (1989). The formation of homosexual identities. In G. Herdt (Ed.), *Gay and lesbian youth* (pp. 43–73). New York, NY: Hayworth.

Willoughby, B. L. B., Malik, N. M., & Lindahl, K. M. (2006). Parental reactions to their sons' sexual orientation disclosures: The roles of family cohesion, adaptability, and parenting style. *Psychology of Men and Masculinity, 7*, 14–26.

Suffering As the Path to Acceptance: Parents of Gay and Lesbian Young People Negotiating Catholicism in Italy

CHIARA BERTONE
University of East Piedmont, Alessandria, Italy

MARINA FRANCHI
London School of Economics, London, England

This article investigates the experiences of parents of gay men and lesbians (GL) as they negotiate the influential Catholic discourse on homosexuality in Italy, and their Catholic belonging and practice. The analysis is based upon in-depth interviews with 46 parents of gay and lesbian people. We explore how parents who are heavily involved in the religious community negotiate their role within it, but also how, more generally, parents frame their notions of what it means to be lesbian or gay in relation to Catholic discourse. Parents draw upon different, and often seemingly contradictory, cultural repertoires in order to combine, negotiate, or integrate what public discourse constructs as irreconcilable positions: acceptance of gay and lesbian lives and identities and Catholic belonging. The notion of the homosexual as being destined to undergo suffering provides room for acceptance of their child's sexual identity whilst preserving heteronormative assumptions. This frame constitutes an alternative to rejection, which is at odds with parents' ideas of the family as being based on unconditional love. It also provides a bridge with therapeutic culture and narratives of liberation from suffering that inform, especially, middle-class family relations and the cultural resources available to them.

INTRODUCTION

Organised religions have, in many contexts, a crucial role in framing sexual orientations outside the heterosexual norm as a social problem and in upholding social hostility. For the Catholic countries of Southern Europe, this conflict has been especially relevant in structuring public debates (Santos, 2013) in which the Catholic Church is commonly identified as a main antagonist of gay and lesbian struggles for a more inclusive sexual citizenship. In the case of Spain, Pichardo Galán (2009) has argued that social and legal change was achieved by challenging the Catholic Church on its own terrain as the guardian of family values.

Parents of lesbian and gay children stand in a critical position with regard to this conflict. Previous research, mainly based in the United States, shows that religion is a central issue for them. It represents a source of tension and difficulty, but is also a resource that provides them with the moral authority to set conditions for the acceptance of their children, and legitimises their engagement in advocating for rights on behalf of their children (Broad, Crawley, & Foley, 2004). In the ways that parents make sense of the relationship between their religious identity and the acceptance of their child's sexual orientation, we can potentially find, on one side, a challenge to current framings of the conflict between religion and gay and lesbian (GL) claims for recognition, and on the other side, a potential for neutralizing the challenges GL experiences may raise for the privileging of heterosexuality that is a founding principle of Catholic power (Fassin, 2010).

The almost unquestioned religious monopoly of the Catholic Church in Italy makes it a very specific context for looking at these dynamics. Based on 46 in-depth interviews with Italian parents of children who came out to them as gay or lesbian between the ages of 14 and 22, this article explores how these parents dealt with Catholic discourses on homosexuality.[1] We investigate in particular which cultural resources these parents mobilize to make sense of their relationship with Catholicism as accepting parents of gay and lesbian children. In so doing we draw upon Swidler's (1986, 2001) notion of culture as a "toolkit" which people use to construct their strategies of action.

The discovery of their child's lesbian or gay identity requires parents to address unexpected problems of action since a taken-for-granted element of their scenario, heterosexuality, has been disrupted. This is emphasised when they have to address this disruption in relation to a religiosity which, as interpreted by Christian Churches, is grounded upon the privileging and naturalisation of heterosexuality itself. As Swidler (1986) argues, actors having to face unsettling situations can engage in innovative interpretations and combinations of action repertoires that are otherwise taken for granted and reproduced. The parents we interviewed have to address this challenge not in terms of an abstract need to adjust their value orientation but in relation to very concrete questions, regarding, for instance, which rules of behaviour to enforce with one's gay or lesbian child, whether and how to come out as a parent of a lesbian or gay child in the local community, and how to modify the forms and meanings of their church attendance.

Parents' strategies show us the possibilities of combining contradictory elements of different cultural repertoires, while helping us to identify the common frames underlying seemingly divergent understandings. Investigating these strategies, therefore, proves useful for looking beyond what appears in public discourse as an irreconcilable opposition between the critical stance of gay, lesbian, bisexual, and transgender (GLBT) movements and pro-gay groups, and the religiously fed homophobia that is particularly associated with the Catholic Church.

PERSPECTIVES ON SEXUALITY AND RELIGION

While embodying the privileges of heterosexuality, the parents we interviewed share with their children a position within the "family closet" (Švab & Kuhar, in this issue), bearing the contagious invisibility and stigmatisation implied by homosexuality. In interpreting their accounts we therefore need to draw on literature and research addressing different issues: first, the strategies that lesbian and gay individuals develop to negotiate their religious and sexual identities; second, how heterosexual religious believers position themselves in relation to inclusionary or exclusionary practices in religious congregations; and third, how parents deal with the discovery of their child(ren)'s lesbian or gay identity.

Negotiating Lesbian and Gay Identities

The growing interest in the conflicting relations between organised religions and lesbian and gay identities and politics in the past few decades has led to a focus on the experiences of those lesbians and gay men that define themselves as belonging to a religious faith. This attention corresponds to the growing visibility of lesbian and gay religious groups and their claims for recognition by, and inclusion within, their religious communities. A wealth of different perspectives investigates both the cultural strategies fostered by support groups and the resources individuals draw on to make sense of the tension between their sexual and religious identities, which are often depicted as irreconcilable positions.

As Thumma (1991) shows in her investigation of an American gay Evangelical group, both religious and sexual identities can be perceived as core identities that are impossible to relinquish. Drawing on the notion of cognitive dissonance, she analyses the material produced by the organisation as well as the experiences of those who came into contact with it. She unveils the cultural resources deployed to reconcile the two previously dissonant religious and sexual identities into a new Gay Evangelical Christian core identity. The process of socialisation into the new identity involves a devaluation of the former state in which the two identities were conflicting and causing individual suffering. By constructing this as preventing people from becoming "whole" Christians, reconciliation is followed by the reward of achieving a truer sense of the integrated multiple self. A sense of truthfulness and righteousness is reinforced through the presentation of the new identity as part of an oppressed minority opposed to both other unwelcoming Christian communities, and to gay communities that stigmatize religious belonging.

The motivations for identity integration provided by the organisation largely resonate with the ones Yip identifies in his work on gay and lesbian Catholics' relations with the Catholic Church (1997b), and on gay Christians (1997a). In investigating the data collected from the postal questionnaires and interviews of 60 gay male Christians in the United Kingdom, Yip (1997a) analyses how his interviewees developed "an alternative vocabulary of moral motives that label their sexuality and lifestyle as compatible with Christianity" (p. 117). Drawing on the notion of stigma management (Goffman, 1963), he identifies four strategies that function not only to sustain his interviewees' identities as gay Christians, but also to undermine the stigmatizing power of the Church.

The first strategy, *attacking the stigma*, consists of an appropriation of the power to interpret and negotiate the Scriptures in order to challenge the condemnation of same-gender sexual behaviour that is based upon them. Basic Christian principles, in particular the value of acceptance of all people and the value of nonjudgement of others, are invoked in opposition to a literal interpretation of the Scriptures. In so doing, the authority of the official Church as sole interpreter of the Scriptures' proclamations on homosexuality is undermined. This corresponds to a second strategy, *attacking the stigmatizer*, in which the Church is deemed unworthy to be "a moral guardian" as its position with regard to sexual minorities is replete with prejudice and incoherence when compared to the position held by welcoming grassroots organizations. However, whilst these two strategies attack one institution, the Church, they do not question one of its basic features, namely the privilege conferred to another institution, heterosexuality. The third strategy consists of *using positive personal experience*, whereby participants define stable loving relationships as complying with Christian values, and assert that partnerships should be evaluated on the basis of their quality and not of their sexual form. The fourth strategy then is to refer to *ontogeneric arguments*, by defining one's sexual orientation as given by God and therefore unquestionable and unchangeable. These strategies, Yip (1997a) argues, imply the rejection of the official Church whose recognition is no longer needed, but not of "Christianity as a spiritual pursuit" (p. 122).

With stronger attention to gender and race differences and to straight church members, McQueeney (2009) draws on Swidler's (1986) notion of "cultural toolkits" to trace three strategies used by lesbian, gay, and "straight-but-affirming" church members to "construct and perform good Christian Identities" in two U.S. Protestant Churches (pp. 157–158). The most common strategy consists of normalizing their sexuality by invoking and enacting Christian notions of manhood, motherhood, and monogamy, thereby accommodating "heteronormative notions (...) while refusing to assimilate (eg. through abstinence, heterosexuality or 'aversion therapy')" (p. 160). This strategy resonates with the one discussed by Yip (1997a) regarding the use of personal positive experience, that highlights a shift in emphasis from "the *nature* of the sexuality" to "the *manner* in which it is expressed" (p. 123). McQueeney (2009) highlights the ambivalence of such a strategy that enables GL members to claim their belonging, which is per se destabilizing for some religious communities, while relying heavily on the exclusion of those who do not comply with this performance. Some black, working-class lesbians minimized their sexual identity, rather than redefining it. In this way, they achieved inclusion but left Church-based discourses on the immorality of homosexuality unchallenged.

Finally, McQueeney (2009) identifies a moralising strategy, consisting of turning the stigma attached to homosexuality from a curse into a blessing by performing a mission to save lesbian or gay souls. It was shared by a few black lesbians and gay men, and by white, middle-class "straight-but-affirming" members, many of them parents of lesbian or gay children, who claimed a moral authority in their "special calling, as straight allies, to make Christianity more inclusive" (p. 167). The implications of the strategies discussed so far in terms of depoliticisation and reproduction of sexual and class hierarchies correspond very much to what research focusing on parents of GL children has argued.

Supporting from the Outside

Research investigating the perspective of heterosexuals has mainly focused on how religion influences their attitudes towards issues surrounding same-gender sexual behaviour (Olson, Cadge, & Harrison, 2006; about Italy, see Garelli, Guizzardi, & Pace, 2003; Garelli, 2011; Barbagli, Dalla Zuanna, & Garelli, 2010), and on their compliance with, or distance from, church doctrine. Deeper and more nuanced analyses are provided by studies exploring how people develop and negotiate their beliefs in everyday life, and how they make sense of the tensions and contradictions which many experience when taking an inclusive stand towards gay and lesbian people (Maher, Sever, & Pichler, 2008; Walls, 2010).

In his ethnographic research on how members of two United Methodist congregations (a liberal and a conservative one) deal with the highly controversial issue of homosexuality, Moon (2004) looks at how people develop their "everyday theologies" through social interaction, by reflecting "on a wide range of inspirational texts, conversations, personal experiences, and understandings of their God" in their daily life, in order to "make sense of a changing world in terms of what they already knew as God's truth" (pp. 13–14). Moon identifies in *narratives of pain* the crucial cultural tool that the people he interviewed draw upon to define their position towards the inclusion of gay men and lesbians in the Church. He highlights how narratives of pain cut across the liberal versus conservative divide, providing the frame for both antigay and pro-gay arguments, by assigning to the Church the duty to provide healing to their suffering. Suffering is recognised as part of the experience of GL individuals, although its causes, and the solutions identified to heal it, are different: for the antigay movement, at homosexuality's core is a pathology that ought to be cured; for the pro-gay movement, homophobia's causes are to be traced to sociocultural (including the Church's) stigmatization and exclusion, and the remedy is an inclusive attitude.

This language of emotions is outspokenly used to deny more conflictual, "political" meanings of issues regarding lesbians' and gay men's lives. The threatening potential of the more defiant and provocative expressions of the GLBT movements is neutralised by interpreting them as symptoms of pain, as a reaction to social rejection. Hence, the language of pain allows the inclusion of gay men and lesbians in the Church, while reproducing the relations of power that provide straight members with a privileged position. It is not by chance, Moon notices, that the language of pain is linked to a "child imagery," representing the role of the Church as that of loving parents towards their suffering children. In a position of relative power, heterosexuals create *feeling rules* (Hochschild, 1979), defining pain as a "moral entrance fee for gay men's and lesbians' admission to the church" (Moon, 2005, p. 332), where they can obtain comfort, not equality. These narratives resonate at the same time with Christian notions of pain "as something which is bad to cause, good to alleviate, and righteous to experience" (p. 331), and with therapeutic culture. The cultural resonance between those two discourses has also been pointed out by other scholars such as Illouz (2008), who has shown the constitutive role that suffering has acquired in narratives of the self shaped by therapeutic culture. She argues, in fact, that therapeutic culture builds upon a paradox: given its imperative to strive for higher levels of self-realisation, despite its apparent vocation to heal, it "must generate a narrative structure in which suffering and victimhood actually define the self" (p. 173).

Parents at the Crossroads

In the scarce sociological literature based on empirical research with the parents of gay and lesbian people, studies have mainly addressed the discourses and experiences of activists within parents' organisations, in particular the U.S. organisation PFLAG (Parents, Families and Friends of Lesbians and Gays). As Broad, Crawley, and Foley (2004) show, representing itself as strongly linked to religious communities allows PFLAG to claim to be the legitimate interpreter of "real family values." The organisation frames an opposition between the Religious Right and its morally illegitimate discourses driving families apart and misinterpreting Christianity on the one side, and its own position as real interpreters of the Christian values of familial and community love and inclusion on the other side. The essentialist explanation of homosexuality is used to legitimate this claim to inclusion, supporting parents' argument that homosexuality is God-given, and therefore cannot be sinful.

In their analysis of advice books for parents of gay and lesbian children, Martin, Hutson, Kazyak, and Scherrer (2010) show how parents' need to reconcile their religious identity with acceptance of their children's sexual identities is addressed as a crucial issue. They argue that a common feature underlies the different strategies to achieve acceptance that are proposed by these books, namely a pressure towards normalisation, which they define as a minimizing of "those aspects of homosexuality that might prove difficult to integrate into the heteronormative family context" (p. 12). Normalisation is set as the condition for reconciliation. This study also identifies in therapeutic discourse a more general frame informing the cultural tools offered to parents both by books taking an antigay position and endorsing change therapies, and by those supporting acceptance of homosexuality. All the books, including those by PFLAG, describe the experience of knowing about a child being gay or lesbian as "a traumatic occurrence for parents" in terms of grief, which is often interpreted by referring to psychological models, like the one proposed by Kübler-Ross (1969), and suggest that parents should seek expert help, or self-help settings, in order to deal with the process of grieving. Although some research on parents has actually questioned its universality (Beeler & DiProva, 1999), the grieving model remains central in framing the shared narrative proposed by parents' organisations and much of the research on parents from the helping professions (Aveline, 2006). Broad (2011) also identifies grief and love as two different "emotional framings of coming out," relating to two aspects of PFLAG's work, namely self-help and advocacy. This shows how "the emotional framing of advocacy as love works because it emotionally resonates for parents coming out of grief" (p. 411), constructing narratives for parents that parallel GL stories.

CATHOLICISM AND SEXUALITY IN ITALY

In order to understand the peculiarity of Catholicism in Italy, we will start by laying out the position of the Catholic Church with regard to homosexuality, and then read it in relation to the presence of representatives of the Catholic

Church within public debates, with particular regard to gay and lesbian rights. The position of the Catholic Church can be traced within the Catechism which defines homosexual tendencies as "objectively disordered" and homosexual acts as "intrinsically disordered" since they are contrary to the law of nature (Catechism: 2357–2358). Lesbians and gay men ought to be chaste; this sacrifice is defined as a way of fulfilling God's will "and, if they are Christians, to unite to the sacrifice of the Lord's Cross the difficulties they may encounter from their condition" (Catechism: 2358). Support to lesbians and gay men ought to be given; however, it must always be stated that same-sex sexual acts are immoral (Ratzinger, 1986). This somewhat ambivalent position is replicated in the Church's condemnation of violence against lesbians and gay men. While homophobic violence is defined as "deplorable," it is also hinted that violent acts can be the result of an increased condoning of homosexuality, since disorderly acts generate disordered violence (Fassin, 2010).

Since the beginning of the twentieth century, while the successes of gay and lesbian movements in terms of rights and public recognition increased in the West, the Catholic Church became more and more vocal in the public arena. The geographical proximity of the Vatican State, the influence it has in Italian politics, and the endorsement of politicians who hold the position of the Church, are peculiar traits of the Italian context (Bernini, 2008; Ross, 2009). In the years 2006 to 2008, when most of the interviews analysed here were collected, in Italy the centre-left government discussed the legal recognition of same-sex cohabiting couples. Such a possibility was met with high levels of criticism from the Catholic Church hierarchies. The traits of the doctrine described earlier migrated into the public debate as uncompromising positions that, translated into the media discourse, became vociferous attacks framed through "homosexuality against nature" and "homosexuality as incest and paedophilia." At the same time, these years witnessed the unfolding of the so-called paedophilia scandal within the Catholic Church, which in Italy broke out following Church pressure to prevent the broadcasting of a BBC documentary (Tulli, 2010).

While the role of the Catholic Church in Italy is undoubtedly strong and Italy remains one of the most Catholic countries in Europe, Garelli (2007) highlights how the process of secularisation has not spared Italy and has resulted in a decreasing number of regularly practising Catholics. Most importantly, it is in the area of the family and sexual morality that it is possible to trace a growing gap between the Church's official positions and the stance of Catholic believers in Italy. This growing divergence from the official position of the Catholic Church, however, is taking the form of more individualised interpretations from within rather than of a search for alternative religious communities (Garelli, 2011). In fact, although a more individualised access to spirituality is gaining ground, it largely remains linked to the cultural heritage of Catholicism (Palmisano, 2011).

With regard to family and sexual morals, Catholic believers distance themselves from the doctrinal position and claim autonomy of judgement and behaviour, but not from the Church as such (Garelli, 2011). People simply live with this contradiction. Socio-demographic differences have to be taken into account, however, since an individualised approach to spirituality is more present amongst the well-educated, younger people, and men.

DATA AND METHOD

The interviews analysed in this article were collected within the project "Family Matters. Supporting Families to Prevent Violence Against Gay and Lesbian Youth," which targeted the parents of young gays and lesbians between the ages of 14 and 22 years old, or those whose child(ren) came out as gay or lesbian within that age range (Bertone & Franchi, 2008; see also Cappellato & Mangarella in this issue). The research comprised a national survey and in-depth interviews.[2]

Participants and Recruitment

We relied on personal networks as well as on the support of various organisations. The main national parents' association AGEDO (*Associazione Genitori di Omosessuali*; Association of Parents of Gay Men and Lesbians) and its volunteers, as well as other GLBT associations at national and local level, have been key resources to get in contact with participants. We also publicised the research on various media and online resources. In this article we analyse the accounts collected from 34 mothers and 12 fathers, who defined their children as either gay (25) or lesbian (10), excluding bisexual or queer identities. We were able to collect interviews with some of these children, who also identified as gay (12) or lesbian (6).

Bisexuality was actually a controversial issue within the parents' organisation through which almost half of our sample was recruited, and an invisible one among the other parents. The prevalence among these parents of an essentialist view on sexual orientation, as we will see, can explain these results. Addressing experiences related to bisexuality and more fluid gender and sexual identities would have required a specific attention that was beyond the scope of our exploratory study.

As expected, we came into contact with a highly self-selected sample of parents who were not only willing to discuss their children's sexual orientation but also whose narratives were very much stories of acceptance. Unlike similar research, however, our sample comprises experiences that are both within and outside support organisations. Only eight of the parents interviewed are active members of AGEDO while 11 never had any contact with the organisation. Twenty-one parents, at the time of the interview, lived in the Centre South of Italy while 25 lived in the north of the country. Information on practice and religious belonging was mainly prompted by questions about participants' religious education and their current relationship with religion, and by their opinion about the position of the Catholic Church with regard to homosexuality. The information allowed us to identify some distinctions in the level of religious attendance amongst the majority who define themselves as Catholic (29): 10 parents (4 of which were fathers) go to Church regularly at least once a week, 6 practice occasionally (5 of which were mothers), and 13 (10 of which were mothers) can be defined as non-practicing Catholics. Finally, 17 parents define themselves as non-Catholic, either atheist or agnostic. While interviews reveal that parents relate differently to religious belonging and spirituality, the issue of the role of Catholicism, in particular in relation to the specific role of the Catholic Church in Italy, is recognised as important by almost all of them.

Data Analysis

The semistructured interviews were aimed at collecting accounts about family practices (Orbuch, 1997), reconstructing their features and meanings, and their changes in time. The interviews were recorded, transcribed, and coded using the ATLAS.ti software. This article is based on a thematic analysis focusing more specifically upon parents' accounts concerning their ways of dealing with spirituality, religion, and the Catholic Church.

LOVE AS THE PATH TO ACCEPTANCE

I got closer to God and in a fight with the Church. Once my son went to confession and the priest told him to see a psychiatrist. So I went [to see the priest] after some days and I told him (...) to get informed, so that they could really help these guys, because they were killing them instead. Then I found a young priest and I asked him to talk to my son, because he needed to be accepted and he told me he would do so. Then I got to know that he told [my son] that being homosexual he was a sinner like the Mary Magdalene and like a drug addict.(...) Then once I confided in an older woman, who told me that it was a God's grace, and I answered her "well..." and she told me that it was something natural. Those words gave me a boost. I can say that it is really through my faith that I found the courage to fight for homosexuality, to come out not giving a damn about anything in order to help those kids.(...) I was also granted absolution from a priest who helped me, a spiritual father.(...) Then one day (...) he gave a homily in which he destroyed homosexuals, saying that they confuse the gastrointestinal tract with the vagina: at that point I saw him as a monster.(...) Then I went to another priest who denied me the absolution.(...) They told me to welcome my son, to love him, but not to accept the fact that he could have a sexual relation. But that was impossible to me, because if I accept him, I accept him as he is. How can I tell someone to repress his sexual instincts? (...) Then I managed to find a priest who welcomed me with open arms and told me that I was doing right, to keep fighting for those kids, that he shared my choice, and he granted me absolution. Really though those have been very difficult years.

This account is from a highly educated mother living in a Southern Italian city. She has a gay son, Alessio. Her account is illustrative of both the struggle with, and the quest for acceptance from, the Catholic Church that only a few of our interviewed parents actually engaged with. At the same time, this mother also plainly states what marks for virtually all of our parents, notwithstanding their different relation with religion, the fundamental source of conflict with the Church. Parents define their acceptance in terms of unconditional love for their child (Bertone, 2013), framing it as incompatible with the official position of the Catholic Church. The acceptance of lesbians and gay men allowed by Catholic doctrine, conditional upon condemnation of enacting one's sexual desires, is deemed impossible. The underlying assumption is that sexuality is a natural and fundamental expression of one's self. Once their children have discovered and disclosed their true sexuality and way of loving, parents cannot but accept this truth and indeed value this unveiling of their children's authentic selves.

What lies beneath this conflict seems to be the opposition Swidler (2001) identifies between two understandings of the self in relation to love. Among the narratives analysed we rarely find a notion of love—and sexuality—based on the control of one's will, a notion that can be ascribed to a "Christian disciplined self" that would position parents in complete coherence with the Catholic Church's catechism. Rather, parents' perception of their child's potential to develop love—and sexual relationships—recalls a notion of the self informed by the "therapeutic ethic": knowing and respecting who you really are is the only way to develop authentic and enduring relationships.

As Illouz (2007) has remarked, the ability to draw upon therapeutic culture to make sense of one's experiences—what she calls "emotional capital"—is not evenly distributed among social classes. Accordingly, the parents we interviewed appear differently equipped with cultural tools enabling them to make sense of their child(ren)'s coming out (Bertone, 2013) and to redefine their position in relation to religious belonging. Some of the parents, particularly those with higher levels of education, talk in terms of a continuity in their reflexive attitude towards both religion and family relations, which they simply apply to deal with the new situation. This attitude allows them to integrate a therapeutic approach to family relations with a notion of Christian love also based upon the value of authenticity:

real love implies letting others express themselves and live according to their authentic needs.

In other narratives, parents represent themselves as having no rules, no roles, and no constructive language (De Vine, 1984) to face the discovery that their child was gay or lesbian. Following a pattern that Swidler (1986) has singled out, as people generally do when their life is unsettled, these parents look for new systems of meanings that can help them establish innovative strategies of action. Expert knowledge, in the form of psychological professional help or self-help material (the latter being used more among middle- and upper-class parents), is one of the main sources of help parents seek out. Another main resource is the encounter with AGEDO, experienced by approximately half of all parents interviewed. AGEDO's advice material (Dall'Orto & Dall'Orto, 2005) and practice are largely informed by therapeutic culture and a notion of authentic love.

Some of the parents in our research, mostly the practicing Catholics, have searched within the Church for a way to make sense of their acceptance of homosexuality. Rather than an autonomous system of meanings, however, they found open-minded priests and other Catholic friends and relatives taking up a discourse on love which resonates with the system of beliefs that these parents have acquired from other sources, mainly from a therapeutic culture. Our sample did not include members of small dissident Catholic communities, often pro-gay, which are operating in Italy (Quaranta, 2008), although the discourse they produce is mentioned as an important inspiration by some of the parents. It is in that material that they appear to find the tools to further confirm their distancing from the official position of the Catholic hierarchies. Our sample did not include parents supporting reparative therapies either; these therapies, often sustained within religious communities, appear in fact incoherent with a narrative based on seeking and accepting the true self embedded in the therapeutic culture that clearly prevails in the accounts we analysed.

A consequence of this narrative that appears unavoidable to the parents we interviewed is that their loving attitude cannot be confined to their own child. It requires that they redefine homosexuality as something generally acceptable, implying that all lesbian and gay children should be welcomed within families and within society at large, allowing them to enact what McQueeney (2009) has described as a moralizing strategy. Because of the strongly exclusionary position of the Church, and its implications in terms of the social stigmatization and social exclusion suffered by gay and lesbian people, same-sex sexual orientation appears a much more conflictual issue than other aspects of sexual ethics, such as contraception. Embracing an attitude of acceptance requires an active engagement in redefining both the meanings of homosexuality, and the meanings attached to one's religious belonging, making the position of parents similar in this respect to that of lesbian and gay Christians.

There are, however, some parents who neither engage in a redefinition of their general position towards homosexuality, nor in a criticism of the Church's role as the guardian of sexual morals. Sharing low levels of education and a greater cultural distance from therapeutic understandings of the self, these parents do not challenge the Church's authority or question their religious belonging; neither, though, do they question their love and support for their children. It does not appear necessary, or possible, for them to address the contradictions that may arise from this juxtaposition. As we have argued elsewhere (Bertone, 2013), however, their children do not necessarily experience them as less accepting, but just as parents letting their offspring take their own road.

REDEFINING CHRISTIAN LOVE AND RELIGIOUS BELONGING

The parents taking a conflictual stance with the positions of the Catholic Church on same-gender sexual behaviour, including some of those who define themselves as non-believers, tend to justify their criticisms by calling upon a notion of real Christian love that requires loving, welcoming inclusion, in opposition to an attitude of inhuman, merciless exclusion ascribed to the Church.

> *... it is one of those instances in which fear prevailed over... over favouring every situation in which there is love; in other words, putting limits instead of fostering good things. (Father of Maurizio, practicing)*

This opposition is also used to narrate experiences of breaking away from other Catholic rules regarding sexual and family morals. Several divorced women indeed recall their personal, painful experiences of stigmatization by the local Catholic community.

Part of parents' criticism concerns the public role of the Church, also censured by a majority of Italian Catholics (Garelli, 2011). The influence of the Church upon public discourse and politics is deemed responsible for gay and lesbian people's lack of civil rights and social recognition. A very direct power to reinforce social exclusion and stigmatisation is also recognised in the Church, especially in smaller local communities:

> *I am upset by the Church, because you should think of a small village, in the inland of the Apennine Mountains in the South of Italy. (...) It should be the Church of love and acceptance. (...) Since today it is argument of discussion, [the Church] should open the discussion, they should be the first that... ehm... I mean, and then attitudes would change.(...) But if the Church is already... discriminates against them, makes them feel*

guilty, etcetera, what is the old lady who lives on the top of the hill going to do? (Mother of Marino, nonpracticing)

The opposition between these parents' stance and the Church position is also defined in terms of honesty versus hypocrisy, which at the time of the interviews was interwoven with the outburst of media attention on the international scandal of paedophilia within the Catholic Church.

Them who cry out for humanity, who want to give to the poor, they don't even know where to find their humanity. (...) I think there is a lot of filth in there (...) in those places there are a lot of gays who have suppressed themselves. (Mother of Riccardo, practicing)

These criticisms of the Church remind us of the techniques of stigma management described by Yip (1997a). Unlike the mainly Protestant contexts that literature on the experiences of gay and lesbian Christians has explored, however, this questioning of Church doctrine does not take the form of an appropriation of the power to reinterpret the Scriptures, but rather of an overall criticism of the Church for not being "attuned with the message of love that underlies the whole Gospel" (father of Alessio, nonpracticing). A resistance to directly questioning the authority of the Church, however, can be found among some of the parents, irrespective of class differences: as the practicing mother of Tommaso says, "I don't agree (...) but I am not entitled to judge the priests."

The chief way for parents to keep recognising the spiritual authority of the Church despite their criticisms of its doctrine on homosexuality is to establish an opposition between the "official Church" and its "base." If the former is clearly identified in the Vatican, and in its most strongly censured form in the current Pope at the time of the study, Pope Benedict XVI, the latter is defined in more diverse ways. Some identify it in the parish context, while others refer to some "open-minded" priests, and still others speak more indeterminately about enlightened members of the clergy. We even found this distinction among some of the non-religious respondents who tend to balance their criticism of the Catholic hierarchy by mentioning positive experiences with local religious people. This is in line with recent research on religion that demonstrates how pervasive the Catholic culture is in Italy, and how esteem towards some charismatic Catholic figures is also widespread among nonbelievers (Garelli, 2011). Even some of the most critical parents we interviewed, in fact, provided their children with a Catholic education, including preparing them for First Communion.

Within this common frame, however, different strategies are enacted. Some of the parents engage in a search for a welcoming parish where they can finally find institutional recognition, which proves especially relevant for those looking for congruence between an acceptance of homosexuality and a strong sense of belonging to the Church. Exploring pluralism within the Catholic Church corresponds to what, in more religiously pluralist contexts, would take the form of choosing between different religious congregations. The quest of Alessio's mother, reported at the beginning of our analysis, allowed her at least temporarily to keep recognising the authority of representatives of the institution, to conform to the institution's rules by obtaining absolution, and to remain part of a Catholic community. Religious pluralism outside the Catholic Church, however, can be traced in our interviewees' narratives: besides a recurrent reference to Don Barbero, a dissident Catholic priest who has been banned from the Church but still leads his local community of faith practicing same-sex marriage (Quaranta, 2008), some of the parents mention as important their encounter with pro-gay Protestant denominations, in particular the Waldensian Church.

A second strategy consists of claiming a direct connection with God bypassing institutional mediation, while often keeping a self-definition as Catholics. An individualised relation with God (Wilcox, 2002), opposed to "bigotry," is invoked by some of the parents in order to justify either why they continue to go to church, or why they have withdrawn from church attendance. Tiziana's mother is an example of this strategy: distancing herself from her "bigot[ed]" education, she defines herself as "still in search because, I mean... to say I am Catholic.... Sure, I go to the mass but I think spirituality and religiosity are also outside of the Church... it is a very personal quest." This individualised relation with spirituality allows her to criticise the Church while continuing to define herself in a loose way as a practicing Catholic: "I think there are too extreme positions there, then for Heaven's sake, it's true that if one is Catholic, one has to abide to them, they are rules, but I find it too rigid, I can't find myself in this."

THE CONDITIONS OF PARENTAL ACCEPTANCE

A further, common strategy consists of reframing the issue of homosexuality itself by subsuming it under a heteronormative family frame. This strategy proves especially crucial for those parents striving to reconcile acceptance of their child's sexual identity and their own Catholic identity, and it appears linked to what Moon (2005) calls a "language of pain." The figure of the suffering homosexual is in fact a powerful resource to challenge the Catholic Church's public stance and its exclusionary implications for gay and lesbian people, in terms of social stigmatization and lack of legal recognition. It enables them to integrate a therapeutic notion of love and of the self and a Christian understanding of their commitment to alleviate their children's, and indeed all homosexuals', pain. An often used symbolic reference in the interviews is Mary Magdalene. She is evoked even when the declared final objective is to support a vision of full equality, as in the case of Fabio's mother, a practicing Catholic:

> *The Church as such doesn't practice what it preaches, because if we take facts into consideration, various readings of the Bible, of the Gospels... even Mary Magdalene herself was a sinner and Jesus forgave her. I mean, if Jesus was here those [kids] who are different would have been welcomed with open arms... because we should not care about diversity, but we should take into account that in front of God we are all the same... we are people... people who deserve respect as people.*

Parents can thereby position themselves as those who can help their child to take the path to a happier life, identified with a place at the heteronormative table (Ahmed, 2010), that is achievable through a romantic, stable, monogamous relationship, and its public recognition. This positioning allows most of the parents to argue for the inclusion of gay and lesbian people in society and in religious communities, while leaving the privilege and naturalisation of heterosexuality unquestioned. It thereby reproduces a hierarchy between them and their children, and entitles parents to establish a hierarchy between worthy (safe/happy) and unworthy (risky/unhappy) (homo)sexual lifestyles (Anderssen & Hellesund, 2009).

A fundamental premise of these hierarchies is the essentialist view of homosexuality, which most of our interviewees believe is inborn (a position shared by 83% of the respondents to the survey and by 88% of those who defined themselves as practicing Catholics). On these grounds, parents can discard the possibility of choice and change advocated by the Catholic Church, opposing to it their narrative about acceptance of the true self. Anchored in naturalization, this narrative of authenticity implies that sexual identities are stable and have clear boundaries, hence upholding a suspicious attitude towards bisexuality.

This narrative also implies conditions for public visibility: these parents are willing to ally with their children for the struggle towards legal and social recognition for an authentic love belonging to the private sphere of the couple. Practising Catholics in particular, among the parents we interviewed, show a concern with the boundaries between private and public space. While they often condemn the open interference of the Church in the public sphere, they also are keen on policing gay and lesbian behaviour beyond the boundaries of family life (see also Cappellato & Mangarella in this issue): from their son's or daughter's public expressions of their sexuality, to what are regarded as the excesses of the GLBT community in the public sphere, including mockery or criticism towards the Church.

> *I am annoyed when I see them [the Church] attack them [the homosexuals] in this way, because I think poor people (...) but I also think that sometimes*

> *homosexuals try to... and their various associations (...) to fight them, but in another way, they should speak about their values (...) they should be able to get into dialogue with them, but in a different way, without showing off....(Mother of Sofia, nonpracticing)*

There are only hints of parents engaging in questioning the hierarchies established by the discourse of suffering by taking up more conflictual framings through the emotion of rage or the language of justice. The mother of Arianna, who has distanced herself from her Catholic background while still feeling a religious "need," finds parallels between her daughter's experiences of discrimination and her past ones as a feminist and Communist. She evokes a turn from suffering to rage in talking about the positions of the Catholic Church on homosexuality:

> *... they made me suffer, a lot (...) a sort of rage has raised in my family; it wasn't there before, our family was never angry with anything, political life was also experienced quite lightly, in the sense that we had different positions (...) I had never thought of having a charge of rage and hatred, but sometimes I rediscover it. Surely I am angry, angry with society, angry with politics especially (...) the rage derives from the fact that I am convinced that we will never get these things [civil rights for gay and lesbian people]. (...) Knowing that the Church does not consider my daughter as normal (...) and that I should be keen on curing her, or I should feel discomfort, it is something that only those who experience it can understand.*

CONCLUSION

In the Italian context the public debate appears saturated with dichotomies that position homosexuality as the "other" to the concept of "family" (Trappolin, 2011) as well as the antagonistic subject to the Catholic Church and as a consequence to Catholicism more broadly. While the number of religious gay and lesbian groups in Italy is growing, their voices are rarely heard in the public arena. Seldom represented, they are treated as an anomaly de facto disempowering them of their disruptive potential (Franchi, 2012). Indeed, gay and lesbian religious groups occupy an ambivalent position that on one side perpetuates the role of an exclusionary institution, while on the other might disrupt it from within (McQueeney, 2009). A similar ambivalence can be traced in the analysis of the experiences of parents of gay and lesbian youths at the core of this work. Parents draw upon different, and often seemingly contradictory, cultural repertoires in order to combine, negotiate, or integrate what public discourse constructs as irreconcilable positions: acceptance of gay men and lesbians and Catholic belonging. When it is not relinquished, religious belonging allows them to develop a narrative of themselves as Catholic welcoming parents. The imperative of love, inspired by a therapeutic understanding and by a Christian notion of mercy, provides the crucial frame that makes these positions compatible. This frame allows them to subsume gay and lesbian lives within the narrative of family values and to reject their construction as "disordered" that is at the core of the official Catholic Catechism, a rejection that is often predicated on one side on questioning the moral authority of the official Church, and on the other on upholding the message of love and acceptance that they see as the core of the Christian faith. Profiting from the plurality of voices which exists among local communities, parents can find inspiration and the possibility of sharing this frame from within their Catholic belonging. Hence, both in their questioning of the authority of the official Church, as well as by repositioning as mandatory the acceptance of their lesbian and gay children, the parents interviewed can be perceived as changing from within the institution. In this respect, recent changes in the Catholic Church may make more space for their voices. The parents we interviewed could clearly identify the exclusionary, rigid position of the Catholic hierarchy as embodied in the former Pope, Benedict XVI. The new Pope's seeming embodiment of a more welcoming attitude towards differences might blur instead the opposition between a detached Catholic hierarchy and the communities of believers. At the same time, we can question to what extent an inclusion of parents' perspectives informed by a therapeutic frame, drawing upon a narrative of suffering and authenticity, can leave some of the fundamental premises upon which the privileging of heterosexuality is established in Catholicism unchallenged.

NOTES

1. Throughout the literature review *homosexuality* and *heterosexuality* will be used either to reflect the language deployed by the Catholic Church or when explicitly used by the authors we refer to. In the analytical section terms such as *homosexual* or *homosexuality* will be deployed when referring to the language and terminology used by the informants.
2. Two hundred thirteen questionnaires were collected.

REFERENCES

Ahmed, S. (2010). *The promise of happiness*. Durham [N.C.]: Duke University Press.

Anderssen, N., & Hellesund, T. (2009). Heteronormative Consensus in the Norwegian Same-Sex Adoption Debate? *Journal of Homosexuality*, 56(1), 102–120. doi: 10.1080/00918360802551597

Aveline, D. (2006). "Did I have blinders on or what?": Retrospective sense making by parents of gay sons recalling their sons' earlier years. *Journal of Family Issues*, 27(6), 777–802. doi: 10.1177/0192513×05285613

Barbagli, M., Dalla Zuanna, G., & Garelli, F. (2010). *La sessualità degli italiani [Italians' sexuality]*. Bologna, Italy: Il Mulino.

Beeler, J., & DiProva, V. (1999). Family adjustment following disclosure of homosexuality by a member: Themes discerned in narrative accounts. *Journal of Marital and Family Therapy*, 25, 443–459. doi: 10.1111/j.1752-0606.1999.tb00261.x

Bernini, S. (2008). Family politics: Political rhetoric and the transformation of family life in the Italian Second Republic. *Journal of Modern Italian Studies*, 13(3), 305–324. doi: 10.1080/13545710802218494

Bertone, C. (2013). Citizenship across generations: Struggles around heteronormativities. *Citizenship Studies*, 17(8), 985–999. doi: 10.1080/13621025.2013.851147

Bertone, C., & Franchi, M. (2008). The experiences of family members of gay and lesbian young people in Italy. In C. Bertone & M. Franchi (Eds.), *Family matters. Supporting families to prevent violence against gay and lesbian youth*. Alessandria, Italy: University of East Piedmont.

Broad, K. (2011). Coming out for parents, families and friends of lesbians and gays: From support group grieving to love advocacy. *Sexualities*, 14(4), 399–415. doi: 10.1177/1363460711406792

Broad, K. L., Crawley, S. L., & Foley, L. (2004). Doing "real family values": The interpretive practice of families in the GLBT movement. *The Sociological Quarterly*, 45(3), 509–527. doi: 10.2307/4120861

Cappellato, V., & Mangarella, T. (2014). Sexual citizenship in private and public space: Parents of gay men and lesbians discuss their experiences of Pride parades. *Journal of GLBT Family Studies*, 10(1–2), 211–230.

Dall'Orto, G., & Dall'Orto, P. (2005). *Figli diversi. New generation [Different Children. New generation]*. Casale Monferrato, Italy: Sonda.

De Vine, J. L. (1984). A systemic inspection of affectional preference orientation and the family of origin, *Journal of Social Work and Human Sexuality*, 2(2/3), 9–17. doi: 10.1300/J291V02N02_02

Fassin, E. (2010). Celibate priests, continent homosexuals. *Borderlands*, 9(3). Retrieved from www.borderlands.net.au

Franchi, M. (2012, December). *On the front line to defend life and (the Italian) family. The debate on the legal recognition of cohabiting couples in Italy (2006–2008)*. Paper presented at the meeting of INED, Paris.

Garelli, F. (2007a). The church and Catholicism in contemporary Italy. *Journal of Modern Italian Studies*, 12(1), 2–7. doi: 10.1080/13545710601132672

Garelli, F. (2011). *Religione all'italiana [Religion, the Italian way]*. Bologna, Italy: Il Mulino.

Garelli, F., Guizzardi, G., & Pace, E. (2003). *Un singolare pluralismo. Indagine sul pluralismo morale e religioso degli italiani [A peculiar pluralism. A study on Italians' moral and religious pluralism]*. Bologna, Italy: Il Mulino.

Goffman, E. (1963). *Stigma. Notes on the management of spoiled identity*. Englewood Cliffs, NJ: Prentice-Hall.

Hochschild, A. R. (1979). Emotion work, feeling rules, and social structure. *American Journal of Sociology*, 85(3), 551–575. doi: 10.2307/2778583

Illouz, E. (2007). *Cold intimacies: The making of emotional capitalism*. Cambridge, UK: Polity.

Illouz, E. (2008). *Saving the modern soul: Therapy, emotions, and the culture of self-help*. Berkeley, CA: University of California Press.

Kübler-Ross, E. (1969). *On death and dying*. London, England: Routledge.

Maher, M. J., Sever, L. M., & Pichler, S. (2008). How Catholic college students think about homosexuality: The connection between authority and sexuality. *Journal of Homosexuality*, 55(3), 325–349. doi: 10.1080/00918360802345065

Martin, K. A., Hutson, D. J., Kazyak, E., & Scherrer, K. S. (2010). Advice when children come out: The cultural "tool kits" of parents. *Journal of Family Issues*, 31(7), 960–991. doi: 10.1177/0192513×09354454

McQueeney, K. (2009). "We are God's children, y'All": Race, gender, and sexuality in lesbian- and gay-affirming congregations. *Social Problems*, 56(1), 151–173. doi: 10.1525/sp.2009.56.1.151

Moon, D. (2004). *God, sex, and politics: Homosexuality and everyday theologies*. Chicago, IL: University of Chicago Press.

Moon, D. (2005). Emotion language and social power: Homosexuality and narratives of pain in church. *Qualitative Sociology*, 28(4), 327–349. doi: 10.1007/s11133-005-8362-5

Olson, L. R., Cadge, W., & Harrison, J. T. (2006). Religion and public opinion about same-sex marriage. *Social Science Quarterly*, 87(2), 340–360. doi: 10.1111/j.1540-6237.2006.00384.x

Orbuch, T. L. (1997). People's accounts count: The sociology of accounts. *Annual Review of Sociology*, 23, 455–478. doi: 10.1146/annurev.soc.23.1.455

Palmisano, S. (2011). Il dio delle piccole cose? Tra cattolicesimo e spiritualità alternativa *[The god of small things? Between Catholicism and alternative spirituality]*. In F. Garelli (Ed.), *Religione all'italiana* (pp. 135–160). Bologna, Italy: Il Mulino.

Pichardo Galán, J. I. (2009). (Homo)sexualidad y familia: cambios y continuidades al inicio del tercer milenio *[Homosexuality and the family: Changes and continuities at the dawn of the Third Century]*. *Política y Sociedad*, 46(1/2), 143–160.

Quaranta, P. (Ed.). (2008). *Omosessualità e Vangelo. Franco Barbero risponde [Homosexuality and the Gospel. In conversation with Franco Barbero]*. S. Pietro in Cairano: Gabrielli editori.

Ratzinger, J. (1986). *Letter to the bishops of the Catholic Church on the pastoral care of the homosexual persons*. Retrieved from http://www.vatican.va/roman_curia/congregations/cfaith/documents/rc_con_cfaith_doc_19861001_homosexual-persons_en.html

Ross, C. (2009). Collective association in the LGBT movement. In D. Albertazzi, C. Brook, C. Ross, & N. Rothenberg (Eds.), *Resisting the tide: Cultures of opposition under Berlusconi (2001–06)* (pp. 204–216). London, England: Continuum.

Santos, C. (2013). *Social movements and sexual citizenship in Southern Europe*. Basingstoke, England: Palgrave Macmillan.

Švab, A., & Kuhar, R. (2014). The transparent and family closets: Gays and lesbians and their families of origin. *Journal of GLBT Family Studies*, 10(1–2), 15–35.

Swidler, A. (1986). Culture in action: Symbols and strategies. *American Sociological Review*, 51(2), 273–286. doi: 10.2307/2095521

Swidler, A. (2001). *Talk of love: How culture matters*. Chicago, IL: University of Chicago Press.

Thumma, S. (1991). Negotiating a religious identity: The case of the gay evangelical. *Sociology of Religion*, 52(4), 333–347. doi: 10.2307/3710850

Trappolin, L. (2011). Quanto e come si parla oggi di omogenitorialità in Italia *[When and how do we talk about homoparentality in Italy]*? In C. Cavina & D. Danna (Eds.), *Crescere in famiglie omogenitoriali [Growing up in gay and lesbian families]* (pp. 117–128). Roma, Italy: Franco Angeli.

Tulli, F. (2010). *Chiesa e Pedofilia [Church and pedophilia]*. Roma, Italy: l'Asino d'oro edizioni s.r.l.

Walls, N. E. (2010). Religion and support for same-sex marriage: Implications from the literature. *Journal of Gay & Lesbian Social Services, 22*(1–2), 112–131. doi: 10.1080/10538720903332420

Wilcox, M. M. (2002). When Sheila's a lesbian: Religious individualism among lesbian, gay, bisexual, and transgender Christians. *Sociology of Religion, 63*(4), 497–513. doi: 10.2307/3712304

Yip, A. K. T. (1997a). Attacking the attacker: Gay Christians talk back. *The British Journal of Sociology, 48*(1), 113–127.

Yip, A. K. T. (1997b). Dare to differ: Gay and lesbian Catholics' assessment of official Catholic positions on sexuality. *Sociology of Religion, 58*(2), 165–180.

"We Are with Family": Black Lesbian Couples Negotiate Rituals with Extended Families

VALERIE Q. GLASS
Virginia Tech, Blacksburg, Virginia, USA

This qualitative work explores Black lesbian couples' experiences with rituals and how the negotiation of these events is predetermined by rules and foundational expectations of families of origin and extended families. Symbolic interaction and Black feminist theories guided the theoretical understanding of the study, while grounded theory methodology was utilized for the data analysis. Eleven couples (22 individuals) from the Southeastern and Midwestern regions of the United States participated in this research. Participants discussed attending and/or creating three distinct types of rituals: (1) family of origin and extended family rituals (e.g., holiday gatherings or family reunions), (2) couples' daily or common rituals (e.g., housewarming parties or family dinners), and (3) couples' wedding or commitment ceremonies. While feeling a sense of belonging in extended family rituals, based on racial identity and connection to family, participants also concurrently de-sexualized their current relationship when taking part in extended family rituals. Couples' daily rituals supported current family experiences and identity. Commitment ceremonies served as the one ritual when partners openly expressed and celebrated their relationship and their lesbian identities as couples and families. The findings indicated that Black lesbian couples negotiated and redefined their roles depending on the type of ritual they attended or created.

Author note: I would like to thank April L. Few-Demo for providing invaluable feedback and constant support for this project. Brandon Bigby provided important suggestions for an earlier version of this manuscript.

INTRODUCTION

Rituals are integral social experiences woven into the fabric of our daily lives. Rituals serve to support and strengthen individual identity, connections to family and community, spirituality, and family identity (Smit, 2011; Viere, 2001; Wolin & Bennett, 1984). There are many typologies of rituals, including large events that celebrate changes or rites of passages (e.g., wedding ceremonies, funerals, baptisms, B'nai Mitzvah, etc.), extended family gatherings (e.g., extended family "Sunday dinner," holiday gatherings, reunions, etc.), and daily events that are ritualized (e.g., praying at bedtime, evening family dinners, etc.) (Wolin & Bennett, 1984). The present study utilized a feminist intersectional framework to understand the way Black lesbian couples negotiate rituals with extended family. Based on qualitative data from interviews, analysis focused on three types of rituals: daily family rituals, gay, lesbian, bisexual, transgender, and queer (GLBTQ) community rituals, and weddings/commitment ceremonies.

In Black families and communities, the meanings behind rituals extends beyond connection to family and community. Black lesbian couples and families must integrate family and community rituals from both Black extended families and GLBTQ community or identity rituals. Historically, rituals for Black families and communities were defined safe places in the face of oppression and racism while concurrently celebrating history and culture (McCoy, 2011). Black community rituals served to challenge and enforce social changes through ritualizing roles and meanings of these roles (Dundes, 1996). For GLBTQ individuals, rituals have served similar functions: building pride in the community, allowing a safe place, providing connections, and challenging social issues of homophobia and heterosexism (Oswald & Masciadrelli, 2008). This current research considers the elements of rituals in the lives of Black lesbian couples, the role of intersectionality in their lives, and how participants negotiate rituals in their families, communities, and personal lives to support and define their identities as Black women, lesbians, and Black lesbian families.

LITERATURE REVIEW

Black lesbian couples often experience a lack of racial support or recognition in GLBTQ communities (Mays, Chatters, Cochran, & Mackness, 1998). In addition, lesbian identity is frequently not supported or even recognized by many Black communities and extended families (Greene, 2000; Mays et al.,

1998; Moore, 2011). This invisibility (Moore, 2011) in both communities poses challenges to Black lesbian couples and families that are working to maintain connections to ritualized experiences. As Viere (2001) described: "Family rituals provide the family and individual members with a sense of identity by creating feelings of belonging. Rituals are the occasions that serve to facilitate social interaction among family members so that families can transmit cultural and normative information as well as beliefs and values across generations" (p. 287). For many Black individuals in the United States, rituals link community, spirituality, history, and extended family (Goluboff, 2011). One example of a ritual in many Black communities is gatherings of extended family (e.g., family reunions) (McCoy, 2011). Family reunion rituals can include "a strong, cohesive family...to provide guidance, education, support" (McCoy, 2011, p. 21). In essence, the idea of experiencing these rituals is a profound and powerful connection to one's racial heritage and promotes an understanding of past, present, and future (Goluboff, 2011).

Daily Rituals

Daily rituals are more second-nature events that are common to all families and can include anything from praying at bedtime, to Sunday dinner at grandma's, to weekly "game nights" (Viere, 2001). These daily rituals both define and validate family roles and relationships. In addition, daily rituals transmit family expectations, morals, and values down to family members (Viere, 2001). The extension of rituals to everyday life has assisted families in defining themselves, connecting to one another, and building a strong cohesive family unit. Daily routines facilitate and dictate the expression of gender roles and family expectations (Suter, Daas, & Bergen, 2008; Viere, 2001).

GLBTQ Community Rituals

GLBTQ community rituals can include public gatherings (e.g., gay pride parades, participation in gay nightlife activities) or private gatherings (e.g., dinners, parties). When faced with a lack of support for their sexual orientation and/or family structures by both extended families and communities, gay and lesbian families often find comfort and support in GLBTQ community functions (Suter et al., 2008). More specifically, GLBTQ community rituals promote a sense of "inclusion" for many GLBTQ individuals and families (Oswald & Masciadrelli, 2008, p. 1070). This feeling of inclusion is based on acceptance and celebration of variations in sexual orientation and chosen families, particularly when biological families or communities are not embracing of their GLBTQ members. Suter and colleagues (2008) researched gay and lesbian couples with children and found that ritualized meetings with other gay and lesbian parents with children was essential for developing a positive GLBTQ family identity. GLBTQ events can provide a place of belongingness for GLBTQ families and help children normalize their family structure. It is important to note that of the 32 participants in Suter and colleagues' (2008) study, only 2 identified as Black. This underrepresented racial category in much GLBTQ research invites a continued discussion on how GLBTQ community rituals are utilized and experienced by Black lesbian couples and families.

Wedding Rituals

Oswald (2000, 2001) explored the role of wedding rituals and the meanings behind extended family weddings, specifically, how gay and lesbian individuals felt about their roles in these rituals. The symbolic discourses around wedding rituals are powerful. Individuals are moving on to a notable stage of life, celebrating love and connection to another human being, are publically announcing this commitment, and receive blessings for this union from family and friends (Oswald & Suter, 2004). This public commitment is recognized as important by larger communities and ultimately creates and defines family identity.

To participate in heterosexual wedding rituals, many gay and lesbian individuals downplay elements of their sexual orientation identity (Oswald & Suter, 2004). Oswald and Suter (2004) reported that lesbian participants often did not bring partners to heterosexual wedding rituals and/or changed other elements of their personally integrated identities (e.g., behavior or appearance) as lesbians to follow established heteronormative ritual protocols. This adaptation allowed them to feel more welcomed and able to provide support at wedding rituals.

The celebratory and ritualized components of weddings often do not become part of similar unions between same-sex couples (Clarke, Burgoyne, & Burns, 2013; Oswald, 2000). Communities and extended family members may resist the ritualistic meanings associated with their lesbian relatives' commitment ceremonies (Baird, 2007). Extended family members that are invited to same-sex unions do not likely feel required to change their identities or appearances to fit a specific ritualistic mold. Gay and lesbian weddings do, at times, follow similar heteronormative ceremonial symbols and meanings (Oswald, 2000). Clarke and colleagues (2013) explored the challenges many same-sex couples have negotiating a ritualistic ceremony, like a wedding or a commitment ceremony, given the heteronormative assumptions placed on the ritual itself. Despite this public assumption of ritualized roles and experiences, many same-sex couples are rewriting this ritual experience to fit their identities as same-sex couples.

There are mixed reactions towards the legalization of same-sex marriage among GLBTQ members and allies (Lannutti, 2011; Shipman & Smart, 2007). On the one hand, this ritualized symbol can be validating to some same-sex couples, but on the other hand, some may argue that the predominant view of weddings should not be the only culturally accepted symbol of commitment or partnering (Lannutti, 2011). Some members of the GLBTQ communities advocate that same-sex unions should not be legalized because of the heteronormative symbols associated with wedding rituals and the expectation of same-sex couples meeting these heteronormative roles (Shipman & Smart, 2007). This perspective identifies that the experience of "marriage" can produce a legitimacy for same-sex couples that fits into previously defined roles and norms.

In Black communities, ritualized symbols are present at weddings that define role expectations of the couples who are getting married and the invited guests. The added components of pride in culture and challenging discrimination are often strong elements of Black wedding ceremonies (Dundes, 1996). One example of the connection to Black identity and history is the "jumping the broomstick" ritual (Dundes, 1996). Historically, enslaved Black couples could not legally marry; despite this, many adapted wedding ceremonies embraced committed Black couples (O'Neil, 2009). The roles of Black churches and Black spirituality have strengthened the role of wedding rituals in many Black communities, by spiritually honoring the unions between heterosexual partners (Goluboff, 2011).

THEORETICAL FRAMEWORK

This research project was designed and analyzed using an integrative theoretical framework of symbolic interactionism and Black feminist theory. Symbolic interactionism placed participants' experiences within the context of their social interactions (Blumer, 1969). The origins of symbolic interactionism identified how individuals define their roles, actions, and identities based on their interactions with those around them and the symbols applied to behaviors and experiences in their environments (Blumer, 1969). In this particular study, the use of symbolic interactionism provided an understanding of ritual experiences, the symbol of rituals, and how participants' roles were influenced or defined by these symbols that were present in their lives (LaRossa & Wolfe, 1985).

Black feminist theory identifies the cultural context that participants interact with (Few, 2007). Smith (2000) claimed that "Black feminism is, on every level, organic to Black experience" (p. xxii). Understanding the context of how participants create a Black identity and a lesbian identity is critical to the process participants experienced defining their selves, their contexts, and their relationships within the symbolic framework (Few, 2007). Black lesbians have unique challenges based on their race, gender, and sexual orientation (Lorde, 1984). For Black lesbians, finding a place for one's complete identity is difficult (Lorde, 1984).

The integrative theoretical framework identified the meaning making related to rituals in participants' lives, while further describing how participants self-created and self-defined symbols and roles expressed through ritual. Black feminism brought in the historical context that added to ritual experiences and the personal adaptations expressed by participants. Specifically, Black feminism allowed this study to be placed within the context of Black experiences: hearing, seeing, and expanding on Black women's thoughts, expressions, and understandings (Few, 2007). Symbolic interaction theory (Blumer, 1969) allowed for an exploration of how meaning and roles of family and community play into ritual experiences of Black lesbian couples. I wanted to see how Black lesbian couples negotiated rituals as lesbian couples and families, based on rituals within Black communities. The integration of Black feminism incorporated Black women's perspectives for a better understanding of the power of ritual in Black communities and the need to bridge safety, acceptance, strength, and community into ritualistic functions (Collins, 2000; Dundes, 1996).

METHODOLOGY

Participants

Study participants consisted of 22 individuals (11 couples). All individuals identified as Black or African-American. Ten of the study participants identified themselves as lesbian and one participant stated her identity was "lesbian by choice." Table 1 highlights some of the demographic information for all of the couples; couples varied in terms of socioeconomic status, career, and education.

All but one of the couples had children living in the home at the time of the interview. Two couples reported conceiving the children through donor insemination (one couple within the course of the current relationship and one couple during a previous lesbian partnership). Eight couples had children who were conceived during previous heterosexual unions. Couples reported an average length of five years in current relationships. None of the couples lived in states where same-sex marriage was a legal institution at the time of the interview. Participants were recruited from Southeastern and Midwest areas of the United States. Recruitment involved a snowball sampling (Heckathorn, 1997) that began with posting recruitment flyers on a GLBTQ family electronic discussion list in North Carolina and attending two Black gay pride events. To participate in this study, participants had to meet the following criteria: lesbian sexual orientation; Black, African-American, or Black-American racial categories; between 25 and 55 years of age; and

TABLE 1 Demographics of Individual Participants ($N = 22$)

Couple	Partner Name	Partner Age	Education	Profession	Relationship Duration	Children (in Home/Biological)	Location
1	Veronica	36	No college	Unemployed	2 years	1	VA (rural)
1	Lora	47	No college	Unemployed	2 years	0	VA (rural)
2	Anna	37	Some college	Therapist	5 years	2	NY (urban)
2	DeeDee	36	No college	Security	5 years	0	NY (urban)
3	Rebecca	28	Graduate school	Teacher/graduate student	1 year	1	DC (urban)
3	Karla	29	Graduate degree	University administration	1 year	0	DC (urban)
4	Betty	44	No college	Factory work	6 years	1	NJ (small city)
4	Chris	49	No college	Factory supervisor	6 years	0	NJ (small city)
5	Candice	27	Undergraduate degree	Social worker	1 year	1	DC (urban)
5	Latasha	31	No college	Security	1 year	0	DC (urban)
6	Tamara	42	No college	Factory work	5 years	1	VA (small city)
6	Lynn	44	No college	Factory supervisor	5 years	1	VA (small city)
7	Crystal	32	Graduate school	Graduate student	2 years	1	NC (rural)
7	Shauna	29	Some college	Nursing assistant	2 years	0	NC (rural)
8	Shay	34	Undergraduate degree	Restaurant manager	9 years	0	NC (urban)
8	Felicia	35	Undergraduate degree	Customer service	9 years	4	NC (urban)
9	Francine	33	Graduate degree	Counselor	10 years	1	NC (small city)
9	Danica	34	Graduate degree	College admin	10 years	1	NC (small city)
10	Hazel	32	Undergraduate degree	Teacher	4 years	1	MD (urban)
10	Andi	28	Some college	Security	4 years	0	MD (urban)
11	Danielle	27	Undergraduate degree	Sales	8 years	0	NC (urban)
11	Geri	27	Undergraduate degree	Teacher	8 years	0	NC (urban)

maintained current committed relationship for at least a year. Because this research was exploratory, both individuals in the couples had to identify as Black, African-American, or Black-American. In addition, couples had to have been dating, in a committed relationship, and living together for at least a year. The purpose of this criteria was to focus on couples who had made some commitment to each other and had been together long enough for family identity dynamics and rituals to emerge, as well as for couples to have had time to connect to and understand how these rituals are situated in extended family relationships.

Interview Structure

Couples participated in dyadic interviews in their homes or private community locations. Interviews lasted approximately one hour. Open-ended questions for these interviews focused on the research questions, which included the following:

- How do participants experience interactions and experiences with extended family?
- How do participants experience the coming-out process with their extended families (both as individuals and as couples)?
- How do couples build family identities as lesbian couples?
- What social supports were available to and accessed by Black lesbian couples?

Data Analysis

Data were analyzed using a modified grounded theory methodology (Charmez, 2006; Glaser & Strauss, 1967). This analysis included a three-tiered coding process of identifying themes within the interview transcript data. Initially, data were coded in general terms. These codes were collapsed to include theory and previous research, and finally, selective codes emerged in a final stage of analysis. Symbolic interaction theory (Blumer, 1969; LaRossa & Wolf, 1985) and Black feminist theory (Collins, 2000) guided the data analysis. Throughout the coding stages, I asked myself: What are participants doing? What are participants telling us? And how does the historical context of participants' experiences shape their understandings of meaning related to ritual?

RESULTS

As a lead into the results, I would like to present the reader with a couple of examples. Take a moment and think about the rituals and experiences in your own life based on community, connection, spirituality, and/or family. What is one important ritual in your life? How does participation in this ritual make you feel? Why do you participate in this ritual? How does this ritual define your family? Consider your personal involvement in this ritual. What is your role in making this ritual happen and what are the expectations of you? Think about the symbol of this ritual in your own life. Now refocus to your thoughts on the participants in this study—Black lesbian women from Midwest and Southern U.S. communities.

For participants in this study, being involved in family or community rituals was essential and part of their identity as Black women. Ritual experiences gave them connection and feelings of strength, similar to feelings you may have identified when considering your own role in rituals. All of participants' multiple roles (mother, lesbian partner, lesbian family member, Black woman, extended family member, etc.) were not recognized or celebrated at external ritualized functions. Participants had to balance their multiple identities (i.e., present one at a time) in order to receive the symbolic meanings and understandings associated with these roles. This adapting of their identity, depending on the ritual and the circumstance, was a result of the intersectionality of race, gender, and sexual orientation.

The most important extended family ritual in my personal life, for example, is a beach trip my extended family takes yearly. This event includes my family of origin and extended family (including current partners and children). My heterosexual sister brings her husband and two children to the weeklong event. Their individual and family identities are embraced, supported, and defined during this extended family ritual. My sister and her husband have romantic dates which the extended family supports by caring for the children. The couple may comfortably kiss each other or express their relationship openly, while we (the extended family) support their coupling. My extended family provides caring feedback, light-hearted joking, and spoken support of their couple relationship. My sister's identity as a white female and heterosexual wife and mother, as well as her roles as daughter, sister, niece, and cousin are all concurrently validated, supported, and defined during this ritualized experience. These types of rituals are fairly common and probably resonate with many readers. Participants in this study, because of the hidden elements of their relationship, did not experience validation from extended family rituals for their roles as lesbian-identified partners, causing a broken acknowledgement of multiple identities.

I, personally, find strength and support, as a lesbian-identified woman, at GLBTQ rituals, including pride festivals or social events. For me there is an experience of personal pride and a connection that I feel when I connect at these ritualized celebrations, especially when there are lesbian families with children. Participants in this study reported not accessing GLBTQ rituals. It is difficult for me to imagine not having GLBTQ community rituals in my life or to feel support for my personal and family identities. I even feel these connections strengthen my child's personal pride in her family identity.

Participants did not discuss racism in the GLBTQ communities as a reason why they were not part of GLBTQ rituals; however, research indicates that there is an understanding of racism in many GLBTQ communities (Lehavot, Balsam, & Ibrahim-Wells, 2009). It is not easy for me to imagine either having a sense that I would not quite feel welcomed or comfortable at GLBTQ functions because of my race (white) or feeling as if I had to downplay my identity as a white female in order to reap the personal and familial benefits of these ritualized symbols.

Overall, ritual experiences were reported by participants in three thematic categories: (1) family of origin or extended family rituals (e.g., holiday gatherings or family reunions), (2) couples' daily or common rituals (e.g., housewarming parties or family dinners), and (3) couples' wedding or commitment ceremonies. These thematic categories closely aligned with the categorical definitions of ritual created by earlier studies on rituals (Wolin & Bennett, 1984). In these three typologies of ritual experiences, participants reported gaining symbolic experiences that validated one aspect of their identity at a time. Therefore, participants adapted their identity at different rituals to gain the defining support of that aspect of their identity. Participants' complete roles were only supported by rituals that occurred in their current homes or through wedding ceremonies.

Family of Origin and Extended Family Rituals

Attending and being part of extended family rituals was of primary importance to most couples and their children. This importance parallels much of the research done with (mostly white) gay and lesbian couples (Oswald, 2000, 2001). Participants in this study reported de-emphasizing any obvious signs of their sexual orientation at these gatherings. To keep their identities less obvious, participants responded in several different ways: (1) by bringing partners to these gatherings and keeping assumptions others had of the relationship vague (e.g., no one talked about it, even if they knew the nature of the relationship); (2) by not inviting or bringing partners to extended family gatherings; and (3) by bringing partners to extended family gatherings while providing space for extended family to perceive them as fictive kin (i.e., extended families were able to embrace partners for their ethnic identity, but did not visualize them or accept them as a partner to their lesbian relative). Participants described feeling welcomed as individuals to these events and their children were always welcomed members, but their roles as lesbian partners were not welcomed.

One couple, Tamara and Lynn, discussed the way they actively integrated into some of Lynn's extended family rituals. One daily ritual that is part of Lynn's family is socializing around bowling. Lynn shared a previous experience of bringing another girlfriend to this extended family ritual:

> *[My mother] told me that, "we know your lifestyle, and we are starting to accept it, but it doesn't mean that you have to put it in my face!" and I was like "okay" because I do not consider that putting it in your face because I was not even like holding her hand or kissing her face, she was just sitting there watching me bowl, but I didn't say anything of course, I don't say things like that to my parents, I just stop what I am doing.*

Lynn felt that her family was not willing to accept any sign of her lesbian identity. Even simply bringing the girlfriend was considered unacceptable and "putting it in (their) face(s)." Lynn's response was to do as her mother said, continue to be part of the ritual, but downplay her lesbian couple relationship. They understood the meaning of their relationship had to be disguised in order to maintain the connection to this ritual that the couple found essential. They continued to attend extended family rituals to gain the symbolic support and understanding of their roles as Black women.

Compared to research on mostly white gay and lesbian couples (LaSala, 2007), Black lesbian couples in this study did not discontinue participation in extended family rituals because of extended families' lack of acceptance or validation of their couple relationship. Often, white gay and lesbian couples will leave family-of-origin rituals if they do not feel acceptance of their partners or their sexual orientation (LaSala, 2007). Crystal and Shauna shared that they did not celebrate the holidays together. Crystal and her biological child would attend with her extended family while Shauna went to her extended family. Crystal explained that her extended family was "real close" and gatherings with her family were "very important" to her. Crystal shared that she sensed there was a lot of negativity in her extended family related to her sexual orientation. The couple presented themselves as "single" women (or "single parents") at these events to maintain their connection to these ritual experiences.

Felicia and Shay presented a slightly different method of negotiating their identities in the face of family rituals. Felicia discussed the importance of her extended family rituals:

> *Every holiday, we are with family, I don't think that a holiday has gone by, even the little crazy holidays that you make up, birthdays, Thanksgiving, Easter, everything. My family is real close, we have family meetings two to three times a month, you know we are just real close, we go there, they come here. It is just one big happy family.*

Despite Felicia and Shay's frequent attendance at ritual gatherings, they felt as if they must leave elements of their lesbian identity out of these experiences. Felicia is aware of tensions among some family members when the couple attends these events. She shared that her older sister and her grandmother have both experienced some struggles they have with Felicia and Shay's relationship based on spiritual convictions. Felicia and Shay both agreed that they are cautious about showing physical affection in front of Felicia's extended family in general. Felicia shared, "I can kiss her goodbye if I need to, in front of my family...there are some things we are not going to do...that is just how we conduct ourselves." Felicia and Shay are similar to other couples in how they make strides and conscious efforts to desexualize their relationship to continue to participate in their Black family rituals. The trend of adapting and changing behaviors to fit into the heterosexual normative molds of ritual experiences and/or removing complete meanings of their identities from ritual experiences has been documented by GLBTQ ritual research (Oswald, 2001).

Another couple, Danielle and Geri, shared that they did go to family gatherings, but it was not comfortable. Danielle stated,

> *I go with Geri to family functions, but it is not that comfortable for me...I am just not seen as a significant part of Geri's life and that makes me uncomfortable...I feel out of place when family events are going on.*

Danielle and Geri were making an attempt to adapt to Geri's need to attend and be connected to her extended family, while negotiating how to build in the couple's relationship and Geri's sexual orientation identity. This adaptation led to discomfort as the couple was unable to express their authentic relationship. This couple felt their relationship was not symbolically recognized by extended family or GLBTQ communities. They later shared their frustration in having to be "role models of committed couples with gay friends." They discussed only having each other to assist in defining their role symbolically as committed lesbian partners.

Couples' Daily Family Rituals

Religion represents part of many couples' daily expressions and behaviors. During interviews, couples expressed their understandings of certain life events, particularly finding their partner, were often based in spiritual beliefs and understandings. Lora and Veronica shared how they met. Veronica stated, "[Our] meeting was not a coincidence, it was just God's plan...at the time, I was going through [a lot] and I had escaped from a two-year relationship." The couple identified that their spirituality defined their roles and connection to each other. Quite frequently during the interview they used spiritualized language to discuss their current lives and family. At one point Lora shared, "being in love, being part of 'the life' [lesbian] is a blessing, a blessed thing." Somehow this couple was able to compartmentalize religion in their home environment as a symbolic and defining ritual, even to the point of using elements of spirituality to celebrate their sexual orientation.

Lora and Veronica shared that they attended the same church with their children and found the rituals of their church community important. At church, however, they carefully presented their identities as Black women while not bringing attention to their identities as lesbians and committed partners. Veronica stated, "they [church community members] do not know [we are a couple]." Their experiences in church provided them with a weekly ritual as individuals. They brought home the messages and connections to explain and understand their relationship. The community connection and celebration of the ritual of going to church actively defines that their roles as lesbians is not part of that ritual.

Anna and DeeDee recounted that they met in the church and their church activities played a significant role in their individual lives. They shared that they were *"raised up in it"* and attend weekly. The couple indicated that they have different roles in the church: Anna "sings in the choir," so they do not come as a couple to church or participate as a couple. DeeDee expanded on this topic: "it is like you are there for a reason and it is not who you sleep with, it is about the main goal, God, your savior." They attend a family (Black) church and reported their coupling relationship was not part of their church experiences.

There was private reflection of spirituality among many of the pairs. This reflection, however, was separate from the ritual of church. In church, couples frequently separated their sexual orientation identity and identity as a couple in order to feel connected to this community and this ritual. Essentially, spiritual rituals defined themselves in two separate spheres, public and private (Moore, 2011). Couples who participated in the public religious rituals of church did not feel that their sexual orientation had a place in this environment. Spirituality, and the ritualized language of spirituality, did have a significant place in most couples' private home environments as lesbian couples and families.

For the holidays, couples reported focusing primarily on the current family. Lora and Veronica shared that they like to have Christmas dinner with just the current family, the two of them and their daughter (Veronica's biological daughter from a previous heterosexual relationship). Lora stated that this past Christmas was "just us, I made a big dinner and then made dessert with our daughter. We like to be with just us." However, Lora and Veronica shared that Thanksgiving rituals include a large group of both nonbiological and biological kin. Veronica shared: "for Thanksgiving we had the lady who I call Mom, and her partner, then, my sister and Lora's friend from childhood, and this other friend...we have this huge extended family." When rituals were on their turf, there were at times slight changes in behaviors. Couples were typically more open about their sexual orientation identities in their homes and invited extended family or community members that showed support and comfort for their roles as lesbian couples. This placing of ritual experiences in their homes allowed for them to define and create their own personal rituals that would identify symbols, meanings, and expectations for their current families and partners. In other words, their identities as lesbian couples and lesbian families were defined and created solely by their current family rituals, in the privacy of their own homes, the exception being weddings and commitment ceremonies.

Weddings

During the interviews, couples discussed their relationships in terms of varied levels of commitment. Most couples ($N = 9$) discussed weddings. Of these, some ($N = 5$) discussed previous ceremonies and some were planning wedding ceremonies ($N = 4$). Most couples used the term *wedding* when discussing these events (as opposed to commitment ceremony). With the lack of legal recognition and the seeming lack of support from larger church communities, extended families, GLBTQ communities, and Black communities, it would seem that couples would have been resistant to plan large, involved rituals that celebrated and defined their unions. Participants' creation of elaborate and pronounced wedding rituals, however, defied this logic. In addition, ritualistic practices of "dating" and "getting engaged" were very much a part of all of the participants' lives despite the frequently heteronormative assumptions placed on these ritualized symbols. Weddings typically included a ceremonial ritual where the couple pronounced their commitment publically to each other. These ceremonies were the one day that participants felt they could be authentic—that they could present themselves as a committed couple and this ritual would define and celebrate multiple identities and roles (lesbian partner, lesbian parent/family, Black woman). Wedding ceremonies were often very detailed, classy, and involved. Invitations were given to families of origin, extended families, church community members, and friends regardless of past feelings of non-support or lack of recognition of the relationship. Participants reported some extended family members struggled with attending these events, but still attended. In addition, participants resumed downplaying their roles as lesbian couples and families immediately after ceremonies.

The ritual process of defining commitment began with dating rituals. Dating was part of some couples' lives, but with the recognition that something to solidify their commitment was coming. Lora shared, "I am in the process of starting to put a ring on her finger." Veronica, her partner, glanced down in a shy and flirtatious way and said, "Yeah, right . . . ." They smiled at each other during the exchange. Later on, Lora shared her ideas surrounding the symbol of marriage. She said, "once we cross the threshold . . . this [will be] my home, we have established and are building a home, not just some floozy to lay up with, this is a relationship." Lora indicated the importance of the marriage ritual for defining their roles as a committed couple to others.

The wedding ritual would create meaning for their couple identity to the outside world; it would define the boundary of their current relationship.

Betty and Chris were in a similar stage of their relationship and during the interview they discussed getting married in the future. Chris came out and said, "Will you marry me?" in a joking way to Betty. Betty replied, "If you ask me to marry you here..." and followed up with an eye-roll that indicated Chris better not attempt a proposal right at that moment. The symbol of engagement was important to Betty and her facial expression indicated to Chris that the engagement ritual should have a specific and important place.

Candice and Latasha shared their sentimental proposal experience. Latasha said, "It was at a BBQ, with some of my friends around...I wrote a poem for her and after the poem, at the end, I said 'will you [Candice] be my wife?'" Candice elaborated:

> *And she had me read the poem with all her friends around me and it was telling me how much she loves me in the poem [and] at the end of the poem it said she wanted to spend the rest of her life with me. And, when I was done reading, she went down on one knee!*

This couple excitedly related their experiences in this public ritual of proposing and explained they had plans for a wedding ceremony the following year. Candice said, "June, we have wedding plans for June of next year...well, we are going to have a commitment ceremony, they do not recognize it as marriage [in Washington, DC]." This couple identified the significance of the proposal and wedding ritual. They also recognized their ceremony did not have the legal validation of heterosexual unions and that, as a result, they have to generate their privatized understanding of the meaning of this ritual.

Out of all the couples interviewed, one couple, Felicia and Shay, shared the most extensive and elaborate wedding ceremony plans. Felicia shared:

> *We got a reception, a big reception, we have spent well over twenty-three grand on this wedding. It is a real big wedding. There are twenty-two in the wedding party and a guest list of over five hundred. I think it will be a big event and an exciting time for us.*

The importance of this ritual to them in defining their relationship is obvious in their plans. Danica and Francine also had a large wedding ceremony; however, Danica elaborated on some struggles she had with her mother surrounding the event. She stated,

> *It was touch and go for a while [if she would even attend the wedding]. She said that she would come, but it was clear that she was not happy about it, up to the moment, I wasn't sure [if she'd come]. She pulled up to the church, and was doing whatever in the car and she took forever to*

come in and so, it was very challenging for her, but she did it. I guess she realized that if she didn't that was pretty much going to be it for me.

Danica's words reflect her understanding of the importance of the ritual and how it was imperative that her mother, being a key important figure in her life, attend this event to add to the defining element of their commitment and the mother's recognition of this definition. Danica defined her mother's role at this event in traditional (heteronormative) ritualized ways (e.g., the mother is an important part of a wedding and her supportive role as "mother of the bride" is essential). Danica's mother was challenged by this clash in her own understanding of these roles and how to balance being a supportive "mother of the bride" while also not making the couple relationship visible.

Weddings and proposals were unique rituals, in that the couples did not leave their full identities as Black women and lesbian partners out of these rituals. Participants created ritualistic space to provide a definition of who they were as couples, as Black women, and as families. Weddings were powerful, defining moments for participants. Participants had this one event, this one day, where they presented themselves as a committed couple despite any negative views from extended family members. It was the responsibility of others to adapt their personal views, if negative, on this one day. It likely was the only moment that participants felt their presentation of their lesbian identity was celebrated; they defined it.

Gay and Lesbian Community Rituals

Four of the 11 couples participating in this study were interviewed at Black pride festivals—a GLBTQ community ritual that celebrates the multiple marginalized identities: Black and GLBTQ. Of these four couples, only one couple shared that they regularly attended "pride festivals." The remaining three couples mentioned infrequent contact with GLBTQ communities. For Betty and Chris, they found feeling supported and comforted by pride festival rituals important to their own acceptance as lesbians (e.g., Oswald & Masciadrelli, 2008). Early in the discussion, Chris reflected on her "main challenge" in her relationship with Betty. She stated,

My main challenge is just being in the life [being lesbian], because, like I said, I can be around anyone and they feel uncomfortable. I can be looking in her [Betty's] eyes and they [those around me] feel uncomfortable. It is just like being a subculture, everyone looks at you and treats you differently.

Later in the interview, Chris reflected on her feelings at the Black pride festival:

This is one of the biggest events we went to alone [as a couple without children], this is the first time we have done something of substance. I am so full right now, we are happy, we are having a good time...just being with each other.

Betty continued: "this right here, I wish we had a chance to do more things like this." It is clear from Betty's comments that this couple struggles with the ritualized support of their couplehood; however, there is a sense of peace and happiness when the couple reflects on their inner experiences of support at the GLBTQ Black pride ritual.

Among the other seven couples that were not interviewed at the Black pride festival, there was a reported need to connect with GLBTQ community rituals. Only one couple of the seven indicated a strong connection to GLBTQ community rituals as a couple or family. The other six mostly indicated they wanted a deeper connection to GLBTQ community rituals. Veronica stated, "I would like to find some more gay and lesbian groups, especially ones with children...a community place or club, some place we can go every day, play pool...have a potluck." Historically, GLBTQ rituals have not necessarily been inclusive of children and families. For participants in this study, children were a focus of their everyday lives and experiences. Participants noted a lack of connection to GLBTQ rituals (pride events, nightlife, bars, etc.) because these did not offer rituals that support their identities as families with children.

DISCUSSION

Participants in this study adapted the symbols and experiences of their current couple and family rituals to provide meaning and identity to their lives. In addition, participants adapted their identities and roles as lesbians and lesbian partners to gain the celebratory connection to their roles as Black family and community members. The participants created a purposeful shift in identity to accommodate the social expectations and stigmas of their multiple minority statuses. Black lesbian participants sensed their lesbian identity is somewhat lesser than or unequal to the heterosexual relationships within Black communities (Lykke, 2010). As a result of this felt sense of inequality, participants fulfilled the expectation by not discussing or bringing their sexual orientation to Black community rituals. It was as if the message received from Black families and communities was, "If you want to be part of these celebrations, you must place the genuine meaning behind your relationship outside this celebration." Participants created meaning from these interactions and complied. Concurrently, participants did not feel they had a place within the GLBTQ community rituals. Although the participants did not cite racism as the reason for not attending these events, there certainly appears to be a sense that these events were not accessible to them based on their roles as mothers.

If GLBTQ rituals are imperative to feelings of social inclusion and acceptance (Oswald & Masciadrelli, 2008) and Black extended family rituals assist Black community members and families in recognizing historical struggles and traditions, as well as providing a sense of safety and inclusion (Dundes, 1996), then what ritualistic experiences are available to Black lesbian families inclusive of their multiple marginalized identities? Black lesbian couples found comfort and solace in their own defined and privatized (Moore, 2011) ritual experiences. Black lesbian couples in this study did not feel comfortable expressing their identity as lesbian partners at extended family rituals; however, they found ways to deemphasize their lesbian identities in order to stay connected to those rituals that gave them a sense of connection based on their racial identity. Participants did not voice a strong connection to GLBTQ community rituals because these did not seem to further define and support their families.

For Black lesbian individuals, participation in rituals with extended Black families and communities is especially complicated. On the one hand, connection to these family rituals can be a crucial element of their lives. Extended family rituals, in general, provide a basis for connection to family members, connection to family history, and connection to spirituality (Dundes, 1996). However, in Black communities, the connection to ritual goes beyond these elements to include safety and refuge from oppression, a place to learn and understand oppression and the role it plays in everyday life, and it becomes a place to express and celebrate Black culture (in addition to family culture). The need to hide or deemphasize one's lesbian sexual orientation was prevalent among participants because of the sense of non-acceptance from extended family and community members. Participants in this current study were very careful about bringing their sexual orientation to family rituals; however, the expanded meaning of family ritual in Black communities makes the ritual experience even more important (Oswald & Masciadrelli, 2008). Participants got the message that if they were to violate the rules of heteronormativity in ritual experiences, they would lose the celebratory power and defining elements these rituals provide them as Black women.

Oswald and Suter (2004) discussed "boundary permeability" (p. 895) at heterosexual wedding rituals. This boundary is the recognition of events and experiences that define typical heterosexual wedding rituals. These definitions are typically heteronormative and can exclude GLBT family members' identities and behaviors. The typical wedding ritual has rules and symbols that urge individuals to adapt to the previously laid foundations of heterosexual experiences (Oswald & Suter, 2004; Oswald, 2000, 2001). Participants in this study found ways to adapt their commitment rituals to include many elements of heterosexual weddings, while still maintaining inclusivity of their own identities (Clarke et al., 2013). Participants' rituals of proposals and weddings suggested the following: (1) the weddings and proposals followed ritualistic protocols of their extended families' and communities' ceremonies (i.e., the wedding rituals adopted many of the same practices as heterosexual members': elaborate proposals, wedding parties, dancing, vows, inviting extended family and friends, and even the clothing was similar to heterosexual counterparts); (2) the participants who discussed weddings and proposals found the wedding (specifically presenting themselves to their families and communities as a committed couple) to be an important and integral component to their identity as a committed couple; and (3) couples, who typically desexualized or deemphasized their sexual orientation to attend family rituals, found this one day to be the day they would be open and "out" about their love and identity. For participants, they created their wedding rituals to solidify their union; however, these ceremonies had a much deeper meaning. This event was the one day that they celebrated and exposed all of their multiple roles and identities. The adaptation integrates new and self-defining elements, much like the "jumping the broom" adaptation where Black enslaved couples incorporated their own elements to legitimize their unions (Dundes, 1986). Participants found a way to validate their relationship based on normative ritualized standards while subsequently celebrating who they were as Black women in same-sex relationships.

Weston (1991) was integral in beginning discussions of how gay and lesbian couples create and identify their family identity. Included in this definition are roles that extended family rituals play in defining and understanding identity (personal identity, family identity, and community identity). Participants in this current study applied meaning to their current family and identified rituals that supported this current family structure. To understand their roles as Black women and mothers, participants took part in extended family and Black community rituals. Participants did not share having their lesbian identity or couple and family relationships supported externally. In essence, many participants indicated developing their own connection to rituals. On top of participating in extended family rituals, participants were able to build and create rituals as Black lesbian families. Previous research has incorporated the idea of language and symbol changes that are non-heteronormative as a way lesbian couples validate and define their lesbian family identity (Suter et al., 2008). Couples' rituals in their home environment took on the symbol of safety and adapted to include extended family and friends that supported their multiple identities. Frequently this involved spirituality and spiritual language. At other times, this included holiday or family gatherings that added to the definition of the current family. Black lesbian couples embraced certain symbols and meanings of rituals in their own lives; however, they adapted them in their own home in a more privatized way to include their multiple identities and strengthen their current commitment to family.

CONCLUSIONS AND FUTURE DIRECTIONS

Limitations of the present study included a narrow demographic. Because of the exploratory nature of the study, I purposefully sought a sample of Black lesbians in committed relationships. In addition, the sample was confined to mostly Southern states. Black couples on the West Coast, for example, would likely have presented very different experiences. In addition, the criteria for committed couples may have limited experiences to couples of a certain age and development. Participants' focus on children and home life, and not on GLBTQ rituals and events, could be partly related to the developmental stage in their lives.

Given the challenges participants in this study at times felt negotiating their multiple minority statuses, it is important to mention the struggles that may occur if participants had labeled themselves "bisexual." The struggles faced by bisexual-identified, same-sex-partnered, Black women would likely add to the struggles intersectionality poses. Research has indicated that bisexual identity and bisexual experiences during wedding and commitment ceremonies pose additional challenges (Lannutti, 2007). Future research could address how these challenges (i.e., biphobia and role negotiation) may play out in Black same-sex-headed family structures.

Future research could explore the dynamic of GLBTQ community rituals and how Black gay and lesbian families utilize these resources. Oswald and Masciadrelli (2008) described a thematic component of gay and lesbian community rituals as existing primarily to provide group support to gay and lesbian members in the face of perceived lack of support by extended families and communities. Given the possible importance of connecting to GLBTQ community rituals, the current research elicits the following question: If Black lesbian couples and families are not accessing the supports of GLBTQ community rituals, where do they get support for their coupling and their chosen families? In addition, participants in this study do not specifically address the reasons Black lesbians are not accessing GLBTQ community rituals.

Participants focused a great deal on weddings, engagements, heterosexual language for coupling (e.g., "wifey"), traditional romance, and dating. Further investigation into how extended families are viewing their biological daughters' movements into couple commitment during these symbolic rituals would integrate a more complete picture. In addition, participants in this current study appeared to place a great deal of power on the commitment ceremony ritual. This ritual defined and solidified their couplehood. A further investigation into the meaning of this ritual for couples and extended families could better define this ritual.

In conclusion, Black lesbian couples in this study found ways to participate in rituals that support their marginalized identities one at a time. The only place that participants defined their multiple minority statuses through ritualized experiences was on their own turf, in their home, or during their commitment ceremonies. Participants adapted to heteronormative behaviors in order to continue to participate and remain connected to extended family. Finally, participants did not necessarily connect to GLBTQ community rituals. The one ritual some attended (Black gay pride weekends) did provide comfort and connection that was recognized as important; however, this was a rare experience for most couples.

REFERENCES

Baird, B. (2007). "Gay marriage," lesbian wedding. *Gay and Lesbian Issues and Psychology Review, 3,* 161–170.

Blumer, H. (1969). *Symbolic interactionism: Perspective and method.* Englewood Cliffs, NJ: Prentice-Hall.

Charmez, K. (2006). *Constructing grounded theory: A practical guide through qualitative analysis.* Thousand Oaks, CA: Sage Publications.

Clarke, V., Burgoyne, C., & Burns, M. (2013). Unscripted and improvised: Public and private celebrations of same-sex relationships. *Journal of GLBT Family Studies, 9,* 393–418. doi: 10.1080/1550428X.2013.808494

Collins, P. H. (2000). *Black feminist thought: Knowledge, consciousness, and politics of empowerment.* New York, NY: Routledge.

Dundes, A. (1996). "Jumping the broom": On the origin and meaning of an African American wedding custom. *The Journal of American Folklore, 109,* 324–329.

Few, A. L. (2007). Integrating black consciousness and critical race feminism into family studies research. *Journal of Family Issues, 22,* 452–473. doi: 10.1177/0912513X06297330

Glaser, B. G., & Strauss, A. L. (1967). *The discovery of grounded theory.* Chicago, IL: Aldine.

Goluboff, S. L. (2011). Making African American homeplaces in rural Virginia. *Ethos, 39,* 368–394. doi: 10.1111/j.1548-1352.2011.01198.x

Greene, B. (2000). African American lesbian and bisexual women. *Journal of Social Issues, 29,* 239–249. doi: 10.1111/0022-4537.00163

Heckathorn, D. D. (1997). Respondent-driven sampling: A new approach to the study of hidden populations. *Social Problems, 44,* 174–199. doi: 10.2307/3096941

Lannutti, P. J. (2007). "This is not a lesbian wedding": Examining same-sex marriage and bisexual-lesbian couples. *Journal of Bisexuality, 7,* 238–260. doi: 10.1080/15299710802171316

Lannutti, P. J. (2011). Examining communication about marriage amendments: Same-sex couples and their extended social networks. *Journal of Social Issues, 67,* 264–281. doi: 10.1111/j/1540-4560.2011.01697.x

LaRossa, R., & Wolf, J. H. (1985). On qualitative family research. *Journal of Marriage and the Family, 47,* 531–541. doi: 10.1111/j.1741-3737.2005.00179.x

LaSala, M. C. (2007). Walls and bridges: How coupled gay men and lesbians manage their intergenerational relationships. *Journal of Marital and Family Therapy, 28,* 327–339. doi: 10.1300/J041v18n02_04

Lehavot, K., Balsam, K. F., & Ibrahim-Wells, G. D. (2009). Redefining the American quilt: Definitions and experiences of community among ethnically diverse lesbian and bisexual women. *Journal of Community Psychology, 37,* 439–458. doi: 10.1002/jcop.20305

Lorde, A. (1984). *Sister outsider: Essays and speeches.* Berkeley, CA: The Crossing Press.

Lykke, N. (2010). *Feminist studies: A guide to intersectional theory, methodology and writing.* New York, NY: Taylor & Francis.

Mays, V. M., Chatters, L. M., Cochran, S. D., & Mackness, J. (1998). African American families in diversity: Gay men and lesbians as participants in family networks. *Journal of Comparative Family Studies, 29,* 73–88.

McCoy, R. (2011). African American elders, cultural traditions, and the family reunion. *Journal of the American Society on Aging, 35,* 16–21.

Moore, M. R. (2011). *Invisible families.* Los Angeles, CA: University of California Press.

O'Neil, P. W. (2009). Bosses and broomsticks: Ritual and authority in antebellum slave weddings. *Journal of Southern History, 75,* 29–48.

Oswald, R. F. (2000). A member of the wedding? Heterosexism and family ritual. *Journal of Social and Personal Relationships, 17,* 349–368. doi: 10.1177/0265407500173003

Oswald, R. F. (2001). Religion, family, and ritual: The production of gay, lesbian, bisexual, and transgender outsiders—within. *Review of Religious Research, 43,* 39–50.

Oswald, R. F., & Masciadrelli, B. P. (2008). Generative ritual among nonmetropolitan lesbians and gay men: Promoting social inclusion. *Journal of Marriage and Family, 70,* 1060–1073. doi: 10.1111/j.1741-3737.2008.00546.x

Oswald, R. F., & Suter, E. A. (2004). Heterosexist inclusion and exclusion during ritual: A "straight versus gay" comparison. *Journal of Family Issues, 25,* 881–899. doi: 10.1177/0192513X04267278

Shipman, B., & Smart, C. (2007). "It's made a huge difference": Recognition, rights and the personal significance of civil partnership. *Sociological Research Online, 12.* doi: 10.5153/sro.1340

Smit, R. (2011). Maintaining family memories through symbolic action: Young adults' perceptions of family rituals in their families of origin. *Journal of Comparative Family Studies, 42,* 355–367.

Smith, B. (2000). Introduction. In B. Smith (Ed.), *Home girls: A Black feminist anthology* (pp. xix–lvi). New Brunswick, NJ: Rutgers University Press.

Suter, E. A., Daas, K. L., & Bergen, K. M. (2008). Negotiating lesbian family identity via symbols and rituals. *Journal of Family Issues, 29,* 26–47. doi: 10.1177/0192513X07305752

Viere, G. M. (2001). Examining family rituals. *The Family Journal, 9,* 285–288. doi: 10.1177/1066480701093007

Weston, K. (1991). *Families we choose: Lesbians, gays, kinships.* New York, NY: Columbia University Press.

Wolin, S. J., & Bennett, L. A. (1984). Family rituals. *Family Process, 23,* 401–420. doi: 10.1177/1066480701093007

Bisexuality and Family: Narratives of Silence, Solace, and Strength

JANET B. WATSON
Deakin University, Melbourne, Australia

This article examines the constellation of factors that come to bear in the family domain for bisexually desiring, behaving, or identifying individuals. Specifically, it interrogates the prevailing conditions that hinder or encourage disclosure of bisexuality and the consequences of such action. It argues that the family is uniquely situated at the interface of private and public domains of sociality, and, thus, negotiation of sexuality is herein constructed through the articulation of the "the family closet." Analysis draws on doctoral research that investigated the sociological nexus of sex, gender, and bisexuality in an Australian sample. Data collected via 47 in-depth interviews comprised a sex-/gender-diverse cohort including men and women, as well as transgender, cross-dressing, genderqueer, and intersex individuals. From this diversity of narratives the family environ emerged as a primary locus of personal and social challenge. Case studies taken from the data demonstrate how disclosure of bisexuality to family of origin was a selective process predicated by a range of sociocultural considerations such as religion, geographical location, and dominant discourses of gender and sexuality. These narratives foreground a spectrum of family responses spanning total estrangement, silence and/or denial, tentative acknowledgement, or complete acceptance and support. Whether encountered as sites of negative resistance or positive acceptance, respondents' stories illuminate the capacity to forge strategies of coping, resilience, and empowerment. A theoretical framework informed by the nomadic philosophy of Gilles Deleuze and Felix Guattari is deployed in order to explain these findings.

INTRODUCTION

Despite the growth of bisexual research over recent decades, literature pertaining specifically to bisexuality and families of origin is minimal (Cohler, 2005; Giammettei & Green, 2012; Power et al., 2012; Short, Riggs, Perlesz, Brown, & Kane, 2007). The limited body of scholarship here underlines that a more comprehensive treatment is warranted (for example Morris, Balsam, & Rothblum, 2002; Orel & Fruhauf, 2006; Pallotta-Chiarolli, 2010; Power et al., 2012). This is largely because existing research generally considers bisexuality in terms of the gay, lesbian, bisexual, and transgender (GLBT) umbrella, which for the most part focuses upon, or defaults to, same-sex attraction. Bisexually identifying or behaving individuals may indeed find common ground with other queerly oriented identities (Diamond, 2008; Leonard et al., 2012; Power et al., 2012; Rust, 2002). However, concerns relating explicitly to those whose sexuality is located between or outside the binary constructs of heterosexual/homosexual categories are likely to be overlooked, glossed, or rendered invisible (Corboz, Dowsett, Mitchell, Couch, & Pitts, 2008; Miller, André, Ebin, & Bessonova, 2007; Rust, 2002; See & Hunt, 2011). Moreover, current research establishes that self-ascriptions of bisexual behaviour, desires, and attractions are tending towards articulations of fluidity and inventive labeling or rejecting conventional idiom of gay, lesbian, bisexual, heterosexual (Owen, 2011; Pallotta-Chiarolli, 2010; Rust, 2009; Vaccaro, 2009). As Rust (2009) has argued, comprehensive examination of bisexuality's fluid, non-linear expressions "cannot be accomplished by 'adding' bisexuals as a third category in the variable 'sexual orientation'; it requires changes in theoretical approaches, measurement, sampling, data collection and analysis" (p. 100).

This article addresses a gap in current knowledge through foregrounding the "B" in GLBT families. It draws on findings from my doctoral research of bisexuality in Australia (Watson, 2012). The principal aim of this study sought to deploy "bisexuality" as an entry point to investigate interplays, diversities, and multiplicities of sexuality and sex/gender. Doing so revealed narratives that reside in between and beyond dominant constructs that inform much GLBT research, particularly statistical analysis (Rust, 2009). Accordingly, this research project principally interrogated the inherent ontological messiness of sexual realities—articulations of desire, attraction, and experience that speak of instability, transformation, experiment, and fluidity.

In recounting their diverse sexual and gendered stories, some respondents revealed detailed portraits of their families of origin, wherein the family locus emerged as a pivotal site in negotiating and coming to terms with their sexual desires and identity formations. I present these particular stories as case studies in order to bring a much needed insight into the relationship between bisexuality and family. My discussion focuses on a dominant theme that emerged in participants' narratives concerning disclosure

TABLE 1 Participant Demographic Profiles

Pseudonym	Age	Sex/Gender	Sexuality	Ethnicity	Relationship/Family	Location
Adele	early 20s	f	queer	Eur	single	urban
Anna	early 30s	f	pansexual	Aust	single	urban
Anthony	late 30s	m	queer	Aust	de facto (m)	urban
Astrid	early 40s	mtf	lesbian	Aust	single	regional
Ben	early 40s	m	no label	Aust	single	urban
Billy	mid 30s	m	no label	Aust	single	urban
Brett	early 20s	m	queer	Aust	single	regional
Cameron	early 20s	m	bi-queer	Aust	single	regional
Carol	mid 50s	mtf	lesbian	NZ	de facto (f)	urban
Cass	late 30s	f	bisexual	Aust	de facto (mtf)	urban
Charlie	late 30s	m/gq	queer	Eur-S Asia	de facto (f)	urban
Charlotte	early 30s	f	bisexual	Aust	mar/chn	urban
Cherie	mid 30s	mtf/cd	queer	Aust	de facto (f)	urban
Cliff	late 60s	m	bisexual	Aust	div/chn/partner (m)	regional
Dan	early 40s	m	bisexual	Aust	single	urban
Dana	mid 50s	f/i	lesbian	Aust	de facto (f)	urban
David	late 20s	ftm	queer-bi	Aust	de facto (m)	urban
Dean	late 30s	m	bisexual	Aust	single	urban
Ewan	early 50s	m/gq	gay-bi	UK	mar/chn	regional
Glenda	late 30s	mtf	bisexual	Aust	div/chn	regional
Graham	mid 40s	m	gay	Aust	div/chn/partner (m)	urban
Helen	late 30s	mtf	queer-bi	Aust	single	urban
James	mid 20s	m	no label	Aust	multi partners	urban
Jay	late teen	ftm	bisexual	Aust	casual partners	urban
Jenna	mid 30s	f	lesbian	Aust	div/chn/partner (f)	urban
Joanne	mid 30s	f	bisexual	Aust	de facto (f)	urban
Jordan	early 40s	m/gq	fluid	UK-S Asia	mar/child	regional
Julia	late 60s	f	primarily lesbian	Aust	div/single/chn	urban
Karen	late 50s	mtf	polymorphous	Aust	single	urban
Kate	mid 30s	f	queer	Aust	partner (ftm)	urban

(Continued on next page)

TABLE 1 Participant Demographic Profiles (Continued)

Pseudonym	Age	Sex/Gender	Sexuality	Ethnicity	Relationship/Family	Location
Lara	early 40s	f	bisexual	Aust	married	urban
Leigh	mid 30s	m	bisexual	Aust	mar/swinger	urban
Lesley	mid 30s	mtf/gq	polysexual	Aust	poly	urban
Lisa	early 40s	mtf	bisexual	Aust	single	urban
Lucy	early 20s	f	bisexual	Aust	single	regional
Matthew	mid 20s	ftm	gay-bi	Aust	de facto (f)	urban
Michael	early 30s	m	bisexual	Aust	mar/poly	urban
Morgan	early 50s	ftm/gq	mostly lesbian	Aust	div/chn	urban
Natasha	mid 30s	f	bisexual	Aust	mar/poly	urban
Paul	late 40s	m	bi-sensual	Aust	div/chn/poly	regional
Penny	mid 30s	f	bisexual	Aust	div/poly	urban
Rachel	mid 30s	f	queer	UK	de facto (m)	urban
Samantha	late 20s	f	fluid	Aust	single	urban
Sarah	late 20s	f	mostly hetero	E Asia	single	urban
Shane	mid 20s	f/gq	bi-queer	Aust	single	urban
Tim	early 30s	m	queer	Aust	single	regional
William	early 60s	m	gay-bi	Aust	mar/chn	urban

Note. f = female, m = male, mtf = male-to-female, gq = genderqueer, cd = cross-dresser, i = intersex, ftm = female-to-male, mar = married, chn = children, div = divorced, poly = polyamorous and/or nondisclosure to family members. This is particularly important given that national survey data of GLBT Australians revealed bisexual men and women reported lower rates of disclosure to family than that of gay men or lesbians (Leonard et al., 2012). Decisions to "come out" or withhold declaring their sexualities often entailed much consternation and measured reflection concerning not only "whether to tell" but also "who to tell." Respondents thus navigated the "family closet"—that is, the varying degrees in which disclosure was negotiated and enacted within the family context.[1] A key figuration of the family closet is, therefore, the construction of family secrets. This occurred in two ways: being withheld *from* family members as well as being kept *within* the family from outsiders (Joos & Broad, 2007). As will be evidenced, such secretive situations were not simply conceived as a negative and linear response to fear and opprobrium, but from a positive standpoint, also generated productive strategies of coping, resilience, and empowerment.

In order to provide a more nuanced reading of these generative spaces of bisexuality and family engagement, I utilize a sociological framework inspired by the philosophy of Gilles Deleuze and Felix Guattari. This approach examines processes of self-actualization as creative or desiring endeavours, which are conceptualized by Deleuze and Guattari (1987) as "becomings" and "nomadism." The *process of becoming* is one of negotiating dominant binary discourses and culturally scripted categories that attempt to nail down the subject as "one," while carving out spaces of heterogeneity and movement (Deleuze & Guattari, 1987, p. 159). This nomadic space of movement dismantles binary regimes (man/woman, gay/straight) that police us as "wholes" (Deleuze & Parnet, 2006, p. 106). Rather than being defined by rigidly predetermined boundaries and limits that "parcel out a closed space to people," nomad spaces are polyvocal and variable (Deleuze & Guattari, 1987, pp. 380, 382). Bisexual subjectivity is accordingly reimagined as an ongoing project of invention that navigates the social field of family and foregrounds how this variously intersects with other structural considerations, such as age, religion, cultural background, and geography.

METHODOLOGY

As sexual minorities often present sampling difficulties in being hard to reach or resistant to being identified, the present study adopted a purposive non-random sampling method (Dowsett, 2007). Via snowball sampling, targeted members of the sample population were asked to distribute the call for participants to their own networks (Neuman, 2006). Participant recruitment sought persons whose intimate partner histories included erotic, sexual, romantic, emotional, and/or psychological connection with *more than one gender*. Furthermore, it solicited beyond the conventional male/female gender divide to include transgender, genderqueer, and intersex individuals.[2] Doing so avoided "naming" individuals as "bisexual," which accorded with the Deleuzian logic that informed the rationale for this study. The sample of 47 individuals (between ages 19 and 67) comprised 15 men and 15 women (who have never questioned their designated sex at birth and subsequent sense of gender), and 17 sex-/gender-diverse persons (for whom conventional notions of the sex/gender binary have in some respect been disrupted either through disavowal, transition, gender-play or biological anomaly).[3] Participants employed various lexica to describe their sexuality: bisexual ($N = 15$); queer ($N = 8$); individualized creative terms ($N = 21$); or rejected labels ($N = 3$).

Given that, as Dowsett (2007) notes, sexual life is not easily measured or quantified, the current study adopted a qualitative methodology in order to reveal multi-dimensions of sexual and gendered lives. Data were collected via individual semistructured, in-depth interviews (face to face or phone, typically one hour). This method is well-suited to the aims of exploring minority populations—eliciting rich information, probing for a deeper understanding of participants' lives, and accessing subjugated voices (Liamputtong, 2007). Interviews were guided by the following topics: self-descriptions and expressions of gender and sexuality; attraction to, and relations with, differing genders; gender preference of partners; relationship styles; social situational experiences; and dominant discourses of gender and sexuality. Interview transcripts were coded to identify and analyse emergent themes.

RESULTS AND DISCUSSION

A key finding from this study was that participants not only *occupy* but also continually *move* within, beyond, and in between the structural boundaries that demarcate conventional understandings of man/woman and heterosexual/homosexual. Such borderland identities—to borrow Pallotta-Chiarolli's (2010) apt phraseology—are not simply confined to sexuality and gender, but also intersect with multiple fields of social interaction. It is in this sense that Deleuze and Guattari's (1987) concept of "becomings" takes on acute salience for an enlarged understanding of bisexuality, particularly in terms of family. For Deleuze and Guattari the "self" is not a fixed or coherent entity, but arises from a creative process as the subject encounters other elements in social, discursive, biological, cultural, and psychological assemblages. Elements infiltrate, disturb, or rupture other elements, producing mobile or nomadic bodies—the body is always in a state of metamorphosing in relation to its shifting surrounds or milieu, becoming something other. As such, the nomadic complexion is a central Deleuzian motif that interrogates how individuals navigate *between* dualisms (man/woman, gay/straight, queer/nonqueer, Western/non-Western). Such dualisms are delimited by borderlines that construct abstract structural figurations of dominant thinking and attempt to curtail multiplicity, rein in unruly bodies, and create a sense of order and homogeneity out of heterogeneous lived realities.

The nomadic body vividly captures the mutable and transient profile of participants' stories, wherein the family represented an ever-present touchstone, a point of reference from which to make sense of the trajectories that their sexual lives and subjectivities had taken. Significantly, participants revealed that disclosure to family members was a selective process entailing dialogue with dominant discourses of not only sexuality but also sex/gender and partner formations. Here, the contemplation or actualization of disclosure to family members was entangled with fearful apprehension of negative reprisal. Such apprehension stemmed from perceived family attitudes towards non-conventional expressions of both sexuality and gender. The social space of the family is, thus, uniquely located at the interface of private and public domains of engagement. Consequently, the "family closet" is drawn in complex ways that sees it as a source of both sanctuary and censorship depending upon family dynamics. As is discussed in this article, such familial encounters invited a spectrum of responses ranging from complete disavowal to unconditional support. The case studies presented here illuminate generative processes of identity formation that emerge from moving fields of lived reality—silences, secrets, and support—in which negative and positive experiences wax and wane in ever-shifting dialogue. I argue that the juncture of bisexuality and family is an experiential and mobile landscape; it is at once informed by, yet contests, the dominant heterosexual template that strives to maintain its hegemonic sway over social formations of family, sexuality, and gender.

Nomadic Trajectories: The Tyranny of Distance

Several narratives traversed multiple borderline crossings that heightened the complexities of familial experiences. Geographic distance provided a barrier of immunity for some respondents who feared the conservatism of their upbringings would cast their non-conventional lives unfavorably. In particular, the stories of Sarah, Jordan, and Charlie straddled border regions of cultural hybridity in tandem with their bisexually emergent sexualities. Although geographically distant, the impress of family of origin figured strongly in their respective articulations of sexual and gendered selves.

Moreover, these narratives highlight the stranglehold of not only heteronormativity in sexual life and relationship formation, but also homonormativity. Heteronormativity refers to the default assumption and privileged status of heterosexuality, and thereby circumscribes opposite-sex relationships as the paradigmatic model of normalcy in Western society (Warner, 1993). Although not equivalent to heteronormativity in terms of hierarchical relations of dominance and oppression, homonormativity upholds the sociocultural legitimation of exclusive homosexual identities (gay and lesbian) over and above sexualities that are more diversely or fluidly conceived, such as bisexuality (Pallotta-Chiarolli, 2010). The potency of homonormativity is actualized in mobilizing mainstream gay acceptability through playing to an ethics of desirable social norms—white, middle-class, monogamous coupling. Predicated by neoliberalism, homonormativity accordingly inoculates the public sphere of gay discourse from radical politics and situates it within the private domain of conventional domesticity and consumption (Duggan, 2002). Hence, a form of gay hegemony solidifies around a particular and morally acceptable version of queer subjectivities and citizenship. The "homo nuclear family" thus emulates the "hetero nuclear family" (Power et al., 2012, p. 534). Consequently, bisexuality is elided from view, stripped of its ontological veracity, ethical virtue, and political potency, and, ultimately, delegitimated as a threat to family cohesion. Bisexuality is not simply caught in a struggle between two cultural worlds—gay and straight (Bradford, 2004). Synchronously quarantined from the private sphere of conventional family ideology and disavowed from the public realm of sexual politics, bisexuality is also located in an awkward juncture between public and private domains.

This emerged as a recurring refrain and is particularly evident in Sarah's narrative as she explained the dilemma that her nascent bisexuality posed in the family context. The antecedents of heteronormativity lay partially in connection to her East Asian homeland, where her family of origin (mother and brother) currently resides, and with whom she maintains close relations. She described her country of birth as "very, very conservative ... gay people just don't exist there, officially." Sarah's relationship history has largely been one of serial long-term heterosexual monogamy, hence, she attaches strongly to a "primarily heterosexual" identity. How to cognize her emergent bisexuality, and the failure of dominant language to adequately capture her circumstances, has thus thrown Sarah's perceived sense of stable sexual self and future vision of heterosexual marriage and children into upheaval. This is despite a significant relationship in her late teens with a male-female couple, and more recently, experiencing a profound attraction for a woman. Sarah explained her quandary:

> *I've had two fiancés in the past ten years, and we were planning children.... But I've recently fallen in love with another woman and broken up with my most recent partner because of it. It's a great unknown. I think it's the sudden switch because I've convinced myself so completely that I'm heterosexual.*

The tyranny of distance from her family of origin has provided some safeguard; thus, Sarah has not felt inclined to disclose this recent development to them. However, she stated that her immediate family "wouldn't care at all" if she had a same-sex partner, explaining that her mother lectures in queer studies and her brother is also bisexual. Conversely, her extended family would view it less favourably. The impress of her conservative East Asian cultural background sits paradoxically alongside what she believes to be the liberal attitudes of her mother and brother, and her own interest in feminist law. But a contradiction emerged when Sarah later reflected that "actually, when I had the relationship [with the male-female couple] the first time around, I told my mother, and she completely ignored me." This type of noncommittal response commonly surfaced in other interviews, as will be discussed shortly. Sarah construed her bisexuality in problematic terms, bemoaning "how much hassle I'm prepared to go through in life."

The family closet evident here, thus, toggles between a private and public struggle, neither wholly one nor the other, but like bisexuality is lodged somewhere in between. The concept of "family" carries with it an abstract image enshrined by state-sanctioned normative ideals, yet it is also an intensely private sphere of specific lived practices. As Bourdieu (1996) wrote, the family is such that "the public is present in the private, and in the very notion of *privacy*" (p. 25). Deleuzian thought provides further elucidation of this conceptual interconnect. Deleuze and Guattari (1987) variously denote the hegemonic macro structures of social organisation (sex, class, ethnicity) as *majoritarian*, *strata*, or *molar* entities. These are constituted by "great binary aggregates" of signification ("man/woman" being the *par exemplar*) that entrench dualist thinking in Western epistemes and, moreover, perpetuate homogeneity, stasis, and rigidity (Deleuze & Guattari, 1987, p. 213). Conversely, lived expressions of bodies and subjects operate at a molecular or micro level. Hence, "family" is at once a molar and molecular structure where there is always a movement or dialogue in the spaces of social production *between* homogeneous groupings (and their named designations, gay or straight family) and the heterogeneities of lived reality (fluid and diverse expressions of sexuality and sex/gender that escape dominant categorization). In other words, the body or subject is constantly in motion—*becoming* something other than a totalizing label (whether lesbian, gay, straight or bisexual) might impute. Sarah's contemplation of bisexuality becomes manifest in a multi-relational field between the private/public realms of family, sexual desires, and normative social formations. Here, she is "swinging between surfaces" of macro structures and micro possibilities (Deleuze & Guattari, 1987, p. 161). Doing so, such pendulous movement slowly erodes the sovereign authority of majoritarian heterosexual and monosexual organization.

Adding a further complication to the bisexual landscape, both Jordan and Charlie were designated "male" at birth, but have struggled with an inner sense of being female or feminine, and the desire to express this outwardly. Neither has transitioned to "female" and they both considered their genders as being somewhere in between male and female. Each has been, or is currently, married. However, their borderline narratives do not attach to dominant polarities of sex/gender and sexuality, but rather, nomadically weave in between. Resisting any recourse to definitive "identity" labelling, their fluid subjectivities are enacted through intersecting fields of gender, sexuality, and culture. Both born to British parents of European-South Asian blended backgrounds, their lives have, therefore, negotiated multiple border regions of cultural, sexual, and corporeal hybridity.

For Jordan and Charlie the notion of family was expressed in two spheres: their relation to family of origin in the United Kingdom, and their role as parent and spouse in their own Australian homes. Like Sarah, neither participant has disclosed to their families of origin abroad any departure from "normal" sexuality or gender. Jordan lives with his wife and child in an Australian rural township, and although predominantly attracted to women, has had casual sexual encounters with men. London's 1980s music scene, in which ambiguities of gender and sexuality were *de rigueur*, provided the backdrop to Jordan's formative years. This cultural milieu afforded a respite from the conservatism of the Sri Lankan community, Christian home life, and English county environ, where, in each of these domains, he felt like "a fish out of water"—triply marginalised by normative decrees of ethnicity, gender, and sexuality. Sri Lankan culture, Jordan explained, is, on the surface at least, very conventional. Any expression of sexual or gender nonconformity, by necessity, is thus covert and hidden. Jordan reflected that his parents were cognizant of his conflicted state around gender and sexuality but, in his words, ignored it:

> *I don't know that they knew the full extent of it. They're fairly conventional people. I didn't really come out to them. I guess I rebelled in other ways and covered it up.*

The incongruent proximities of the exotic and domestic cultivated a vacillating movement between repression and expression of inchoate bisexuality and transgressive gender. As Jordan commented, this was synchronously troubling and transformative:

> *My sexuality probably was confusing and problematic because of my upbringing and being a quite straight environment. Certainly in a suburban county it's still seen as a weird thing.... I probably used drugs and alcohol [during] my teenage years [and] came at it in a negative way, generally struggling with the whole idea that you had to be straight or gay.... In my teens, playing around in the London band scene, luckily, it was very trendy to be bisexual.... It allowed me to express myself a bit more, like wearing makeup and going out in a frock; it was kind of liberating.*

Now in his forties, the London scene and the attendant secrets of Jordan's gender and sexuality that were withheld from his parents' knowledge have long been forsaken. Although his parents are no longer living, the vestiges of Jordan's family closet remain. Here, Jordan recounted not feeling comfortable about opening up to his sister in the United Kingdom, anticipating a negative response, which he did not want to affect his child and wife. However, within the sanctity and privacy of home, Jordan's queerly oriented gender and sexuality finds a liberation of expression—a comfort and safety of not having to edit "his" preferred androgynous embodiment to conform to heteronormative expectations of being "masculine," "husband," and "father." As full-time carer of his child, Jordan explores border region possibilities, noting, "I love being a mummy-daddy, which is what I'm called by my son."

Likewise, Charlie embraces a labile genderqueer status, shifting between and often melding self-presentations of masculinity, femininity, man, and woman in ways that blur and question the boundaries of sex/gender and problematize the master categories of sexuality—lesbian, gay, straight, and bisexual. Attracted to men, women, and those who sit somewhere in between, Charlie's preferred self-description is "queer," and he explained that his sexual desire exceeds the limits of binary gender. A father to a teenage son, twice married, and partnered predominantly to "straight" women, Charlie's relationship history appears conventionally "heterosexual." However, Charlie's bisexual desires and genderqueerness prevent his partnerships from deferring to a hetero-/homonormative model. In particular, his second marriage to a lesbian-identifying woman clearly problematized positioning his relationships according to the dominant categories of gay or straight. Charlie's Anglo-European-Indian genealogy, like Jordan, presented a cultural barrier to ever disclosing his "authentic" sexual and gendered self to traditionalist family members in the United Kingdom. He mourned his conservative family upbringing in the United Kingdom, recalling the necessity to conform to what Connell (2005) refers to as hegemonic masculinity: "I was pretty much to look at, an average, young heterosexual male, playing football on a weekend and going to the pub." However, from 12 years of age Charlie recognised something unusual in himself and began covertly cross-dressing, borrowing his sisters' clothes without their knowledge.

Since leaving the United Kingdom a fear of difference looms in long-distance phone calls with his mother or siblings: "When I have conversations on the phone with my family or my mum, she'll tell me about something going on in the U.K., and something homophobic comes out." Charlie acknowledged profound feelings of isolation from his family, which he conveyed with an affective sense of bereavement or loss. His "lesbian" marriage, now ended, permitted a sense of sexual and gender freedom denied to Charlie by family of origin. He explained how it offered a space of sanctuary that afforded a safe space for him to flourish and salve the psychological wounds of prior social and familial isolation:

It's probably the period of time where I've been able to express myself the most and really feel more comfortable with my identity and my gender, how I present myself. It opened up all sorts of opportunities.

The queer family is hereby located on the cusp of private and public spheres, such that the private space contests social institutions, formations, and ideologies that prescribe a heteronormative template of familial functioning. It is, therefore, a space of retreat or deterritorialization forged by lines of flight in Deleuzian language. Jordan's and Charlie's "becomings" are, thus, relentless productions that steer between conforming to public scripts of family and intimate relationships and seeking ways that loosen these binds in order to liberate their private desiring selves.

Navigating Silences

The stories of Sarah, Charlie, and Jordan underscore that a conservative upbringing played heavily into their respective decisions concerning nondisclosure of sexual preference to family of origin. Indeed, this was the case for approximately one-third of my respondents, whose parent/s remained uninformed. In these narratives, conservative milieu commonly dovetailed with religious affiliations and/or rural locale. Here, respondents spoke of homophobic sentiments and a lack of understanding and willingness to embrace difference or diversity of sexuality and gender. While a sibling might often be privy to revelations of bisexual identity or desires, parents were left in ignorant silence. For the remaining two-thirds of participants who came out of the family closet to parents and/or siblings, eight experienced significant negativity. Such circumstances frequently gave rise to a protective cloak of silence. A parent and/or sibling would lapse into silent denial on the matter of bisexuality, or conversely, a participant sought refuge in refusing to raise the issue again in the family context. Navigating these troubled and troubling bisexual landscapes, families thus invoked the strategic use of secrecy and silence (Orel & Fruhauf, 2006). The poignancy of silence—that which is left unstated, unutterable, or non-signified in its mournful absence—was a central motif that permeated participants' stories in this study. As is evidenced, it was not merely a mechanism of repudiation, but also a coping strategy in its capacity to provide a safeguard or safety net.

SECRET LIVES

Lara and Rachel—both of whom have de facto male partners—considered their bisexualities as private matters. Both have negotiated an open relationship agreement that allows the inclusion of female partners within the spousal context, which is sometimes referred to as "gender monogamy" (Gustavson, 2009, p. 418). Lara and Rachel did not feel comfortable disclosing such non-conventional intimate arrangements to their parents, particularly as dominant representations of bisexuality perpetuate stereotypes such as promiscuity and infidelity (McLean, 2008). Lara attributed this to being a "men's sexuality thing" in which the perception of her father as "quite homophobic" has acted as a filtering system in her life. Lara claimed that her mother "certainly wouldn't have a drama," and although she has a close mother-daughter relationship there is a reticence to talk about personal sexual matters. "Mothers don't need to know those things about their daughters," Lara opined. Lara attributed these attitudes and responses to the conservative small community of her rural farm upbringing:

> *I developed a need-to-know basis on a lot of aspects. Some people say I compartmentalize life in a lot of ways, but that's always worked really well for me. And yes, a very homophobic father in lots of ways, he would just say awful things.*

However, Lara's family closet, like many others in this study, is partial, as she has disclosed to her brother and sister. Both have responded openly in ways that reflect their social settings and personal encounters. Lara stated that her sister is also bisexual, and although her brother is straight "he's gone to the Rubber Ball."[4] She further added, "his best mate is bi, so he's [a] very open and positive kind of person." Similarly, Rachel confided in one of her sisters, who she discovered was "on the same page."

Such partial disclosure sees bisexual subjectivity as being "half in and half out" of the family closet (Karlson, 2007, p. 4). Selective disclosure to family members commonly occurs in nonheterosexual populations (Weeks, Heaphy, & Donovan, 2001). Natasha's story provides further elucidation of the complexities posed by living a bisexual lifestyle. Natasha is multi-partnered to two men (one of whom is her husband) and a woman. A Catholic family upbringing, coupled with conservatism and a "homophobic father," have presented the possibility of a profoundly negative reaction, one that she is not willing to entertain despite a professed desire for honesty. As with several other respondents, Natasha is open about her bisexuality with her siblings and has experienced no ill will. Regarding her parents, however, Natasha's domestic arrangements have necessitated disclosing her polyamorous lifestyle but not her bisexuality, whereby her parents are "as accepting of it as they can be, given their religious beliefs."[5] She explained that while such acceptance is couched in terms of disapproval, both parents treat her other male partner with respect and friendship.

Similarly, Paul is less inclined to reveal his bisexuality to family of origin or adult children than acknowledge his two primary female partners (who live in separate households). A committed Christian for many years, Paul has since severed ties with the Church, but nevertheless, is haunted by the vestiges of family ideology and heteronormativity that religious doctrine encoded as part of his early life:

> *There's this feeling that bisexuality is like playing around, sexual perversion for the sake of it, the whole vice thing ... like you're queer in a bad sense.*

Anthony also refrains from discussing his diverse sexuality with his Catholic family of origin. His situation is somewhat the reverse of the usual "coming-out" story, in that Anthony's family knows about, and supports the fact of, his "gay" lifestyle. Identifying as "queer" to encapsulate that his attractions are "broader" than "gay," he nonetheless felt unable to discuss the reality of his bisexual attractions with his family. He believed that it would "confuse" them, citing "Catholic sex guilt" as a further reason for finding bisexuality "too difficult" to discuss in the family domain. Others also cited non-disclosure of bisexuality to family of origin for reasons of not wanting to "complicate" their families' lives.

"The Elephant in the Room"

For those who disclosed their bisexuality to family of origin, in some cases secrecy was reconstructed via a tacit understanding that the topic was relegated to the unspoken or unheeded. Younger unpartnered participants found it easier to adopt or partake in such silencing strategies. Samantha reported a complete lack of acceptance from her mother and brother, and a more moderate response from her father, who was "a little more accepting." She described her mother as holding to "paranoia about pedophiles" in relation to homosexual males. Upon "coming out" to her family of origin as bisexual at age 20, Samantha recalled their stated belief that "I don't care if you are gay, but just pick a side." The imperative that resides within the idea of having to "choose" to be either gay or straight, hence, adds a complicating dimension to negotiating the family closet beyond that of fearing homophobic refusal. In other words, a common theme in this study is that the family closet is frequently constructed through sentiments of biphobia, which are predicated by dominant stereotypes of bisexuality previously discussed. As witnessed in Anthony's belief that it was easier for his family to accept his gay lifestyle rather than "confuse" them by acknowledging his bisexual desires, this belies both the heteronormative and homonormative assumptions that attach to the now mainstream construction of the "good gay subject" (Agathangelou, Bassichis, & Spira, 2008, p. 126). Public discourse thus infects the private domain of family. Premised on such confusion and lack of understanding, particularly from her mother and brother, Samantha now does not discuss her sexuality with her family.

Brett's and Kate's experiences were typical of the "elephant in the room" syndrome. Brett's mother knew of his bisexuality by virtue of "someone else telling her" and "didn't take it particularly well." Her initial response was intensively emotional, making comments like, "Are you going to be alone forever?" Although she "got over it fairly quickly," Brett lamented that it was because "we just don't talk about it." Kate similarly encountered muted reaction from most of her family. While a close relationship with her sister has fostered a supportive attitude, her mother, father, and brothers convey what she terms "an invisibility factor—they don't say anything." Kate has found this very frustrating, especially on occasions when bringing a female or trans partner to the family home. In these instances, her family's actions were somewhat paradoxical and disingenuous, which have had profound ramifications on how Kate relates to her parents and brothers.

They kind of bent over backwards to overcompensate, to show that they were really okay with it all, with her [Kate's partner]. But then they'd say fucked things to me later, which they didn't think were that bad, but we had debates about.... Like "Can you please refer to her as my partner rather than my friend?" And Mum couldn't understand why it was such a big issue. And with my trans partner [female-to-male], somehow I found myself having this conversation with my mother about phalloplasty [surgical construction of a penis] ... and it's not appropriate to discuss this stuff. So in terms of how it affected my family, it affects trust and how invested I feel in asking about their lives. Because if I can't talk about my issues then why would I want to engage with them? It becomes an uneven relationship.

The "invisibility factor" surfaced more explicitly in Michael's interactions with his father. Brought up in a Christian-dominated country environment, Michael recounted profound negativity towards homosexuality; it was "never talked about in a positive manner." His father's response to Michael's self-declared bisexuality was thus one of self-admonishment and apology for having "gone wrong" in raising his son, and a subsequent absence of acceptance and acknowledgment. Michael maintains contact with his father, but said,

He never discusses my male partner; he pretty much makes out like he doesn't exist and he really doesn't want to be aware of that part of my life.

Beheld in such silences and secrets, bisexuality is seemingly circumscribed as an unwanted and undesirable truth that must remain hidden from view. However, the secretive aspect of bisexuality exudes a residual potency in its capacity to disturb, yet, reconfigure dominant social templates and the moral underpinnings that weld monosexuality (heterosexual/homosexual, gay/straight) to familial ideology. For Deleuze and Guattari (1987) secretive behaviour is given a form (such as covert bisexual behaviour) and is thereby replaced by an "envelope or box" in which the empirical content is hidden and preceded by paranoid judgement, such as moral transgression, guilt, and shame (p. 286). This, then, is the locus of negative stereotyping that circumscribes aberrant bisexual bodies. But, as Deleuze and Guattari argued, the secret secretes: "the content is too big for its form" and, hence, "something must ooze from the box" (pp. 286–287). The secretive aspect of bisexuality is, therefore, not static but actuates becomings of self that contest negative ascriptions of fear, revulsion, internalised homophobia, risk, and gender stereotyping.

Eliminating the Negative

Respondents' narratives commonly related a struggle with emergent feelings of bisexuality in juxtaposition with conservative family and sociocultural contexts. However, these are also journeys that move beyond silences and disavowals, forging other avenues of solace, new pathways of possibility. Such movement is a productive enterprise that repeals the dominant overcoding of societal norms, structures, and organization, and generates "becomings" of subjectivities and social formations (Deleuze & Guattari, 1987). Deleuzian analysis thus foregrounds how elements of the socius (which are always partial and multiple) function—that is, what is produced or constructed in the relations *between* elements. Hence, the "minoritized" self is a creative project of emergent subjectivity that traverses the lines of binary demarcation—in-between spaces that rupture molarities of gay/straight, and man/woman. In doing so, strength, resilience, and positivity are cultivated from this often dubious vantage point of what Hemmings (2002) has dubbed "the middle ground" of bisexuality (p. 2).

Strength and resilience are, therefore, energizing or affective forces of agency and empowerment. But this is not to romanticise bisexuality as a utopian ideal or panacea for social ills and inequity. Rather, the landscape of bisexuality is a constantly moving field of encounter, contestation, and embattlement—one that is contoured in dialogue with a mosaic of dominant discourses. The most conspicuous cases of this are witnessed in the accounts of Tim, Joanne, and Matthew, who each suffered profound negative reprisal from family members. Self-describing as a liberal queer Christian, Tim lives in what he describes as a "redneck" regional centre, coloured by extreme attitudes of homophobia, religious conservatism, and macho sporting culture. Tim "came out" to his family origin with "disastrous consequences" in which he was shunned by all except his father. Tim's brother physically attacked him, and his sister refuses to accept him into her home or allow contact with his niece if he is in a same-sex relationship. His mother's reaction surprised him the most:

QUEERYING FAMILIES OF ORIGIN

It took Mum about two years to accept it. I was quite stunned by that; I expected her to accept it straight away.... Because her friend was a lesbian and my mum had a one-nighter with her, I expected my mum to be more accepting, not so bloody judgmental.

Much of his teenage youth was fraught by internal struggles over his same-sex desire and attempting to reconcile this with Christian dogma that decried homosexuality as deviant. Conversations with a sympathetic gay priest eventually resolved his sense of internalized homophobia and precarious relations with family of origin. He is now comfortable with his bisexual attractions and desires, and has had monogamous relationships with both men and women. Tim's resilience manifests in a passion for social justice, and commitment to community sector GLBT and youth organizations.

As a rebellious teenager, Joanne "locked horns" with her "homophobic and prejudiced" Catholic father and assumed the provocative stance of a "cool, gay-friendly" person. However, his unjustifiable prejudice "lifted a veil" for Joanne as she became aware of her own bisexuality. No longer simply an ally of sexual radicalism, Joanne actively and openly participated as a member of the queer community. Consequently, Joanne's father "disowned" her and remains alienated from his daughter. This extreme response led Joanne's mother to be more supportive and open-minded, and hence, she "double-parented" Joanne. Joanne is now partnered to a genderqueer trans person (female-to-male) and actively engages in bisexual and queer politics.

Travelling differently to the hegemonic norms of sexuality, gender, and monosexuality, thus, effectuates multiplicities of self and subjectivity, which for Deleuze are "micro-politics" of becomings (Deleuze & Parnet, 2006, p. 13). Such micro-political becomings reveal heterogeneities of desire that slowly erode and rewrite molar or dominant scripts of family, sexuality and gender. For Matthew (trans man), the hegemonic family scripts of his upbringing were enacted through the ordinance of fundamentalist Christianity, which inflicted much pain and suffering on his then "lesbian female" identity. Coming out as lesbian as a teenager, he was "kicked out of home." Matthew's decision to transition to male was "equally well received" and he remains estranged from his parents. The impact of excommunication from family and church was devastating. Matthew recalled recurrent suicidal ideation and "horrendous nightmares" of impending doom and Armageddon. Over time, and with the benefit of counselling and establishing queer friendship networks, Matthew has rescinded such extreme religious beliefs and is now actively involved in queer and state politics. Matthew's story is testament to the creative forces of self-actualization. He is partnered to a lesbian-identifying woman with whom he plans to start a family. In carving out a queer path that contests both heteronormativity and homonormativity, Matthew's story demonstrates the revelatory capacity that issues from negative experience:

> *After being unceremoniously booted out of my religion I had to decide how to construct my own moral/ethical framework of right and wrong. When you're making that up yourself, and basing it on some basic premises like "do no harm," then your horizons are considerably extended. And all of a sudden you can.*

Accentuating the Positive

For almost half the participants in this study, family of origin has, overall, variously offered solace, comfort, encouragement, and support. That family has not presented an initial hurdle to social acceptance of non-conventional sexualities and genders, their journeys appeared somewhat less troubled. Cass' observation that "it was really scary telling them; you just don't know what reaction you will get" was a typical experience. Cass was previously married, but is now in a long-term partnership with a trans woman. Despite the positive acceptance of family members, Cass added that family comments suggest "they actually still just never get it [bisexuality]; they don't ever quite understand." Cameron encountered similar incidents with his parents where habitual reference to him as "gay" is predicated by an assumption that any partner will be male. The impress of dominant binary thinking accordingly holds sway through reiterating a persistent occlusion of those who straddle the border regions.

In comparison to participants who either endured negative responses or remained silent about their sexuality due to perceptions of conservatism, biphobia, or homophobia, positive experiences were largely situated within family contexts variously described as liberal, progressive, and nonjudgmental. A keen sense of social justice and equality were often accorded primacy in such settings. Family support, however, sometimes came attached to certain caveats. James, for instance, described his sexuality as "complex," rejecting identity labels as none adequately captured his preference for "ambiguity" and predominant attraction to bisexual and trans individuals. Currently partnered to a transgender female-to-male, James lives with his mother and teenage brother, who are supportive of such complexity. James explained the family dynamics in relation to his mother:

> *She is not entirely accepting, but is supportive. She has been supportive of my relationships from the outset. One of her recent comments—in a dry humor—was that she was already having enough trouble dealing with [my] Asperger's and I had to throw this into it. Having to be reserved at home around my younger brother is starting to grate—Mum requested that we [James and his partner] be discreet. He likes my partner, and asks, "When is he coming back? He is fun."*

James' narrative traverses several border-zone subjectivities—bisexuality, transgender, Asperger's—which brings to light micro-realities of those who live in between the dominant categories that construct one-dimensional views of queer versus non-queer identities. Bisexuality opens up new vistas of non-conventional possibility that challenge assumptions upon which traditionalist representations of family structure and relationality are grounded. Bauer (2010) denotes this affective field as the "the domino-effect of perversion" such that "once you have crossed a certain line and start to question society's norms around gender and sexuality, you may proceed further to question the validity of other norms, becoming more open-minded to new options and less dependent on culturally available scripts" (p. 151).

Bauer's concept resonates with my respondents' stories wherein ethical processes of living are produced through rewriting and inventing their own scripts. While moral systems seek to rule and judge, ethical modes are enacted through sets of relations that challenge normative constructs. Hence, participants generated an "ethics of responsiveness" through "openness to interferences" in how they conceptualised their family relationships (Bogue, 2007, pp. 12,14). Participants' constructions of bisexual relationships within the family setting actively produced an ethics of multiple becomings that suspends the tyranny of hierarchical dualisms, and thereby exposes "hidden possible worlds" (Bogue, 2007, p. 13).

The "hidden" private world of bisexual swinging, which is dominantly constructed around moralising and sensationalist discourses of risk, infidelity, and promiscuity, cultivated the positive ethical framework within which Charlotte's family structure operated. Charlotte, a self-identified bisexual swinger, is twice married with two primary school-aged children. Relinquishing the heteronormative model in her second marriage, Charlotte and her husband have embraced a swinging lifestyle that allows for sexual freedom with both men and women within the marital domain. Moreover, the private sphere of swinging converges with her public professional role as a relationship coach, in which Charlotte advocates for, and writes about, sex positivism and sexual health awareness. As a result of her public persona, Charlotte's mother, father, and sister are aware of and support her alternative lifestyle without prejudice. The success of this lifestyle choice has been based around building an ethics of honesty, open communication, respect for each other's needs, and mindfulness towards continued relationship strength and vitality. It is an ethics of both affective and corporeal dimensions that overflows onto a nonjudgmental value system, detached from conservative morality, which Charlotte encourages in her daughter:

> *My daughter [has] learnt about sex education at school. I've had a conversation with her and asked, "Do you know what gay means?" She told me and I was quite impressed that she knew. I asked if she knew what bisexual*

is and she didn't, so I explained that. I'm in a position now where I can be myself and I want her to have the same choice.... What I'm teaching is very sex-positive and accepting.

CONCLUSION

The narratives discussed here demonstrate that the family domain is pivotal to becomings of ethical bisexual selves. Such subjectivities are drawn here as creative endeavours that emerge through both negative and positive experiences of negotiating the family closet. As evidenced by participants in this study, these experiences are contingent upon, and move through, intersecting domains of engagement—religion and value systems, geographic location, cultural background, and dominant discourses of sexuality and gender. What I term a generative ethics of bisexual becomings, howsoever named by self or others, thus emerges from flows of desire that interweave through self, family, and social fields of encounter. In seeking to rupture the hegemony of monolithic discourses, social structures and bodies, the kernels of revolutionary process are uncovered in "composing a more powerful body" (Deleuze & Guattari, 1987, p. 257). It is this powerful body, in its micro-movements and diverse constituencies, which progressively gnaws at the binary delineations of gender and sexuality. Importantly, positioning participants' familial experiences as "becomings" allowed analysis to take account of their narratives as a dialogue between self and wider socio-discursive contexts. Doing so, individuals are accorded agency and empowerment, rather than being circumscribed as docile receptacles of social forces, structures, and ideologies.

The case studies presented in this article are stories of pathos, struggle, courage, and resilience. Experiential realities that emerge from the interstitial spaces of sexual and gendered production demand to be heard and seen beyond the silences and secrets that frequently contour family experiences. As evidenced, family of origin sits at the juncture of intersecting spheres of the private and public, in which personal biographies are framed in and through a complex nexus of relations with intimate others and family members. The navigation of such domains is often drawn as battlelines, some more easily won than others. This article has presented cases from my data, but more empirical research is needed. Respondents' stories have opened up questions for future exploration, especially regarding the selective disclosure to family members, which constructs the family closet as partial and paradoxically protective and prohibitive. Participants related widely differing experiences in their responses with, and encounters between, mothers, fathers, siblings, daughters, and sons that indicates more comprehensive research is required here. Bisexuality must be further demystified in this primary sphere of sociality—that of family—where the seeds of understanding are first sown, in order that it may seek to flourish unhindered elsewhere in the sociocultural and political world, and accordingly liberate desire from the hegemonic binds of dualistic constructs and moral ordinance.

NOTES

1. The dominant usage of "family closet" in literature generally denotes hiding one's sexuality from family members without further conceptual explication.

2. Transgender embraces all those whose gender identity is not congruent with their sex designation at birth. Genderqueer persons variously straddle, play with, or reject the gender binary of man/woman. Intersex denotes *physical* diversity or anomaly pertaining to biological sex characteristics (hormones, chromosomes, gonads, and external anatomy) and may be either/neither/both/in between male and/or female.

3. Sex-gender diverse participants variously adopted a range of treatments, including hormone therapy and surgical procedures, in order to present in their preferred genders.

4. A social event that celebrates fetish subculture and sex/gender/sexuality diversity.

5. Polyamory indicates relationships in which individuals have multiple romantic, sexual, and/or affective partners. It emphasises long-term intimacy premised on an ethics of full disclosure and honesty.

REFERENCES

Agathangelou, A. M., Bassichis, M. D., & Spira, T. L. (2008). Intimate investments: Homonormativity, global lockdown, and the seductions of empire. *Radical History Review*, *100*, 120–143. doi: 10.1215/01636545-2007-025

Bauer, R. (2010). Non-monogamy in queer BDSM communities: Putting the sex back into alternative relationship practices and discourse. In M. Barker & D. Langdridge (Eds.), *Understanding non-monogamies* (pp. 142–153). Hoboken, NJ: Routledge.

Bogue, R. (2007). *Deleuze's way: Essays in transverse ethics and aesthetics*. Aldershot, UK: Ashgate.

Bourdieu, P. (1996). On the family as a realized category. *Theory, Culture & Society*, *13*(3), 19–26. doi: 10.1177/026327696013003002

Bradford, M. (2004). The bisexual experience: Living in a dichotomous culture. *Journal of Bisexuality*, *4*(1/2), 7–23. doi: 10.1300/J159v04n01_02

Cohler, B. J. (2005). Life course social science perspectives on the GLBT family. *Journal of GLBT Family Studies*, *1*(1), 69–95. doi: 10.1300/J461v01n01_06

Connell, R. W. (2005). *Masculinities*. Berkeley, CA: University of California Press.

Corboz, J., Dowsett, G. W., Mitchell, A., Couch, M., & Pitts, M. (2008). *Feeling queer and blue: A review of the literature on depression and related issues among gay, lesbian, bisexual and other homosexually active people*. Melbourne, Australia: La Trobe University, Australian Research Centre in Sex, Health and Society.

Deleuze, G., & Guattari, F. (1987). *A thousand plateaus: Capitalism and schizophrenia*. Minneapolis, MN: University of Minnesota Press.

Deleuze, G., & Parnet, C. (2006). *Dialogues II*. London, England: Continuum.

Diamond, L. M. (2008). Female bisexuality from adolescence to adulthood: Results from a 10-year long study. *Developmental Psychology, 44*(1), 5–14. doi: 10.1037/0012-1649.44.1.5

Dowsett, G. W. (2007). Researching gay men's health: The promise of qualitative Methodology. In I. H. Meyer & M. E. Northbridge (Eds.)., *The health of sexual minorities: Public health perspectives on lesbian, gay, bisexual and transgender populations* (pp. 419–441).New York, NY: Springer.

Duggan, L. (2002). The new homonormativity: The sexual politics of neoliberalism. In R. Castronovo & D. D. Nelson (Eds.), *Materializing democracy: Toward a revitalized cultural politics* (pp. 175–194). Durham, NC: Duke University Press.

Giammattei, S. V., & Green, R. -J. (2012). LGBTIQ couple and family therapy: History and future directions. In J. J. Bigner & J. L. Wetchler (Eds.), *Handbook of LGBT-affirmative couple and family therapy* (pp. 1–22). Hoboken, NJ: Taylor and Francis.

Gustavson, M. (2009). Bisexuals in relationships: Uncoupling intimacy from gender ontology. *Journal of Bisexuality, 9*(3/4), 407–429. doi: 10.1080/15299710903316653

Hemmings, C. (2002). *Bisexual spaces: A geography of sexuality and gender.* New York, NY: Routledge.

Joos, K. E., & Broad, K. L. (2007). Coming out of the family closet: Stories of adult women with LGBTQ parents(s). *Qualitative Sociology, 30*(3), 275–295. doi: 10.1007/s11133-007-9064-y

Karlson, M. (2007). Bisexuals exist—and so do bisexual parents! *Bi-Victoria Newsletter*, August/September, 1–4.

Leonard, W., Pitts, M., Mitchell, A., Lyons, A., Smith, A., Patel, S., Couch, M., & Barrett, A. (2012). *Private lives 2: The second national survey of the health and wellbeing of GLBT Australians.* Melbourne, Australia: La Trobe University, Australian Research Centre in Sex, Health & Society.

Liamputtong, P. (2007). *Researching the vulnerable: A guide to sensitive research methods.* London, England: Sage Publications.

McLean, K. (2008). Silences and stereotypes: The impact of (mis)constructions of bisexuality on Australian bisexual men and women. *Gay and Lesbian Issues and Psychology Review, 4*(3), 158–165.

Miller, M., André, A., Ebin, J., & Bessonova, L. (2007). *Bisexual health: An introduction and model practices for HIV/STI prevention programming.* New York, NY: National Gay and Lesbian Task Force Policy Institute, The Fenway Institute at Fenway Community Health, and BiNet USA.

Morris, J. F., Balsam, K. F., & Rothblum, E. D. (2002). Lesbian and bisexual mothers and nonmothers: Demographics and the coming-out process. *Journal of Family Psychology, 16*(2), 144–156. doi: 10.1037//0893-3200.16.2.144

Neuman, W. L. (2006). *Social research methods: Quantitative and qualitative approaches* (6th ed.). Boston, MA: Pearson/Allyn and Bacon.

Orel, N. A., & Fruhauf, C. A. (2006). Lesbian and bisexual grandmothers' perceptions of the grandparent-grandchild relationship. *Journal of GLBT Family Studies, 2*(1), 43–70. doi: 10.1300/J461v02n01_03

Owen, M. (2011). Still sitting on fences: Reflections on "Overstepping the bounds: Bisexuality, gender, and sociology." *Journal of Bisexuality, 11*(4), 493–497. doi: 10.1080/15299716.2011.620844

Pallotta-Chiarolli, M. (2010). *Border sexualities, border families in schools*. Plymouth, UK: Rowman and Littlefield.

Power, J. J., Perlesz, A., Brown, R., Schofield, M. J., Pitts, M. K., McNair, R., & Bickerdike, A. (2012). Bisexual parents and family diversity: Findings from the work, love, play study. *Journal of Bisexuality, 12*(4), 519–538. doi: 10.1080/15299716.2012.729432

Rust, P. C. R. (2002). Bisexuality: The state of the union. *Annual Review of Sex Research, 13*, 180–240.

Rust, P. C. R. (2009). No more lip service: How to *really* include bisexuals in research on sexuality. In W. Meezan & J. I. Martin (Eds.), *Handbook of research with lesbian, gay, bisexual and transgender populations* (pp. 100–130). New York, NY: Routledge.

See, H., & Hunt, R. (2011). Bisexuality and identity: The double-edged sword: Stonewall research into bisexual experience. *Journal of Bisexuality, 11*(2/3), 290–299. doi: 10.1080/15299716.2011.571995

Short, E., Riggs, D., Perlesz, A., Brown, R., & Kane, G. (2007). *Lesbian, gay, bisexual and transgender (LGBT) parented families: A literature review prepared for the Australian Psychological Society*. Melbourne, Australia: The Australian Psychological Society.

Vaccaro, A. (2009). Intergenerational perceptions, similarities and differences: A comparative analysis of lesbian, gay, and bisexual millennial youth with Generation X and baby boomers. *Journal of LGBT Youth, 6*(2/3), 113–134. doi 10.1080/19361650902899124

Warner, M. (1993). Introduction. In M. Warner (Ed.), *Fear of a queer planet: Queer politics and social theory* (pp. vii–xxxi). Minneapolis, MN: University of Minnesota Press.

Watson, J. B. (2012). *Re-visioning bisexuality: Rhizomatic cartographies of sex, gender and sexuality*. Unpublished PhD thesis, Deakin University, Melbourne.

Weeks, J., Heaphy, B., & Donovan, C. (2001). *Same sex intimacies: Families of choice and other life experiments*. London, England: Routledge.

"It's Always the Mother's Fault": Secondary Stigma of Mothering a Transgender Child

SUSAN L. JOHNSON
Bright Horizons Family Solutions, Cary, North Carolina, USA

KRISTEN E. BENSON
North Dakota State University, Fargo, North Dakota, USA

This instrumental case study (Stake, 2003) explores the process of transition and secondary stigma experienced by a white single mother who is parenting her six-year-old transgender daughter. Using an online chat interview format, a mother living in a rural U.S. community was asked to describe her parenting experiences as well as her perceptions of support services involving her child. Specifically, the aspects of mental health services that she deemed both helpful and not helpful are explored, as well as other contextual factors that contribute to the overall experience or impression of the therapeutic environment for a family with a transgender child.

INTRODUCTION

Parents of transgender children may seek support and information as they face parenting a child who challenges the dominant two-gender cultural system. In a culture that allows little flexibility in regards to gender norms and children, there are currently few already known gender-flexible affirming resources available to these parents (Lev, 2004), yet the establishment of support may increase parental acceptance of their gender-nonconforming child,

---

The authors extend their sincere appreciation to Sarah for her participation in this project. Portions of these findings were presented at the 2012 meeting of the National Council on Family Relations, Phoenix, Arizona.

and consequently the child's well-being (Brill & Pepper, 2008; Ryan, 2009). Likewise, clinicians find that some cisgender parents seek supportive and comprehensive therapeutic and health care services (Ehrensaft, 2011; Lev, 2004) as they navigate a phenomenon unfamiliar to them. Parents often face negative social judgment for their parenting decisions and secondary stigmatization for raising a transgender child (Menvielle & Tuerk, 2002). Moreover, due to the social reinforcement of strict binary gender roles, mental health care providers may often question parents' decision to affirm and encourage the transgender identities of their children. Single parents, specifically single mothers, face further stigmatization due to the common societal notion that they are less competent at parenting their children (DeJean, McGeorge, & Carlson, 2012). Furthermore, single mothers are more likely to perceive less social support compared to married mothers, and also experience more stress and depression (Cairney, Boyle, Offord, & Racine, 2003).

The focus of this study is on a middle-class, white mother's experiences raising a transgender child as well as her perceptions and experiences of therapeutic services. Her parenting experiences were explored in-depth, as well as the aspects of mental health services which she deemed both helpful and not helpful, and other contextual factors that contribute to her overall impression of the therapeutic environment for a single mother with a transgender child. Previous studies have typically focused on the gender-nonconforming individual (Lev, 2004) rather than on the experiences of someone who holds a significant relationship, such as a mother.

The needs of gender-nonconforming individuals are unique and deserve attention within social science research. While gay, lesbian, bisexual, transgender, and queer (GLBTQ) populations are similar in that they are marginalized groups, sexual orientation is often the focus of social science research. Literature is just starting to address gender identity from a non-diagnostic lens (e.g., Ehrensaft, 2011; Grossman, D'Augelli, Howell, & Hubbard, 2006; Malpas, 2011; Vanderburgh, 2009), yet these issues present relevant and important considerations for gender-creative people and their families. As more research emerges that focuses on the needs and experiences of gender-creative people, better support and advocacy efforts can be made on their behalf, which in turn may lead to a better understanding by their loved ones. Relationally focused research in particular will be helpful as there is little guidance available for the families and loved ones of transgender people (Lev, 2004).

LITERATURE REVIEW

Parents of transgender children often experience secondary stigmatization which may intensify negative feelings such as isolation and shame (Menvielle & Tuerk, 2002). These parents may face multiple struggles stemming from their own personal acceptance of their children, to advocating for their children in spite of social stigma, to the seeking of acceptance from others of their commitment to advocate for their children (Johnson & Best, 2012), in a culture that privileges whiteness and class status (Rothenberg, 2008). Single parents face further negative stigma, and single mothers are viewed more negatively than single fathers. Single mothers are perceived as less secure, less fortunate, less responsible, less satisfied with life, less moral, less reputable, less of a good parent, and less economically advantaged when compared to single fathers (DeJean et al., 2012). It is important to consider the multiple layers of oppression a single mother who is parenting a transgender child experiences.

Transgender children may rely heavily on their home environments for acceptance since they are constantly told they do not belong in many public settings such as their school environment (McGuire, Anderson, Toomey, & Russell, 2010). A child's home environment may or may not be supportive; many parents may be ill-equipped to empower their transgender child, and they may even perpetuate the social oppression associated with transphobia (Burdge, 2007). The quality of transgender individuals' family relationships is related to their life satisfaction (Erich, Tittsworth, Dykes, & Cabuses, 2008); furthermore, parental attitudes shape children's self-worth. Many parents believe that the best way to help their gender-nonconforming child is to change the child's self-ascribed gender identity so that it may match the child's assigned sex at birth (Brill & Pepper, 2008), which matches socially ascribed identification. Even though these parents may have loving intentions, a child oftentimes experiences this as rejection. Rejection of a transgender identity may be experienced as rejection of a child's entire identity (Ryan, 2009). Many transgender youth live in fear of parental and familial ostracism and ridicule (Grossman et al., 2006).

While a majority of the research has focused on parents' negative responses to their transgender child, research is beginning to demonstrate encouraging findings. Transgender youth who feel supported and valued by their families experience advantageous benefits such as higher self-esteem, a more positive sense of the future, lower risks for mental and physical health issues, and greater life satisfaction and well-being as compared to youths who do not feel supported and valued (Ryan, 2009). Indeed, one of the most important factors in the lives of transgender youth is the presence of an adult who is interested in their well-being and accepts them unconditionally (Ryan, 2009).

Many parents, after accepting and embracing their child's transgender identity, believe that their child has made them better people through the experience of being "different" (Menvielle, 2009). Parents of GLBTQ children may also develop critical thinking about the reality and impact of discrimination (Gonzalez, Rostosky, Odom, & Riggle, 2013). Gonzalez and colleagues

(2013) found that parents of GLBTQ children reported psychosocial benefits including personal growth through open-mindedness and awareness; positive emotions such as pride; activism; and new social connections with the GLBTQ community and allies.

Parents who are unfamiliar with gender nonconformity may seek services from an experienced and affirmative therapist for a multitude of reasons. They may be confused about whether their child has a mental illness, they may be unsure about what to do regarding their child's nonconforming actions, or they may wish for help understanding the ramifications of a transgender identity (Vanderburgh, 2009). In addition, they may desire education about transgender identity, the process of transitioning, gender in a cultural context, consequences of disclosure, referrals or introductions to other families with similar experiences, advocacy for the gender-nonconforming child within her or his school or community, or help with developing support systems (Vanderburgh, 2009).

There is an overwhelming need for mental health professional training programs to educate clinicians on working affirmatively with transgender youths and their families in order to address and reduce this distress that society has placed on them (Benson, 2013; Grossman & D'Augelli, 2007). Unfortunately, counselor training often does not include any extensive information on gender identity, which may serve to further negative stereotypes or at the least leave practitioners unprepared to work with this population (Carroll, Gilroy, & Ryan, 2002). Many transgender people who seek therapy are likely to be the first transgender client their therapist has ever worked with (Lev, 2004). However, therapists must be prepared to work with transgender youths, as they are at risk due to the stigmatization they experience. For instance, almost half of transgender youths report having had serious thoughts about taking their lives (Grossman & D'Augelli, 2007). As a highly stigmatized group, transgender children are subject to social isolation, mistreatment, and ostracism by their peers (Brooks, 2000). These reasons, combined with the social stigma and bias associated with transphobia, provide strong support for the therapeutic needs that a transgender youth may have in terms of care, support, and affirmation of identity.

Due to societal expectations based on gender-normative binaries, disclosure to family, friends, and significant others can often be a very frightening and painful process (Lev, 2004), so the rapport and trust built with a counselor or therapist is necessary in the process of therapy. As there is little cultural support for transgender children to actualize their true identity, the therapist's role in the child's life may become essential (Vanderburgh, 2009). The environment that the therapist creates should be respectful and safe, and allow the child and family to explore the child's gender identity and promote a positive sense of self (Grossman et al., 2006).

RESEARCH QUESTIONS

This study focused on a mother's experiences raising her transgender child, and her understandings, experiences, and perceptions of mental health services and other forms of support. The primary research questions that guided this study were "How does a parent describe her experiences raising a gender-nonconforming child?" and "How does a parent describe her perception of mental health services regarding her gender-nonconforming child?"

METHODOLOGY

The current project used a single-case study approach informed by a queer feminist lens, which explored the phenomenon of mothering a transgender child, and her perceptions of how mental health services promote her family's well-being. The use of queer theory allows researchers to examine how socially enforced binaries, such as girl/boy, construct normality and therefore deviance, and how the classification of "normal" and "deviant" serve to regulate and punish members of society (Oswald, Kuvalanka, Blume, & Berkowitz, 2009). Queer theory helps us understand the "deviant" classification that is placed on transgender children and their parents for living beyond gender-normative categories and the social expectations that have created harmful effects on the well-being of the participant and her family. The very nature of parenting a gender-nonconforming child essentially queers the dominant discourse surrounding parenting and family. The scope of feminist research emphasizes remaining outside of the limitations that society may place on groups without dominant social power, as well as centering on a group's gendered marginalization and the institutions that create the situation (Olesen, 2003). We identified the phenomenon of mother-blaming, which is a sexist bias that mothers are ultimately responsible and to blame for the actions, behaviors, mental health, and overall well-being of children (Jackson & Mannix, 2004), specifically with a transgender child.

Feminism and queer theory together attempt to address and deconstruct categories of gender, and both have explored the ways through which gender and sexuality are performed within contextual environments (Oswald et al., 2009). This lens also guides discussion regarding mother-blaming and the perception of mothers who support and advocate for their transgender children. We maintained an awareness of the social construction of gender and family, and the marginalization that stems from the distribution of social power (van Eeden-Moorefield, Martell, Williams, & Preston, 2011). More specifically, we continually remained aware of the social context which reinforced gender norms for the child and parental expectations of a white mother, and how this context affected the participant and her family. This project is intended to help researchers and mental health clinicians move toward social change and freedom from ideologies that have historically been oppressive through analyzing dominant discourse (Hesse-Biber, 2007).

Method

The purpose of a case study is to obtain comprehensive information in rich detail about a case of interest, resulting in an organized and systematic product (Patton, 2002). A case study is a useful methodology for encapsulating the meaning derived from a complex story into a finite report (Stake, 2003). The instrumental case study approach can produce unique information about a phenomenon that other methods cannot (Creswell, 2007). This case study explored the phenomenon of a mother parenting a gender-nonconforming child, her lived experiences, and her perceptions of how and to what extent mental health services and providers promote her family's well-being.

We used purposeful sampling to recruit the participant for this single-case study project by inviting organizations that support and/or advocate for GLBTQ families (i.e., PFLAG, Gender Spectrum) to post research announcements and flyers on electronic discussion lists, Web sites, and social networking Web sites. Parents and caregivers of a gender-nonconforming or transgender child were invited to participate in an interview conversation, because they are usually responsible for seeking out therapy services or take on the role of gatekeeper for their child's health care needs. More specifically, we used criterion-based sampling (Creswell, 2007), which encompassed the selection of a single parent who is raising a transgender child ages 6 through 18, prepubescent through age dependency. The second criteria required that the participating parent have the child reside in her home a majority of the time. The third criterion for the study was that the participant had to have sought some sort of support related to her child's gender identity personally or professionally. This research study was reviewed and approved by the North Dakota State University Institutional Review Board.

Data Collection

Data were collected via online chat sessions. Online qualitative methodology can be beneficial to reach marginalized groups, who often connect online and maintain member electronic discussion lists for the exchange of information (Mustanski, 2001). This study follows an online interview model developed by van Eeden-Moorefield, Proulx, and Pasley (2008), who designed a study in which gay male participants were interviewed individually online and participated in online focus groups. Marginalized populations, such as the parents of gender-nonconforming youths, may participate in online research due to the safety and anonymity that this method provides (Mustanski, 2001; van Eeden-Moorefield et al., 2008). Online methodology can give researchers access to underrepresented populations that might not be reached otherwise (Mustanski, 2001).

Only chat services with published privacy statements who comply with federal regulations to protect users' personal information were considered for use for online interviews. When the participant registered to use the online chat program, she was required to indicate that she read and agreed to the Terms of Service, which included the privacy policy of the program. We were mindful that in the event of a technical problem, an employee of the company (i.e., Yahoo Messenger technical support) who is bound by confidentiality obligations may access the user account. The participant was instructed to create a user account for the interview and delete the account after the interview was complete to minimize the likelihood of access by technical support. We prepared additional information about security for the preferred program to address questions or concerns about privacy protection (i.e., Security at Yahoo; http://info.yahoo.com/privacy/us/yahoo/security/).

After the participant responded to recruitment materials via e-mail, we contacted her by phone to answer questions about the study and set up an interview time. She completed informed consent and a demographic questionnaire online. The online interview took place as scheduled, lasting for approximately three hours. There were two remaining questions, which the participant requested to answer via e-mail. She responded within three days with a total of two more e-mail correspondences. We then combined and edited the transcript for grammar and formatting purposes, identified areas that were in need of clarification, and asked follow-up questions through e-mail and a brief phone interview, as it was most convenient to her. A semistructured interview guide with open-ended questions guided the online chat interview and subsequent correspondence. In addition to online transcripts, field notes and reflections were maintained throughout the interview process.

Data Analysis

After the interview, a completed transcript was e-mailed to the participant to ensure that the interview accurately captured her words and experiences. She was invited to make corrections or clarify points in the transcript. After she responded, we organized the data into a case record by including all of the edited and reordered information important to the final case analysis (Patton, 2002). The case record was then organized to form initial codes, develop primary themes and patterns, and finally, present an in-depth and organized picture of the case (Creswell, 2007). Trustworthiness (Patton, 2002) was established by use of member checks with the participant, ongoing reflexive writing of the researchers, and cross-checking codes between multiple coders during data analysis.

FINDINGS

Case Description

Sarah is a 40-year-old, white, middle-class, divorced single mother who lives in a small Midwestern U.S. city with her 6-year-old, white, transgender daughter, Lee. Sarah is divorced from Lee's biological father, and while they share co-parenting responsibilities, Sarah is responsible for the majority of parenting and maintains physical custody of Lee, who is a first-grade student at a public school. Their local community is not aware that Lee was assigned male at birth and transitioned to her affirmed gender at age five, as Lee presents as a girl and is currently enrolled as a female at her elementary school, thus they are non-disclosing about her male birth sex and only know her as a girl. Therefore, in order to protect their privacy, Sarah did not disclose details about her profession and employment beyond reporting that she attended some college, plans to return to school, and is employed full-time. In an effort to honor Lee's self-ascribed identity as a girl, which is affirmed by Sarah, we will refer to her by female pronouns throughout this article.

During the interview conversations with Sarah, we asked a variety of questions about her experiences and perspectives as a single mother parenting a transgender child. She highlighted her Unitarian faith and liberal political views, as well as the lack of support she received during her own childhood, which seem to influence her perspectives on parenting. In an effort to provide a clear and accurate portrayal of Sarah's parenting experiences, we describe the following themes that emerged: Gender Identity: She Is a Girl in All Aspects; Facing Adversity: "It's Always the Mother's Fault"; Distant Dad: "I Will Keep Trying to Help Them"; Professional Help: "They Wanted to Be Supportive"; Support: "They Saved Us... Her..."; Educator and Advocate: "We Are Modern-Day Pioneers"; and Being Mom: "The Toughest Job I Will Ever Love."

Gender Identity: She Is a Girl in All Aspects

When asked about her child's gender identity, Sarah stated that Lee is female and transgender. As mother and child, they have embarked on a journey to better understand gender and gender identity. In talking about Lee's gender, Sarah stated,

> *Lee is female and she sure KNOWS it. Seems to have always known it. Made sure everyone around her knew it even if it meant negative feedback from others. Unfortunately her identity does not match the body she was born into. So, I feel, she was incorrectly identified as male at birth. I almost feel like my child was born with a birth defect.*

Sarah described her experience discovering that her son identified as a girl at a young age. She perceived her son as gentle and found that he had a strong preference for feminine clothing, hairstyles, and toys. The child she viewed as a little boy preferred to spend time with girls rather than boys. She said,

> *When she started preschool around three, she noticed a distinct difference between girls and boys, how they wore their hair and their clothing. [Lee] started expressing a very strong preference for all things typically girl....*

Sarah's attempts to persuade Lee to pursue more masculine interests backfired, resulting in frustration, anger, and depression. Sarah described one of her first memories of her realization that Lee saw herself as a girl:

> *Around that time I was reading a bedtime story that had a line: "Some of us are boys and some of us are girls." That is the first time she broke down into tears and started expressing fears of growing up into a man with a man face and a beard. It was a little scary.*

Sarah had never thought about gender identity; however, she began researching online when Lee was approximately three or four years old. This research led her to believe that gender identity is "complicated and multidimensional." Based on the majority of information she discovered about children and gender identity, Sarah allowed Lee to begin determining her own gender presentation. Sarah reported that Lee embraced her transformation and became an "amazingly happy, spunky, and outgoing young girl who wears her hair long, has an all-girl wardrobe, and a bubblegum pink bedroom." She eventually legally changed Lee's name from a masculine name to the name of her choosing and enrolled her in school as a girl.

Facing Adversity: "It's Always the Mother's Fault"

Sarah's willingness to allow Lee to live as a girl elicited accusations from her family suggesting child abuse or neglect. Her uncle made phone calls to family members to voice his discontent, they aren't invited to certain family events, and Lee doesn't get invited to her cousins' birthday parties, even though they are the same age. Sarah learned that organizations like Focus on the Family, led by James Dobson, and well-known gender specialists such as Ken Zucker, advocated for reparative therapy, which focuses on rejecting the trans identity, can be ineffective and dangerous (Vanderburgh, 2009). Her family still encouraged her to pursue these practices. Sarah stated,

> *It was obvious that Lee wasn't expressing herself as a "typical" boy.... Everyone flipped out. The family is still fractured. My mother and her*

husband are conservative Christians who refused to support in any way, kept shoving Dr. Dobson and Zucker information at me. Were talking to Lee about right and wrong, heaven and hell and changing her clothing during visits, etc. Lee would come home from visits and be very upset.... It was just awful.

As a reaction to the judgment Sarah faced from family members, she began to question her parenting and blame herself for Lee's girl gender identity. She said,

I went from patting myself on the back for being such a progressive parent... to being really concerned that I must be doing something terribly wrong to cause this gender "confusion." EVERYONE, mostly my mother and ex-husband told me I was being too permissive, I should try to affirm his maleness and not allow all the girl stuff. I started to wonder if perhaps I was doing something wrong and am embarrassed to say that I did start to try getting her interested in typical "boy" stuff.... It really just made things much worse.

Sarah began to realize that she was being blamed for Lee's gender identity and expression. She was told that somehow her "feminist" beliefs caused her son to be feminine and it was her responsibility to fix what family members perceived as problematic. She explained,

My family liked to tell me that I must be doing something wrong to make my son loathe his maleness. I was too permissive and supportive with all his girly interests. It's always the mother's fault, don't you know?

Sarah's ex-husband's family became more vocal about their lack of acceptance and contacted legal counsel along with child protective services, claiming that allowing Lee to live as girl was neglectful. Sarah stated,

In the very beginning, when I allowed Lee to socially transition, some family members were trying to band together to get an attorney to "save this boy" from me. I know [my ex-husband] was having conversations with them regarding this, but also that he didn't go so far as to think that was the answer, nor reparative therapy thank goodness.

While she has developed ways to deal with critics in her family, Sarah described her ongoing concerns for Lee. She knew she had created a safe home life for her, yet the outside world is often not kind to transgender people or their supportive parents, especially mothers.

I worry about her future. I worry about her safety. I worry sometimes about doing the right thing in order to keep her healthy, happy, and emotionally

secure. I worry about people who don't understand or bigots who may want to have her taken away from me.

Distant Dad: "I Will Keep Trying to Help Them"

Although Sarah and Lee's father are divorced, she believes it is important for him to have a nurturing and supportive role in Lee's life, so she continues to encourage his relationship with Lee. She explained her role in maintaining her ex-husband and daughter's relationship by saying:

I go overboard probably trying to get together with him for her sake. My/our therapist says it's not my responsibility, but I can't help myself. I guess I'm trying to shield her for as long as possible and feel that if I don't do something to help them nurture a relationship and stay in contact no one will. I see her intently watching other children with their fathers, especially daughters and it breaks my heart that she will probably never have a close relationship with him. I will keep trying to help them though.

While custody arrangements allow Lee's father to have visitation with her every other weekend, Sarah reported that he does not see Lee regularly. She described feeling sad for her daughter and frustrated with her ex-husband due to the discomfort in their father-child relationship since Lee's transition. Sarah described Lee's father as a "manly man" who holds fairly conservative and homophobic beliefs, which she believes contributed to his secrecy about Lee. For example, Sarah stated,

He is still very much grieving the loss of a son. No one in his life knows either... friends, coworkers, etc., still ask him how his boy is doing.

Sarah provided Lee's father with an immense amount of research to look through, and attempted to take him to therapy appointments. She wants to keep Lee's father educated, involved, and "on her side" so that she and Lee will always have him as an ally.

Professional Help: "They Wanted to Be Supportive"

Sarah has seen several mental health professionals in the hopes of learning how to best support her transgender daughter, and to ensure that Lee has professional support. When asked about her overall impression of the field of mental health in regard to helping gender-nonconforming individuals and families like hers, Sarah's response was that it is "crappy." She has seen therapists that have been somewhat supportive, but most do not seem very educated on gender-nonconforming children and how their families should be supported. She held the impression that professionals wanted to help, but did not know how. For example, one therapist suggested that Lee live how she wanted at home, but present as a boy to the rest of the world, which Sarah knew would not work for Lee based on her experiences. She said,

> I think everyone I saw did seem like they wanted to be supportive. ... I guess I wanted "professional" confirmation that I was doing the right thing by allowing Lee to live as a girl. I also was terrified of having CPS show up at my door one day and wanted proof that I wasn't just some crazy mother who wished she had a girl instead of a boy. I felt I needed proof that I was seeing a therapist/doctors and had confirmation that this was the best course for Lee.

GLBT resource centers generally provide GLBTQ-friendly referrals to therapists and health care providers. Sarah initially went to a local therapist, who was referred by her GLBT resource center, and was discouraged to learn her parenting was again scrutinized by professionals who she had hoped would be helpful. She described her experience with the therapist:

> She knew nothing. Was good to talk to but had some really unappealing ideas, didn't know anything about trans youth what-so-ever, made us jump through hoops before she was willing to write a support letter. ... .and told me the lesbians in charge at the LGBT center thought I was a crazy mother who was doing the wrong thing!

She then traveled out of town a few times to see a psychiatrist, but the distance was a deterring factor for continuing. They traveled to a large city nearby to see a therapist who specialized in working with youths in counseling who they were hopeful would be helpful since this therapist also had a gender-variant son, but reported that therapy with this provider did not work out. When asked about who they currently see for therapy, Sarah replied that a therapist in a nearby town works with other transgender youths. She described that both she and Lee like the therapist because:

> She just seems to "get it". ... She also just seems to be exceptionally supportive. Thinks Lee just seems like a normal kid.

In Sarah's experiences, the most helpful aspect of therapy has been the inherent knowledge that a therapist understands gender identity and children specifically. The importance of education and prior experience with gender-nonconforming youths holds a high value to her. She stated that therapists should:

> LEARN FACTS! [Remain aware of the] updated research regarding what it means to be transgender/gender-nonconforming. Know which course

of medical treatment might be necessary as a child/teen grows. Knowing about transgender/transsexual adults and their issues is not even close to being enough information for helping trans/gender-variant youth and their families.

Support: "They Saved Us... Her...."

The Internet served as a tremendous resource to Sarah as she sought information to better understand her child. Since her early discoveries, Sarah has kept up-to-date on research regarding transgender children that includes both medical and critical queer frameworks that promote transgender child health, advocacy, and inclusion. She connected with other parents through an online support group she found by conducting a Google search for transgender children. Peer support has allowed Sarah to correspond with parents who have asked the same questions and sought support for their transgender and gender-creative children. She stated,

> Oh my. I seriously don't know what would have happened without [a support network]! I had no idea [we] could be helped in such a way! It's amazing! Wonderful! Also, being able to compare notes with other parents going through the exact same experiences. Learning from those who have gone before you. Being able to offer support to those just beginning and in so much turmoil.

Connecting Lee with peer support was also important to Sarah. She wanted to ensure that Lee knows she is not alone. Since locating the online and subsequent in-person support groups, Lee has had the opportunity to meet other transgender and gender-creative children, which Sarah believes has created significantly positive experiences. She stated,

> Lee knows that she is not alone. She is not the only transgender kid out there. She gets to see pictures and videos of other kids. Other normal little girls like her. They saved us... her....

Trusted friends have been an ongoing source of social support for Sarah, which is critical as she and Lee are non-disclosing about Lee's birth gender in their community. She exclaimed, "My friends are the best!" and described a friend who sent Lee a Dora the Explorer lunchbox to show her support. Sarah shared that friends have accompanied her to therapy and attorney visits, and have been there during difficult times. Yet support eventually came from an unexpected family member: time and information have helped Sarah's mother, who initially struggled with Lee's gender identity, to become understanding. Sarah said,

> *My poor mother has been through a lot and come such a long way. She seems to be fully supportive now... even bought Lee a top the other day that was bright pink and sparkly that says GIRLS ROCK.*

Support also came from another unexpected source based on Sarah's concerns about religion. Sarah explained,

> *I expected [my grandmother] to react negatively because, you know the God thing. She ended up being pretty nonchalant though. It was really amazing. She said not to listen to all the Christian people criticizing me because who were they to speak for God, and how many of them had been divorced or done other things supposedly against God. She also said that she may not understand everything, but wanted to and also wanted to be and stay in our lives. We've had many conversations since and she says she feels better and better the more she learns about this whole trans thing.*

Educator and Advocate: "We Are Modern-Day Pioneers"

Sarah described her process of learning and becoming an advocate for her daughter:

> *I spent so much time in the beginning with extreme anxiety. I spent many nights crying myself to sleep. There have been some very scary times. I worry still sometimes. It was just awful. Now though, I feel strong. I feel educated. I feel that I can be an advocate and supporter of my child 100%. I see myself (and Lee) as somewhat modern-day pioneers regarding how we are choosing to deal with gender issues.*

Sarah was discouraged to discover that the director of Lee's former preschool disclosed Lee's gender identity to staff but did not offer subsequent education to them. It became so uncomfortable that she eventually removed Lee from that preschool and was beginning to consider homeschooling. Sarah has since worked to develop awareness about gender identity to multiple institutions and various professionals within the medical and mental health community. She explained what happened when she advocated for her daughter with their family doctor:

> *Our family doctor thought back to concerns I had had years earlier about my son wanting to be a girl. She apologized to me about blowing me off and telling me it was just a phase. She told me she would take any and all information I had, would be sure to study it all and would be sure her staff used proper names and pronouns and were respectful.*

Being Mom: "The Toughest Job I Will Ever Love"

When asked to describe her daughter in three words, Sarah responded, "creative, dramatic, [and] loving." Sarah maintained the perspective that her child is happy and healthy, and it is other people who take issue with her parental decisions regarding her child's gender. She expressed her love and support for her daughter throughout the interview.

> *[Parenting Lee is] the toughest job I will ever love.... It's challenging, but I love it. I love her so much and feel incredibly blessed to have such an absolutely amazing little being in my life.*

While support groups and online research have been helpful, Sarah explained her position as a mom by saying,

> *I see myself as being exceptionally lucky to have somehow been chosen to be Mom to the most amazing person I have ever met. My child is/has been my greatest teacher. I also see myself as just a normal parent trying to get through and do the very best I can for my child and her future.*

DISCUSSION

Sarah's lived experience reinforces much of the existing literature and research regarding transgender youths and their families. Some of the parallel themes throughout her interview and relevant professional literature include harsh social judgment of parenting decisions when choosing to support her transgender child and the subsequent secondary stigmatization parents face, family disruption, pride regarding open-minded parenting, and frustration with inexperienced health care providers. Her experiences reflect the multiple layers of discrimination a single mother of a transgender child faces. Sarah took the initiative to educate herself about gender identity and sought out a support network to advocate for Lee within the family and health care community.

Sarah experiences secondary stigmatization, which was highlighted by the belief of others who judge her as too permissive or "crazy," a theme shared by parents of gender-nonconforming children (Menvielle & Tuerk, 2002). As transgender individuals are often highly stigmatized and subject to social isolation (Brooks, 2000; Lev, 2004), their loved ones are certainly prone to feeling affected by this judgment. Being a single mother, Sarah faces gendered stereotyping, as negative attributes are imposed on single mothers more so than single fathers (Haire & McGeorge, 2012). This intersection of stigma only further complicates the social message of deviation; Sarah has repeatedly received the message that she has done something wrong in parenting Lee, and this message has, at times, caused her much anguish and doubt.

Conversely, Broad, Alden, Berkowitz, and Ryan (2007) describe activist parenting as protecting GLBT children by challenging the traditional definition of parenting and responding to bigotry with activism that is both political in nature and relational within a community. They conceptualized this idea from the experiences of poor mothers of color, who resisted racism and poverty in the early 1990s by challenging traditional meanings of parenting and politics (Broad et al., 2007). Similarly, Sarah has responded to societal discrimination by her ongoing advocacy for her child as well as herself. Oftentimes parents believe that their gender-nonconforming children make them better people through living the experience of being "different" (Menvielle, 2009), which we see as a strategy to resist and counter stigmatization. Similar to Gonzalez and colleagues' (2013) findings that most of the parents of GLBTQ children in their study experienced positive outcomes, Sarah described how she has personally grown thanks to her transgender daughter. It was apparent that Sarah cares deeply for Lee's well-being, and she is doing everything in her power to ensure that Lee leads a full and healthy life through the nurturance of her identity.

This study sought to understand social and therapeutic supports; however, Sarah also demonstrated that her political stances and ability to think critically led her to access her primary resources, such as her ongoing self-education about gender identity, and the development of a supportive community, which exist outside of therapy. Results support the limited yet current literature demonstrating that parents of gender-nonconforming children are in need of support (Lev, 2004) as their decisions are subject to much scrutiny (Menvielle & Tuerk, 2002). This mother illustrated the ways in which her parenting has been called into question by family members and gender-normative mental health professionals, and how she has developed supports and remained resilient as a mother throughout her daughter's transition. Sarah's middle-class status allowed her to access therapists, legal representation, and her choice of preschools, which underscores how class privilege grants access to resources. Notably, race was not brought up as an issue central to the experience of this family, which is reflective of the racial invisibility of most white people who do not face racial oppression (Rothenberg, 2008). While Sarah may not realize it, her whiteness allows her advantages even in the face of adversity. Her experiences markedly highlight the multiple layers and complexity of concerns mothers of transgender children face, and help us conceptualize how this experience is further complicated as we consider the intersections of gender, race, and class.

Sarah experienced both positive support from therapists and the misuse of therapy as a form of social control, which has the potential to further stigmatize mothers of transgender children. There is a need for mental health professionals to be aware of mothers' abilities to self-organize and develop knowledge relevant to parenting their transgender child in order to help counter stigmatization. Yet it is still necessary for therapists to be educated and reflexive when working with mothers of transgender youths in an effort to reduce the distress that society has placed on them, to affirm, and provide care for their families. For example, research shows that mothers are disadvantaged post-divorce and frequently continue in the role of primary caregiver (Kelly, 2007). While current literature addresses mother-blaming to some extent (e.g., Jackson & Mannix, 2004), scholarly research has not yet addressed mother-blaming specific to parenting queer children.

Mental health professionals would benefit immensely from more graduate-level training on the subject of affirmative practice with transgender individuals and their families (Benson, 2013). The Association for Lesbian, Gay, Bisexual, and Transgender Issues in Counseling (ALGBTIC) outlines competencies for providing counseling to transgender clients. These include the use of transgender-affirmative language, maintaining a belief that all persons are able to live healthy lives while embracing the full spectrum of gender diversity, an acknowledgment of the fact that the oppression of transgender people pervades this culture, and an understanding that therapists must seek consultation or supervision to address personal biases (ALGBTIC, 2009).

An affirmative therapeutic environment can be helpful to families (Benson, 2013), particularly mothers who may benefit from helpful explorations and discussions about the fear of condemnation, grief over lost dreams, and regrets or self-blame (Brill & Pepper, 2008). Family therapy may help parents focus on their love for their child, and parents who hold love paramount fare best in accepting their gender-nonconforming child (Brill & Pepper, 2008). This acceptance is related to positive emotional outcomes that persist over time (Ryan, Russell, Huebner, Diaz, & Sanchez, 2010). Therapists need to be aware of the stigma single mothers face (Cairney et al., 2003); specifically discrimination based on gender, race, and class. Therapists should address the importance of supporting single mothers specifically in family therapy with a transgender child, and they should be considered advocates for supportive parents, empowering their decisions in spite of negative social messages (Brill & Pepper, 2008).

Families have a tremendous impact on children's well-being, so discussing a gender-nonconforming child's family life in therapy is crucial to providing comprehensive mental health services (Ryan, 2009). An important aspect of this therapy includes addressing which family patterns serve to promote the healthy development of a child's transgender identity, and which serve to pathologize the child's identity (Vanderburgh, 2009). Ehrensaft (2011) refers to helping parents and professionals "untangle gender" and listen to the unique experiences of their children so they are able to be their true and authentic selves (p. 10). A therapist can help parents to move beyond social messages that are experienced as, and/or are, non-affirming and defeating, thereby creating space for more positive emotional possibilities and relationships within and outside of the family (Ehrensaft, 2011). More specifically, therapists must be aware that mothers' secondary stigmatization is real; it is essential not to trivialize these experiences as her being oversensitive or paranoid. In addition, therapy for the parents and families of transgender children should address physical and emotional safety concerns, particularly for children in school; educate family members; support each family member emotionally; and serve as a safe place where the family can receive referrals to other professionals (e.g., medical doctors, school administrators, and even legislative support) (Riley, Sitharthan, Clemson, & Diamond, 2011).

Sarah's experience of never having questioned gender-normative identity reflects the initial lack of information that many parents of gender-creative children experience (Riley et al., 2011). Many parents, particularly mothers, notice their children's gender preferences and look to the Internet for answers. They may find resources such as TransYouth Family Allies (imatyfa.org), which includes educational information for parents, educators, youths, and helping professionals, as well as online discussion groups and information about in-person support groups across the United States. Parents, Families, and Friends of Lesbians and Gays, more commonly known as PFLAG (PFLAG.org), hosts the Transgender Network (TNET) which provides educational and support information online along with a search function to locate one of their 350 chapters in the United States. Gender Spectrum (genderspectrum.org) offers education and support online, and hosts an annual conference for families with gender-nonconforming and transgender young people.

LIMITATIONS AND FUTURE DIRECTIONS

There are certain limitations associated with this study. One limitation of the online chat format is the absence of face-to-face contact, which limited our ability to make observations such as facial expressions and other types of nonverbal communication. It is traditional to include these observations in the form of field notes, thereby allowing readers to assimilate certain descriptions into their memories (Stake, 2003); therefore, we tracked subtleties such as which questions elicited a longer pause before the participant typed her response. There are undoubtedly differences between field notes from an online interview and a face-to-face interview.

Another limitation presented itself when the chat session timed out before all of the questions were answered. The last few questions of the interview took place via e-mail correspondence, which restricted our ability to follow up with probing questions or ask for clarification on the spot. E-mail format tends to produce broken conversation rather than a smoother flow, as with instant messaging. Furthermore, conducting a study that requires a participant to have access to the Internet may limit the available participants since there are certain class issues associated with owning a computer and having Internet access. As the Internet has become a primary source of information and networking for mothers of transgender children, it was deemed worth the limitation to conduct the study online.

In the present study, Sarah's responses to interview questions almost completely supported current research and professional literature regarding transgender parents and their children and families. Her immersion in literature and research also serves to inform her experience. While Sarah faces many challenges, she also benefits from race and class privilege; thus, additional research is needed to understand how racism and class informs parenting experiences. We also encourage researchers to look specifically at the roles of fathers in parenting gender-creative children. As such, more research is needed regarding other, more diverse, queer family structures that do not reflect heteronormative and gender-normative family structures. Another major area for further research involves gaining multiple perspectives by interviewing other family members. For example, siblings of gender-nonconforming children have received very limited attention in professional literature (Lev, 2004) and would offer interesting and important perceptions regarding family therapy, family well-being, and ways to best support families such as their own.

REFERENCES

Association of Lesbian, Gay, Bisexual, and Transgender Issues in Counseling (ALGBTIC). (2009). *Competencies for counseling with transgender clients*. Alexandria, VA: Author.

Benson, K. E. (2013). Seeking support: Transgender client experiences with mental health services. *Journal of Feminist Family Therapy, 25*, 17–14. doi: 10.1080/08952833.2013.755081

Brill, S., & Pepper, R. (2008). *The transgender child: A handbook for families and professionals*. San Francisco, CA: Cleis Press Inc.

Broad, K. L., Alden, H., Berkowitz, D., & Ryan, M. (2007). Activist parenting and GLBTQ families. *Journal of GLBT Family Studies, 4*, 499–520. doi: 10/1080/15504280802191749

Brooks, F. L. (2000). Beneath contempt: The mistreatment of non-traditional/gender atypical boys. *Journal of Gay & Lesbian Social Services, 12*, 107–115. doi: 10.1300/J041v12n01_06

Burdge, B. J. (2007). Bending gender, ending gender: Theoretical foundations for social work practice with the transgender community. *Social Work, 52*, 243–250. doi: 10.1093/sw/52.3.243

Cairney, J., Boyle, M., Offord, D. R., & Racine, Y. (2003). Stress, social support, and depression in single and married mothers. *Social Psychiatry & Psychiatric Epidemiology, 38*, 442–449. doi: 10.1007/s00127-003-0661-0

Carroll, L., Gilroy, P. J., & Ryan, J. (2002). Counseling transgendered, transsexual, and gender-variant clients. *Journal of Counseling and Development, 80*, 131–139. doi: 10.1002/j.1556-6678.2002.tb00175.x

Creswell, J. W. (2007). *Qualitative inquiry & research design: Choosing among five approaches* (2nd ed.). Thousand Oaks, CA: Sage Publications, Inc.

DeJean, S. L., McGeorge, C. R., & Carlson, T. S. (2012). Attitudes toward never-married single mothers and fathers: Does gender matter? *Journal of Feminist Family Therapy, 24*, 121–138. doi: 10.1080/08952833.2012.648121

Ehrensaft, D. (2011). *Gender born, gender made: Raising healthy gender-nonconforming children.* New York, NY: The Experiment.

Erich, S., Tittsworth, J., Dykes, J., & Cabuses, C. (2008). Family relationships and their correlations with transsexual well-being. *Journal of GLBT Family Studies, 4*, 419–432. doi: 10.1080/15504280802126141

Gonzalez, K. A., Rostosky, S. S., Odom, R. D., & Riggle, E. B. (2013). The positive aspects of being the parent of an LGBTQ child. *Family Process, 52*, 325–337. doi: 10.1111/famp.12009

Grossman, A. H., & D'Augelli, A. R. (2007). Transgender youth and life-threatening behaviors. *Suicide and Life-Threatening Behavior, 35*, 527–537. doi: 10.1521/suli.2007.37.5.527

Grossman, A. H., D'Augelli, A. R., Howell, T. J., & Hubbard, S. (2006). Parents' reactions to transgender youths' gender nonconforming expression and identity. *Journal of Gay & Lesbian Social Services, 18*, 3–16. doi: 10.1300/J041v18n01_02

Haire, A. R., & McGeorge, C. R. (2012). Negative perceptions of never-married custodial single mothers and fathers: Applications of a gender analysis for family therapists. *Journal of Feminist Family Therapy, 24*, 24–51. doi: 10.1080/08952833.2012.629130

Hesse-Biber, S. N. (2007). Feminist research: Exploring the interconnections of epistemology, methodology, and method. In S. N. Hesse-Biber (Ed.), *Handbook of feminist research: Theory and praxis* (pp. 1–26). Thousand Oaks, CA: Sage.

Jackson, D., & Mannix, J. (2004). Giving voice to the burden of blame: A feminist study of mothers' experiences of mother blaming. *International Journal of Nursing Practice, 10*(4), 150–158. doi: 10.1111/j.1440-172X.2004.00474.x

Johnson, J. L., & Best, A. L. (2012). Radical normal: The moral career of straight parents as public advocates for their gay children. *Symbolic Interaction, 35*(3), 321–339. doi: 10.1002/SYMB.23

Kelly, J. B. (2007). Children's living arrangements following separation and divorce: Insights from empirical and clinical research. *Family Process, 46*(1), 35–52. doi:10.1111/j.1545-5300.2006.00190.x

Lev, A. I. (2004). *Transgender emergence: Therapeutic guidelines for working with gender variant people and their families.* Binghamton, NY: Haworth Press.

Malpas, J. (2011). Between pink and blue: A multi-dimensional family approach to gender nonconforming children and their families. *Family Process, 50*(4), 453–470. doi: 10.1111/j.1545-5300.2011.01371.x

McGuire, J. K., Anderson, C. R., Toomey, R. B., & Russell, S. T. (2010). School climate for transgender youth: A mixed method investigation of student experiences and school responses. *Journal of Youth & Adolescence, 39*, 1175–1188. doi: 10.1007/s10964-010-9540-7

Menvielle, E. (2009). Transgender children: Clinical and ethical issues in prepubertal presentations. *Journal of Gay & Lesbian Mental Health, 13*, 292–297. doi: 10.1080/19359700903165357

Menvielle, E., & Tuerk, C. (2002). A support group for parents of gender nonconforming boys. *Journal of the American Academy of Child and Adolescent Psychiatry, 41*, 1010–1013. doi: 10.1097/00004583-200208000-00021

Mustanski, B. S. (2001). Getting wired: Exploring the Internet for the collection of valid sexuality data. *The Journal of Sex Research, 38*, 292–301. doi: 10.1080/00224490109552100

Olesen, V. L. (2003). Feminisms and qualitative research at and into the millennium. In N. K. Denzin & Y. S. Lincoln (Eds.), *The landscape of qualitative research* (pp. 332–397). Thousand Oaks, CA: Sage Publications, Inc.

Oswald, R. F., Kuvalanka, K. A., Blume, L. B., & Berkowitz, D. (2009). Queering "the family". In S. A. Lloyd, A. L. Few, & K. R. Allen (Eds.), *Handbook of feminist family studies* (pp. 43–55). Thousand Oaks, CA: Sage Publications, Inc.

Patton, M. Q. (2002). *Qualitative research and evaluation methods (3rd ed.)*. Thousand Oaks, CA: Sage Publications, Inc.

Riley, E. A., Sitharthan, G., Clemson, L., & Diamond, M. (2011). The needs of gender-variant children and their parents: A parent survey. *International Journal of Sexual Health, 23*, 181–195. doi: 10.1080/19317611.2011.593932

Rothenberg, P. S. (2008). *White privilege: Essential readings on the other side of racism (3rd ed.)* New York, NY: Worth Publishers.

Ryan, C. (2009). *Supportive families, healthy children: Helping families with lesbian, gay, bisexual, & transgender children.* San Francisco, CA: Marian Wright Edelman Institute, San Francisco State University.

Ryan, C., Russell, S. T., Huebner, D., Diaz, R., & Sanchez, J. (2010). Family acceptance and the health of LGBT young adults. *Journal of Child and Adolescent Psychiatric Nursing, 23*, 205–213. doi: 10.1111/j.1744-6171.2010.00246.x

Stake, R. E. (2003). Case studies. In N. Denzin & Y. Lincoln (Eds.), *Strategies of qualitative inquiry* (pp. 134–164). Thousand Oaks, CA: Sage Publications, Inc.

Vanderburgh, R. (2009). Appropriate therapeutic care for families with pre-pubescent transgender/gender dissonant children. *Child & Adolescent Social Work Journal, 26*, 135–154. doi: 10.1007/s10560-008-0158-5

van Eeden-Moorefield, B., Martell, C. R., Williams, M., & Preston, M. (2011). Same-sex relationships and dissolution: The connection between heteronormativity and homonormativity. *Family Relations, 60*(5), 561–571. doi: 10.1111/j.1741-3729.2011.00669.x

van Eeden-Moorefield, B., Proulx, C. M., & Pasley, K. (2008). A comparison of Internet and face-to-face (FTF) qualitative methods in studying the relationships of gay men. *Journal of GLBT Family Studies, 4*, 181–204. doi: 10.1080/15504280802096856

The Influence of Psychiatric and Legal Discourses on Parents of Gender-Nonconforming Children and Trans Youths in Spain

RAQUEL (LUCAS) PLATERO
Universidad Complutense de Madrid, Madrid, Spain; Universidad Nacional de Educación a Distancia, Madrid, Spain

In recent years there has been an increasing interest in transgender issues in Spain, influenced by the growing acceptance of sexual minorities and gender equality. Despite growing media attention, new legislation allowing name and sex changes in all documents, and budding literature, progress in the areas of family relationships and assistance to children and youths is insufficient. For instance, the links between family responses and social change are understudied. Interviewing 12 parents and 8 education, health, and social work professionals provides a closer look into the situation of gender-nonconforming children and trans youths, and highlights families' and professionals' mutual influence and the journey narratives take between them. These families face shock and uncertainty and lack assistance and information, which makes them feel isolated from the external world and alone, as in having no peers or social networks of other parents going through the same experiences. In addition, parents often report feeling guilty. They seek assistance from professionals who often also feel they lack

---

This article was produced with the support of two projects: HERMES European Project (2011–2013), Fieldwork at the Grassroots Level with the Involvement of Children, Young People, and Women, funded by the Daphne III Programme of the European Commission. It has also been supported by the Spanish research project DER 2012-34320, "The Boundaries of Law in Time of Crisis: Excluded Groups" (2013–2015), directed by Patricia Laurenzo Copello. I am extremely grateful to the professionals in the public service for homosexual and transgender people in Madrid, Ana Gómez, Lola Martín, and Manuel Ródenas, who have made this research possible and who are generously helping many families and GLBT individuals.

sufficient training and are reluctant to work with these youths, fearing children may grow up to be gay instead of transgender, or may not show gender nonconformity in their adult life.

INTRODUCTION

In recent years there has been an increasing interest in transgender issues internationally, and Spain is no different.[1] Transgender people are out in politics, professional positions, and in the media. They take part in TV talk shows, and news outlets from all over the world report on trans people who achieve success and get attention. Invisibility is no longer mainstream. Stories of trans people doing *incredible* things are aired, such as becoming pregnant, getting important jobs, or denouncing transphobic violence. The representation of transgender people includes different degrees of stereotyping, and often links transgender people to show business, gay pride, prostitution, or homosexuality.

In addition, the literature on transgender issues in Spain is still in its initial stages and often exploratory, when compared to gender or gay, lesbian, bisexual, and transgender (GLBT) studies. Most of the literature focuses on research describing a clinical transgender sample or takes a medical and pathological stance (e.g., García Siso, 2003; Becerra-Fernández, 2004; Sosa et al., 2004; Gómez-Gil and Esteva de Antonio, 2006; Gómez-Gil, Trilla, Salamero, & Godás, 2009; Gómez-Gil et al., 2010; Iglesias Hernández et al., 2010). Some authors' interest lies in the current legal situation and the implementation of new legislation (Galofre Molero, 2007; Bustos Moreno, 2008; Espín Alba, 2009; Martínez Vázquez de Castro, 2010). There is also important work being carried out within an anthropological framework (Mejía, 2006; Nieto Piñeroba, 1998, 2008). Other approaches discuss the social, legal, and cultural aspects of transgenderism, and mostly concentrate on social movements, activism, and the narratives of trans individuals (Martínez, 2005; Mejía, 2006; Platero, 2008, 2011; Soley-Beltran, 2007; Missé & Coll-Planas, 2010; Soley-Beltran & Coll-Planas, 2011; Missé, 2012, among others). In addition, there is a growing set of authors that discuss the normative pathological approach from a critical point of view (Garaizabal, 1998, 2006; Ramos, 2003; Martínez, 2005; Galofre Molero, 2007; Ortega Arjonilla, Romero-Bachiller, & Ibáñez Martín, 2014; Platero, 2010, 2011; Missé & Coll-Planas, 2010; Missé, 2012). Some exploratory studies describing the nuances of Spanish transgender people have also been conducted (Martín Romero, 2004; Coll-Planas, Bustamante i Senabre, & Missé i Sánchez, 2009; Zaro Rosado, Rojas Castro, & Navazo Fernández, 2009; Domínguez Fuentes, García Leiva, & Hombrados, 2011; Osborne et al., 2011), though they are clearly still insufficient to establish transgender people's needs. Last, there is some research starting in the field of education, where transgender youths are treated as a new topic that requires further research (Platero & Gómez, 2007; Coll-Planas et al., 2009; Platero, 2010, 2012; Casanova, 2011; Hurtado García, 2011; Moreno & Puche, 2012; Puche Cabezas, Moreno Ortega, & Pichardo Galán, 2012).

Little has been discussed regarding trans youths or gender-nonconforming children in family relationships (Gómez & Esteva de Antonio, 2006). Two decades after the successful achievement of sexual rights in Spain, the intertwined relations between family responses and social change are still insufficiently studied. Most studies and research on transgender issues have been conducted either by experts or activists, with a strong focus, in the former case on documenting pathologies, and in the latter on legal innovations and social movements. Professionals, families, and trans people lack easily accessible information on what gender nonconformity and transgenderism is for youths and young adults. Apart from the materials offered by GLBT organizations, little information is provided on public policies, how to cope and act, how to prevent transphobia, what resources are required by the community, or what kind of support can be provided by institutions and professionals.

My interest lies first of all in how families talk, behave, and feel about their children and youths, and about themselves; second, in how professionals such as teachers, social workers, and doctors relate to, act with, and influence parents and their relationship with their offspring. In this article, the mutual influence between parents and professionals will be highlighted, showing how most of them frame gender nonconformity and transgender youths within the normative medical discourses embedded in mental disorder manuals such as the *Diagnostic and Statistical Manual of Mental Disorders* (*DSM*-IV) or the *International Classification of Disease* (*ICD*-10). Parents also, however, develop different coping strategies in which they maximize the benefits of this framework, developing as much agency as they can to be able to support their children and adopt suitable parenting roles. This article presents a qualitative study in which interviews are used to introduce research questions that may be useful for future analyses.

Transgender Rights in Spain

In this section, I present a short introduction to the social construction of transgender rights in Spain, which allows a better understanding of the present socio-legal situation of families with gender-nonconforming children and trans youths.

The recent past has played a relevant role in constructing how we feel and act towards those that were once considered sick, sinners, and criminals. The historical context for sexual rights in Spain is a fruitful legacy of discrimination and dissidence, where written norms and social control dictated punishment. Nonetheless, even in this context, some found ways to make their lives possible by using different strategies (Platero, 2011). Before democracy (1978) and throughout the dictatorship (1939–1975) homosexuality was prosecuted, under several laws.[2] During this long period, non-normative sexualities and alternative gender identities were disciplined through the use of formal control, set not only in legislation, but also using the knowledge produced in medicine, along with the moral control imposed by the Catholic Church. Several segregated institutions articulated formal control (e.g., schools, army, sport clubs, women's institutions such as "*Sección Femenina*" or "*Auxilio Social*," etc.). Gender and sexuality were also regulated through informal control, produced by different institutions such as family and neighbors and priests. The dictatorship kept under close surveillance and punished masculine women, feminine men, transvestites, and anyone who did not fit in the masculine/feminine division.

Using *homosexuality* as an umbrella term, all kinds of gender non-conformity and sexual dissidence were punished and were included within the legal notions of "social dangerousness" or "slackers and delinquents" (Platero, 2011). These notions are now outdated, but still influence today's collective imagination, especially for those that grew up with these values.

During the early stages of democracy, in the 1970s and 1980s, transgender people could be taken to court under Article 431 of the Penal Code, accused of "public scandal," which allowed the police, up until 1988, to arrest anyone involved in "immoral behavior." Public scandal was often used against transgender sexual workers. In 1995 a new Penal Code was approved which introduced sanctions against homophobia.[3] These reforms were needed, but transphobia was still alive and present throughout society, especially in the labor market, schools, and media. Meanwhile, court rulings were the only way transgender citizens could change their new name and sex in all documents but birth certificates. In 1987, the first victory was achieved through litigation, allowing a transsexual woman to change name and sex, but also limited her right to marry. Judges were reluctant to fully recognize transsexual women as "real" women, stating that they were "fictional females" ("*una ficción de hembra*") (de Verda y Beamonte, 1999). Transgender individuals continued fighting for their specific rights into the late 2000s, when the political scenario evolved.

As the international context changed concerning lesbian, gay, and transgender rights, but also regarding women's rights (especially in the European area of influence, where directives were approved), so did Spain. A number of slow and progressive changes took place, shifting problems around sexuality and gender from the margins to the center of policy making. This was made possible by social movements' continuous struggle, especially that of GLBT and feminist organizations, along with the influence of these movements on left-center political parties, their previous experience of lobbying for the achievement of rights for same-sex couples, etc.

Spain is often portrayed as being at the forefront of sexual minority rights internationally, especially following the approval of same-sex marriage in June 2005 and the recognition of transgender rights in the Gender Identity Law of 2007. Over the past two decades non-normative sexuality entered the agenda, first with the demand for "domestic unions" ("*parejas de hecho*") for same- and different-sex couples (1992–2000), soon to be followed by the demand for same-sex marriage (2000–2005), and last, focusing on transgender rights (2004–2013). This rhetoric of success and progress is challenged by the current economic crisis and conservative backlash, in which relevant civil rights (such as abortion, same-sex marriage, or the access to universal health care) are under threat, either by appeals to the Constitutional Court or through ongoing law reforms by the conservative government of Mariano Rajoy.

According to current Spanish law (Act 3/2007), the access to recognition of the name and sex of choice in all documents is open to all Spanish citizens of 18 years of age or older, after two years of medical treatment (usually interpreted as hormone treatment), who have been diagnosed as "gender dysphoric" by a doctor or psychologist, in the absence of other mental health disorders. Interestingly, gender reassignment surgery is not mandatory, and being sterile is not a requirement, though it can be argued that after two years of hormonal treatment, fertility is affected. In addition, Act 3/2007 does not require divorcing a spouse in a prior heterosexual marriage. Inspired by a notion of gender identity as irreversible, the new name must be unambiguous with respect to gender. This is controlled by the local registry office, where people register births, deaths, marriages, divorces, adoptions, etc. The approval of Act 3/2007 can be related to several factors, including the existence of an active trans movement since early democracy, European and international influence on domestic legislation and the recognition of new rights for women and lesbian and gay couples in Spain, along with the implementation of gender equality policies.

The national identity card has been the locus of transgender struggle, since it is the most relevant form of legal documentation and is constantly used to establish a person's identity, including their gender identity. In most Anglo-Saxon countries, transgender people have focused the struggle to change names and identities on birth certificates or driving licenses. However, in Spain, the ID card is compulsorily used in all transactions. The ID card associates a person's geopolitical and ethnic origin with an ID number and establishes kinship with a biological family, but it also ties a person's image to a specific gender, presented as one out of two possible options (Platero, 2011).

Furthermore, identification and regulation of gender identity is relevant to research into children and youths, where the connection between legislation and psychiatric categories is quite literal. The legal requirements of Act 3/2007 fit well with the descriptions in diagnostic manuals (*DSM*-IV and

ICD-10). The diagnosis of Gender Identity Disorder is a prerequisite to change name and sex on legal documents, and to be recognized as a transgender person and have access to some rights. Transgenderism is defined by Act 3/2007 as "the existence of dissonance between the morphological sex or physiological gender initially assigned and the applicant's gender identity or psychological sex, and the stability and persistence of this dissonance." In the regions of Navarra (2009) and the Basque Country (2012), new acts have been passed which have a slightly different focus, shifting slowly towards antidiscrimination and the depathologization of transgenderism, at least in their rhetoric.[4,5] Now let's examine the specific situation of gender-nonconforming children and trans youths in Spain.

Gender-Nonconforming Children and Transgender Youths

What attention and rights are Spanish gender-nonconforming or trans minors and youths getting? For those under 18, gender reassignment is only granted under court ruling, based on individual circumstances. This was the case of a 16-year-old trans girl from Barcelona made public in 2010, which attracted relevant media attention. The judge listened to her case, which included her parents' support, and allowed gender reassignment surgery, which finally took place at a private clinic. A whole new debate arose regarding the age of consent for transgender youths, the lack of assistance for families, and the emerging field of specialized professionals.[6]

The 41/2002 Act regulating patients' health rights sets 16 as the age when a person is old enough to decide about medical procedures and be able to give consent for medical treatment. This medical age of consent has three exceptions: assisted reproduction, abortion (banned until 2010 under the Law 2/2010 on abortion) and sexual reassignment. So, a youth can consent to open-heart surgery, or even plastic surgery, but not make other choices regarding his or her body such as gender reassignment treatment.[7]

In addition, not all Spanish regions offer gender reassignment treatment within the public health system, at the so-called Gender Identity Disorder Units.[8] Therefore, some are forced to attend private clinics. There is a heterogeneous landscape of services in the public health system: not all units offer full gender reassignment surgery and they do not share the same standards and requirements.[9] Most units follow the World Professional Association for Transgender Health (WPATH) standards, but interpret these differently and pose local requirements concerning residence. The regions that once did offer gender reassignment surgery now lack funding, due to the conservative government's decisions, using the economic crisis as an argument for austerity.

Finally, most Gender Identity Disorder Units are reluctant to treat youths under 18 years of age, and restrict their assistance to documenting children's or youths' gender nonconformity to better ground a later Gender Identity

Disorder/Gender Dysphoria diagnosis. Units also help children, youths, and their families to better adjust by explaining the disorder, asking schools and other socializing institutions to use their name of choice, etc. They start the "Real-Life Test" once they are sure these children and youths meet the criteria for being a "real transsexual."

Although it is known that these units are reluctant to provide hormone blockers, there are no shared protocols for treating minors; the scope of the assistance to children, youths, and their families is still understudied. Another area that requires further research is the gender reassignment treatment provided by private clinics, in both adults and youths. It can be anticipated that a relevant number of trans adults and minors are choosing these private clinics, as they provide resources such as immediate assistance, well-known surgeons, and privacy.

Therefore, it is likely that families with children or youths who do not conform to gender norms, or claim that they are transgender, experience shock and not knowing what to do, and lack assistance and information, which makes them feel isolated from the external world and alone, as in having no peers or social networks of other parents going through the same experiences. In addition, parents often report feeling guilty and responsible for their children's gender nonconformity. These parents face new challenges, due to their awareness of gender nonconformity and trans youths in their own homes, and not only as part of the stories portrayed by the media. They are often under a great deal of distress and lack relevant knowledge. Less commonly, they are supported by public GLBT programs (Madrid, Basque Country, Catalonia, etc.), where they are told that under the current legislation they need to wait until their children are 18, or older, to be able to change their names in all documents and access gender reassignment treatment. There are a few emerging organizations of parents of GLBT people, such as Associació de Pares i Mares de Gais i Lesbianes (AMPGIL; www.ampgil.org and CHRYSALIS Asociación Estatal de Familias de Menores Transexuales, The association of families of transgender minors; http://chrysallis.org.es), that provide support and information in several regions, pioneering the discussion over gender-nonconforming children and trans youths.

If we consider both Spain's historical background concerning new sexual and gender rights, and the current situation of families of gender-nonconforming and trans youths, as well as that of the professionals who assist them, it is clear that there is an emergent area of research and public health training and resourcing that requires further attention. In this research, parents and professionals are the target instead of children and youths. This shift is due to a number of reasons: first, gender-nonconforming children and trans youths are over-monitored. Such levels of attention may be disturbing, and research ethics need to be discussed in depth. More importantly, there is a lack of research on how parents, teachers, doctors, psychologists, and social workers think, talk, behave, and feel in their roles and how their discourses impact on children, youths, and their families.

METHOD

This study was carried out from 2010 to 2013. I interviewed parents and professionals within a qualitative research approach. Their experience is by no means representative of the experience of all parents in Spain. My goal was rather to create awareness of the lack of knowledge and spark an informed discussion.

Participants and Study Recruitment

Twelve parents volunteered to participate in long interviews. Participants were parents who contacted me through my teaching activities in master degrees in different universities, looking for advice on what do to with their offspring. Another part of the sample was found through the public Service for Homosexual and Transgender people in Madrid, who explained my research and offered parents an interview with me. Therefore, the sample was developed through a snowball technique, in which participants were selected among those willing to talk to me. They already had a positive attitude towards supporting their gender-nonconforming children or trans teenagers and were actively seeking help.

Out of these 12 interviews with parents, 9 interviewees were mothers and only 3 were fathers, from different regions in central Spain (Madrid, Salamanca, Toledo, Guadalajara), of ages ranging between 35 and 56. Their children were ages 4 to 19, and all of them had siblings. There was a clear gender imbalance in parents' participation that I was not able to balance by interviewing more fathers. According to one psychiatrist interviewed, "most people who attend 'Gender Identity Units' have some family support, although not always from their fathers, mostly from their mothers," which is consistent with Connell's approach to hegemonic masculinity and how it is confirmed in fatherhood, for which the heteropatriarchal constructions of masculinity and fathering would be linked to attitudes of homophobia and transphobia (Connell, 1995/2005). This would also be consistent with the difficulty I had finding fathers to interview. Regarding race, one family was Roma and lived in a housing project in Madrid; the rest did not present any relevant information concerning ethnic background or migration. As regards social class, the sample was mixed, ranging from people who own several properties and businesses, to those living in working-class suburbs and earning modest incomes. In terms of relationship status, all had lived in partnered relationships; four mothers were divorced, two of whom had a new partner, and the other two regarded themselves as single. The rest were married or living with a partner. None reported having a disability. In addition, 1 father had attended a 12-step therapy program at Alcoholic Anonymous.

As for professionals, the sample in this study included eight participants from Madrid, Andalusia, and the Basque Country, contacted through an announcement made at the Confederation of Workers in Education (STES), and personal contacts through my professional activities. It included two psychiatrists, four teachers, one social worker, and one expert in social integration. Again the sample was made up of people who were sensitive to trans issues and volunteered to share their experience; their motivation can be traced back to their experience as activists in unions, queer and feminist organizations, left-wing parties, and other social movements. Their ages ranged from 32 to 63 and they belonged to different social classes. This sample is also gender biased (five women and two men).

Interview Method

The interviews were conducted in different locations in Madrid, face to face, along with a few telephone interviews (three). The interviews lasted between two and four hours. All were recorded, transcribed, and analyzed using codes of themes, which identified relevant events, explanations, and participants' attributions.

RESULTS

There is a relevant psychological and legal influence on parents of gender-non-conforming children and trans youths, which transfers in how parents deal with their feelings and attitudes towards their offspring. Some parents' narratives on realizing their children were transgender seem to fulfill the actual requirements of psychiatric manuals for Gender Identity Disorder and Gender Dysphoria. Nonetheless, parents are not passive actors, and instead show certain agency when acting in benefit of their children. Professionals are less likely to be influenced by parents or trans infancy, who on the other hand, are able to identify clearly their current needs. The current crisis situation in Spain makes it even more difficult to meet professionals' and parents' identified needs.

Parents and Their Relationship with Professionals

In the 12 interviews conducted, parents indicated that most of the information they received, other than through the Internet, was provided by hospitals, psychologists, and medical staff. Only some were given information at the Homosexual and Transgender Services (public services available in cities like Madrid, Barcelona, Bilbao), or more infrequently, through social services, parents' organizations of GLBT, or schools. In most interviews, the first issue that arose was families' lack of information. They narrated their search, which yielded different results. Finding professionals, peers, and some relief from doubts and lack of knowledge was their primary goal.

The lack of information was not exclusive to families. Interviewees reported facing professionals that not only provided incorrect information, but also told them to correct their children's gender expressions and that they had somehow caused their children's behavior ("over-loving" mothers, "weak masculinities" in fathers); parents often found professionals knew less than themselves about transgender and gender-nonconformity issues.

I think acceptance is harder for me than for him [her husband]., I feel I have to justify myself much more as a mother. I am told that I wanted a daughter instead, so often, I feel the pressure, something I must have done.... I am blamed somehow. In fact, wherever I go they always tell me to come with my husband.... (Mother talking about her 8-year-old daughter)

Therefore, parents often reported that they had to "educate" the professionals around them, such as kindergarten and primary teachers, general practitioners (GP), and social workers.

We didn't know what information to give a three-year-old, so we decided to go to a psychologist. (...) It was an ordeal and a disappointment. He started to draw a nice picture of a house and as the psychologist started talking, he started to cross out the drawing. (...) What she [the psychologist] said was making my son feel terrible. According to her, boys cannot dress like girls and boys cannot play with girls' toys. I couldn't believe it! I asked her, what if he wants a doll for Christmas, what am I to do? Her answer was that children need to learn to deal with frustration. (Mother talking about her 6-year-old daughter and her relationship with the psychologist)

The pediatrician first referred us to the public mental health clinic in our area, and the psychologist had five or six sessions with D, who cried endlessly after therapy. Finally, one day D told me that the psychologist asked if he was a boy or a girl, and asked if he was gay, whether he liked boys or girls. He was only six! I had a big argument with the psychologist and thought about writing a complaint. We never went back to the clinic. (Mother talking about her 9-year-old daughter)

Narrating the first time that they became fully aware of their children's gender nonconformity, describing feelings that it was not just a phase, and the sense of their children belonging to the opposite sex were relevant parts of the interviews. These parents have told these stories again and again, to many different professionals and relatives, showing similarities that were shocking. Some authors have argued that there is a retrospective sense making, when parents are reexamining the past to fit the information they have in the present, showing a second-level interpretation of gender nonconformity or gender identity of children (Aveline, 2006). It may be the case that these similarities are a product of retrospective sense making in the interaction with professionals. This can be seen in these two extracts from different mothers:

When he was three years old he started saying that he was going to cut off his willy, and we told him not to, but we didn't know what information to give him, so we decided to go to a psychologist. (Mother talking about her 6-year-old daughter)

When D. was eleven or twelve months old, we could see he chose dolls instead of cars... I have pictures that show this.... One day I found him crying in front of the mirror, saying he didn't want "that," pointing at his genitals, and he would cut it off. I realized that I needed to do something right away. I couldn't put my son at risk. (Mother talking about her 9-year-old daughter)

Most parents could remember the precise event, the age of the child, the impulse they felt to seek help, and how the journey to find a psychologist or a GP started. Interestingly, one of the parents strayed from this narrative, and focused on their denial to acknowledge what was happening:

I didn't want to see it [that my daughter was a boy]. It was the psychologist who finally told me: "A. is transgender, and she was born that way." So many problems at schools, so many visits to different specialists and now the psychologist was telling me what I didn't want to know. (Mother talking about her 19-year-old teenager)

In this case, gender identity becomes a revelation in which a mother retrospectively makes sense while reexamining the past of her trans son; some information from the past was missed or interpreted as having other meanings (Aveline, 2006, p. 792). Parents talked about their resistance to acknowledging that gender non-conformity was not only really taking place in their children's lives, but also that it was not temporary. More importantly, they discussed what these breaks away from gender norms meant within their social imagery and how they linked it to homosexuality, transvestites, prostitution, social exclusion, unhappiness, etc.

I asked for advice, went to a children's psychiatrist, and told her, that J. wanted to be a girl, and she suggested I bring the kid in to see her. But my husband refused. (...) He didn't want to take him anywhere; he said that it was a way to "put ideas in his head." The psychologist said that the biggest problem was that my husband had to accept that our child may be different. She gave me some articles with statistics on children's behavior, and he read them. (...) My husband had an upbringing that will make it difficult for him to overcome the influence of patriarchal values. He listened, but didn't speak. This is painful, but I have to tell you that he has a gay brother, doesn't accept him. (Mother talking about her 8-year-old child)

So not only is how and when a child becomes visible to parents and relatives as rebelling against the gender norms assigned at birth important, but the process of finding a professional is also crucial to making sense of their personal experience. Most parents searched long, and often unsuccessfully, for professionals that could provide adequate information, sometimes travelling to different regions (Madrid, Barcelona, etc.). Another source of information was the Internet, which was not always reliable. Some parents, even parents living in large cities, reported that the search for a professional who gave them accurate advice took one to four years. Having early bad experiences clearly conditioned their later contacts with health professionals.

I was so scared of going to a psychologist, after the bad experience we had. At the hospital [Gender Identity Disorder Unit at Ramón y Cajal Hospital, in Madrid] they don't want to assess younger children, in case they change in the future, which is logical. Even if there is only a remote possibility. I think they will give us a report so we can have the name changed, and then we will see. [In the hospital] They aren't going to do anything else. (Mother talking about her 6-year-old child)

Although it was clear that not all first contacts with mental health professionals were positive, if a good relationship was established, parents were likely to include in the interviews remarks and perspectives on their children that appeared to be taken from psychologist and psychiatrist feedback. Parents seemed to adopt a medical perspective, using medical language and knowledge without questioning it. Interviews showed that after a period of shock of differing lengths, parents used different coping strategies, sometimes showing great acceptance, such as wanting to help other parents; meeting other parents and their children; reading as much as they could on the issue; becoming members of organizations; being extremely involved in their children's transition; and choosing a different school or playground to have a fresh start.

A different coping strategy was denial, showing different types of resistance, which could be summarized as wanting to wait for these behaviors to pass once children grew up. This strategy was adopted by most parents for a short period of time, and for others, was the main answer to their children's discomfort. Not listening to their children's demands often evolved into problematic behavior at school, such as passivity, low grades, dropouts, and suicide attempts. Other families even chose girls' Catholic boarding schools; sending the child abroad during the summer; changing to stricter schools; and enrolling the child in several after-school activities to keep him or her busy. Luckily, in our interviews some families stated that they evolved from punishing and correcting strategies to acceptance and support, having tested most of them through trial and error.

For some parents, discovering the concept of "transgender" as separate from "homosexual" was a relief. They thought of gender nonconformity as a genetic problem that required their support as parents through medical treatment. Some even expressed their disagreement for the joint nature of the services for homosexuals and transsexuals in Madrid, and found a lack of trans- and child-specific assistance. Other parents wished their children were gay or lesbian instead, since discrimination is less for them and they are better known in Spanish society.

> *Before we got married, I used to say "please, if we have a son, I don't care if he's gay, but I don't want him to turn out transgender." And now, it is my fate. I didn't say it for any reason other than the suffering.... We both agree, he knows we accept her, we just want her to be happy.* (Mother talking about her 7-year-old child)[10]

According to the interviewees, family relationships clearly improved once parents accepted their children's gender nonconformity and agreed with their choices. Acceptance meant children not only improved their relationship with siblings, schools, and family members, but it also meant they became more flexible in their choice of games, toys, and other childhood materials.

> *So much has changed since we started attending the Madrid Service for Homosexuals and Transgender people and we spoke to the psychologist. Our child has gained space. This means we are not going to question she's a girl. Before she would overact, she was so stubborn. She would not play with anything that was not girl-specific. She didn't negotiate anything. After a while, she even started playing football with her brothers. We couldn't believe it.* (Mother talking about her 6-year-old child)

Accepting the child's gender was seen as the turning point, when relationships evolved and improved. A deeper level was reached within families, where they all felt closer and more prepared to come up with strategies to face external relationships where gender was an issue. Some of the interviewees were clear in this respect:

> *Every Saturday we take D. to a different park, dressed like a girl. He's got everything, bikinis, girl's underwear.... Here [this neighborhood] if people see him dressed feminine.... My partner Antonio, starts the car and parks by the door, with the car door open, and tells D. "come out," and D. runs out of the building. My partner and D. have a great deal of understanding.... Sometimes, D. goes outside to play and comes back*

saying "someone called me faggot." Antonio replies, "Look, who are you? You're this way, right? So people have to accept you the way you are, otherwise tell them to go to hell."(. . .) None of us is telling D. that everything is going to be just fine. D. will have to fight and struggle in the future. (Mother talking about her 9-year-old child)

Once we were at a park, and he started playing with a little girl, who came to ask me what was her name? I didn't know what to say, didn't know what the deal was. . . . The little girl said that my daughter told her that she could not remember her own name. I replied, she is Leila, and she smiled at me. I hadn't given her away. (Father talking about his 7-year-old child)

She asked me to quit Catholic school and in the end I accepted. At the new high school she goes to now, the very first day she went to talk to her tutor, and said that she wanted to be called Samuel. Then all teachers met, she was under age, and they said "if she's coming in with such clear ideas it's because they already know at home." And then, everyone called her Samuel, even her friends, and they are hugely supportive of her. (Mother talking about her teenage child)

Sometimes parents made decisions that they acknowledge would have been wrong in a different situation, only because they couldn't find a better option at the time. For example, one family felt their son was at high risk of suicide, after a long period of bullying at school. They allowed him to stop attending school for a while. They moved out to the countryside, and no institution contacted them while he was missing school. Two years later, he started attending a distance school program, where he could avoid having to face being called a girl's name, and the dissonance with his masculine appearance and attitude.

One of the interviews presented racial intersectionality. A Roma couple explained that they faced not only rejection for being perceived as different, but also had to challenge the dominant perceptions in Roma communities.

It is tough; we are Roma and we live in a Roma housing project with a lot of sexism. When people see a child that is different, he is attacked. D. cannot be by himself in our neighborhood. (Roma mother talking about her 9-year-old child)

Even accepting professionals around them often had stereotyped perceptions of how Roma people would react.

We had a wonderful primary school teacher, Loli, and one day I could see she was so nervous. She started saying "I have observed that D. plays with girls, and this is not a problem, but I think he is so sensitive, and his tendencies are more. . . I am just telling you in case you haven't noticed."

> *I was aware that Loli had had bad experiences with Roma people, and she didn't know how to tell me. Not because she didn't know me, but because I was Roma. (...) She probably knew how to tell a non-Roma family, but she had a tough time telling me. (...)* (Mother of a 9-year-old child)

It became apparent in all of the interviews that the way families dealt with the medical and social processes of gender reassignment was decisive in their acceptance of, and their feelings towards, their children. Although for some it meant thinking that there was a genetic or a congenital problem, they became aware of how important their support as parents was. For others, it was not a matter of identifying a problem, but of finding ways to address their children's needs in the present and near future. Acceptance was present to varying degrees in all parents interviewed. They all demonstrated ways of gaining agency over the situation through the use of different strategies that evolved over time. They reported that changing attitudes and finding support improved the quality of their family life.

Talking to Professionals about Gender-Nonconforming Children and Trans Youths

Professionals such as doctors, psychologists, teachers, and social workers have a clear impact on how parents deal with their children's gender, as they are a source of authority, as well as providing meaning to families' experience. Medicine and/or religion are often called upon as the cause and the solution for gender nonconformity and transgenderism. These narratives reach even children:

> When our child was about three, he started asking questions and once said, "why didn't you tell the doctors to make me into a girl?" By the time he was six, he asked, "Who's to blame for what's happening to me? The doctors? God?" *(Mother talking about her 6-year-old daughter)*

One consistent finding was that dealing with gender and sexuality is uncomfortable for professionals, who think "the problem" will go away once children grow up; or that it is someone else's problem (e.g., family, specialists, counselors); and that "doing something" will bring trouble. This is what this special education teacher reported, talking about an 8-year-old:

> *She was a girl with a sight problem. She was adopted and she was very masculine, and was telling everyone she was a boy, and was called "Jose Mari," which made all the teachers laugh. Her mom was really nice and told me: "I know one day she will have to go through surgery" [as gender reassignment surgery]. When I became aware of this problem I spoke to the teachers and suggested we get training, and one teacher said, "Is*

it necessary? It makes me so uncomfortable. I don't want to get in any trouble." At least she was honest.

The interviewed professionals who were aware of transgender issues often reported isolation and lack of guidelines in their professional environment. The lack of training and protocols had an impact on the pace of their intervention, which often came too late if at all. They described their despair over the lack of appropriate actions.

> We contacted a twelve-year-old Romanian boy living in the suburbs who wanted to be girl, but his father sent him back to Romania so that he would be cured of "that." Not only was he harassed at school, but at home his father also beat him horribly. At the height of it, we were about to request the father's legal custody be taken away, after his father found him looking at photos of naked men on the Internet. But we couldn't do anything. His father put him on a bus to Romania. *(Social worker talking about a 12-year-old gender-nonconforming child)*[11]

Other informants reported that the ignorance on transgender issues was such that some colleagues could find no explanation to the situation. They did not acknowledge the source of the problems and focused exclusively on the problem behavior or the lower school performance that occurs when students feel isolated, stressed, or excluded.

> She was a girl in sixth grade; I couldn't tell if it was a boy or a girl. Teachers could see that all of a sudden she was so nervous, having a bad time. I asked if they had thought the girl might be having identity issues. This teacher didn't even think it could be an identity problem. The girl was a very good student, and suddenly, she was so nervous. The staff was avoiding the issue, not even asking her why she was feeling terrible. Children get through the school year and then it's someone else's problem. I don't know what happened, since I was transferred to another school; I haven't seen any school in the Basque Country do anything about problems related to gender identity and we all feel that we are already doing things around equality, sexuality, but we don't do anything really. *(Teacher of a 12-year-old gender-variant child)*

Most teachers interviewed were used to having gay students, but were not so familiar with gender-nonconforming and trans youths. Two teachers stated that trans youths sometimes acted violently and defensive towards their peers, who actively ignored, excluded, or discriminated against them.

> That school year at the PCPI program was complicated; in addition of the typical issues there were bad relationships among students.[12] The girls wanted to study or at least try, but the boys were very immature and created a violent environment. The transgender girl in my class chose one survival strategy: attack. She would talk back all the time, threatened

students using her brother as defense. In my opinion, she was becoming obsessed; she thought everyone was looking and laughing at her. Sometimes it was true, but sometimes it wasn't and her reactions were disproportionate. *(Female teacher talking about a 15 year-old trans girl)*

One of the interviewed psychiatrists reported,

there is a growing number of children attending the units. In Madrid there are around thirty. We provide assessment but we do not treat them. (...) We do not provide hormone blockers since they have an effect on bone growth, and we use this to avoid providing treatment to youth under 18.

If the situation in Madrid is replicated in other regions, there are a number of children and families who are provided with public counseling but no other services.

Children and families reported bearing a secret that needed to be kept and only revealed to someone they trusted, like a qualified expert, and that this was too much of a burden for small children and their families. Furthermore, the framework embedded in the *DSM*-IV, *ICD*-10, and Spanish law assumes sexuality is something pertaining to adults. This is consistent with the widespread notion that gender identity is somehow resolved once adulthood is reached, so not much can be done besides documenting gender dissonance during childhood and adolescence (interview with a psychiatrist, 2012). This common approach puts children at risk, ignoring the needs of today and trusting professionals' good intentions, whereas this area requires training. Parents demand specific support, specialists, and guidance. The health professionals interviewed were cautious not to label gender-nonconforming behavior in terms of identity or sexuality, which contrasts with parents' reports around their bad experiences with other professionals.

Somehow, gender nonconformity and transgenderism are both invisible and hypervisible. At schools, youth clubs, sports, etc., children's and youths' bad or passive behavior becomes undeniable, along with the visibility of the "improper" masculinity/femininity displayed by the student. These students opted for different coping strategies at school, such as high performance and fitting in with the expected behavior; choosing to maintain a "low profile," trying not to be noticed and participating as little as possible; pretending nothing is happening and passing as cisgender; or becoming extremely rebellious and creating trouble (Platero, 2010).

The lack of information and professional training contributes to the conflation of homosexuality, gender variance, and transgenderism, therefore not providing specific attention to different types of problems. Both professionals and parents often reported professional bad practices, and the influence of specific moral ideas, such as blaming fathers' masculinity or mothers' care and attachment. They stated that this bad practice went unreported, and was continuously repeated.

In sum, further research needs to be carried out in different professional areas (mental health, pediatrics, social work, teaching, non-formal education, vocational training, counseling, etc.) to identify specific needs and best practices already developed in Spain. Nonetheless, our small sample was useful in identifying some professionals' growing awareness. They were able to make sense of the experience of some children, youths', and families in their work practice. These professionals tell us that inaction is wrong and waiting may mean higher risk, including for suicide, self-harm, dropping out of school, and bullying. They reported actions that included advising parents to contact local GLBT organizations, GLBT public services, and Gender Identity Disorder Units, and provide constant support to their offspring, rather than punishing unexpected gender expressions. To other professionals, this was a mental health disorder with a specific process and intervention meaning follow-up and support into adulthood, when decisions would be made.

CONCLUSIONS

Despite growing acceptance and the development of new legislation for sexual and gender minorities, Spanish society is also concerned with the gender ruptures, which are labeled as problematic, evidence of disorders, and linked to sexual minorities. The influence of the international framework where transgenderism is seen as a disorder has permeated Spanish legislation. As a result, gender-nonconforming children and trans youths lack assistance and proper information. Therefore, we need to reflect on the impact of psychology/psychiatry and legislation in shaping citizens' feelings and understanding of their bodies, gender expressions, and how society relates to them. Even in a context of growing acceptance, normative discourses generate meanings and influence how individuals think and behave, especially when it comes to their children, students, or clients.

Sexuality and nonconforming gender identity are perceived as an adult matter, which creates a context of ignorance and risk for some children and their families. It also bans professionals from prevention and intervention when needed. Lacking specific research and professional training allows bad practice, as well as the emergence of different moral ideas towards sexual dissidence, influenced by Spain's repressive past. The lack of adequate knowledge paves the way for those who support discipline and suggest correcting inappropriate gender behavior. The current shift in Spain towards austerity and conservative positions may reflect an understanding of transgenderism as transgressing upon well-respected notions of family and gender norms linked to the concept of "nature" that are vigorously promoted by the Catholic Church.

There are social costs to presenting gender nonconformity and transgenderism as individual problems. Gender norms, the gender binary, or children's sexuality are issues that are not tackled. This framework perpetuates and reinforces sex and gender norms. Furthermore, since Spanish legislation relies on diagnosing a disorder, Gender Identity Disorder, to grant rights to transgender people, how is the new *DSM*-5 vision of transgender people and gender-nonconforming children going to impact future legislation? Will a new mental health framework impact on the triangle of morality-legislation-medicine that determines how society relates to transgender individuals?

In the interviews, participants identified needs that may guide future action, such as providing services for families and children, specific training for professionals, creation of shared protocols across disciplines, coordination of services and professionals, peer groups, transphobia prevention, etc. Interviews also revealed that parents are able to find some agency even within a medical framework, and decide upon their children's well-being even to the point of making decisions that they consider wrong, such as disagreeing with professionals or allowing a child to drop out of school for a while. One research question can be derived from this work: "What agency can be gained out of having a 'disorder'?" Some of the parents interviewed did find the pathological notion of Gender Identity Disorder comforting, since it implied children were not responsible for choosing transgenderism, or gender nonconformity. What is missing in this reaction is wondering what is and will be the cost of presenting children as suffering a disorder, as victims of a random situation. We could also ask how parents can escape the notion of disorder, help their child avoid feeling like an outcast, as well as how we can support them when experts tell them that transgenderism is the result of being born in the wrong body. This paradox requires further reflection. It may be useful to remember that many of life's conditions, which are not disorders, such as pregnancy, aging, menopause, growth, etc., also require biopsychosocial intervention. Therefore the argument that transgender people (or youths) can only be offered assistance if transgenderism is considered a disorder is strongly challenged, and can be used to gain support for both families and transgender individuals of all ages (Araneta, 2012; Garaizabal, 1998, 2006; Missé & Coll-Planas, 2010; Missé, 2012; Platero 2011; Suess, 2011).

Also, regarding future research and the limitations of this study, it is clear that including parents from different sources in the sample, especially those who are not as accepting of their children, or even not linking myself with a perspective of acceptance, might have yielded different results. The lack of fathers in the sample did not allow me to establish gender differences in acceptance and denial of their children's gender nonconformity and transgenderism. Therefore, further research is needed concerning parents and relatives of gender-nonconforming children and trans youths in Spain.

Last, I would like to pose another question. What is the role of researchers in the area of gender variance and transgender studies in terms of providing data? My concern is that better knowledge of this situation may be used to essentialise gender, instead of providing arguments to better understand gender constructions in different societies, along with improving families' and children's lives, which is, after all, the goal of many professionals in this field.

NOTES

1. In Spanish, the term *transsexual* is broadly used without making a distinction between pre- or post-operative status, whereas this distinction is relevant in other contexts. We must also note that in countries of Anglo-Saxon influence as well as Latin America, the term *transgender*, as enunciated by Feinberg (1992), is widely used. *Transgender* intends to avoid this distinction regarding transition and surgery, and has different meanings and contexts (Hausman, 1995; Nieto Piñeroba, 1998; Valentine, 2007). However, this term has not had the same predicament in Spain. Taking these distinctions into account, I will use the English term *transgender* when referring to the term *transsexual* as used in Spanish (Platero, 2011).

2. See 1954 Slackers and Delinquents Act (Ley de Vagos y Delincuentes, 194) and 1970 Social Danger and Rehabilitation Act (Ley de Peligrosidad y Rehabilitación Social, 1970).

3. Ley Orgánica 10/1995, November 23, del Código Penal. BOE, November 24, pp. 33987–34058.

4. Navarrean 12/2009 Act, November 19, on nondiscrimination on the grounds of gender identity and the recognition of the rights of transgender people. BOE, December 22, pp. 108177–108187.

5. Basque 14/2012 Act, June 28, on nondiscrimination on the grounds of gender identity and recognition of the rights of transgender people. BOE, July 19, pp. 51730–51739.

6. Público/Efe (2010). Elcolectivotransexualpidequelosmenorescambiendesexosinpermisojudicial (Transgender organizations demand the minors' access to gender reassignment without court permission). *Publico*, January 12, 2010.

7. It is relevant how the age of consent is different in every country. For instance, in Spain the sexual age of consent is 13, marriage is possible at 14, work is allowed at 16 as well as criminal responsibility, but adulthood starts at 18. The current discussion (2013) over sexual age of consent if pushing for a more conservative approach, suggesting the age of 16 in line with the general backlash in sexual rights.

8. Currently, there is no national "Gender Identity Unit," and the regions have uneven service provision. Since June 2012 gender reassignment surgery has been limited due to austerity cuts (Corcuera, 2012).

9. In 2010, a number of professional and activist organizations were consulted by the government in search for a common ground standard that could homogenize treatments nationally (interview with Marina de la Hermosa, resident psychiatrist at the Madrid Gender Identity Disorder Unit, December 30, 2012).

10. Often parents use mixed pronouns; in the translation this mixture is respected.

11. I would like to thank David Berná for this interview.

12. PCPI stands for "Programas de Cualificación Profesional Inicial" (Initial Professional Qualification Program). These programs address student diversity and are aimed at 15- to 16-year-olds who do not meet mainstream standards. In Spain education is free and mandatory for 6- to 16-year-olds. This program was designed as an alternative for those that drop out of regular courses.

REFERENCES

Araneta, A. (2010). Transfronteras: Un nuevo activismo mundial por la despatologización trans [Transfrontiers: A new global activism for trans depathologization]. In L. Puche Cabezas & O. Moreno Cabrera (Eds.), *Transexualidades, adolescencias y educación: Miradas multidisciplinares* [*Transgenderisms, adolescents and education: Multidisciplinary perspectives*] (pp. 89–109). Madrid y Barcelona: Egalés.

Aveline, D. (2006). "Did I have blinders or what?" Retrospective sense making by parents of gay sons recalling their son's earlier years. *Journal of Family Issues, 27*(6), 777–802. doi: 10.1177/0192513x05285613

Becerra-Fernández, A. (2004). *Transexualidad*. Madrid, Spain: Díaz de Santos.
Bustos Moreno, Y. (2008). *La transexualidad*. Madrid, Spain: Dykinson.
Casanova, E. (2011). Trans-formar la educación primaria. Reflexiones de un maestro transexual [Trans-forming elementary education: Reflections of a transgender teacher]. *Cuadernos de Pedagogía, 414*(July), 84–86.
Coll-Planas, G., Bustamante i Senabre, G., & Missé i Sánchez, M. (2009). *Transitant per les fronteres del gènere: Estratègies, trajectòries i aportacions de joves trans, lesbianes i gais [Transiting the gender frontiers: Strategies, trajectories and contributions of trans, lesbian and gay youth]*. Barcelona, Spain: Generalitat de Catalunya, Secretaria de Joventut.
Connell, R. W. (1995/2005). *Masculinities*. Berkeley, CA: University of California Press.
Corcuera, L. (2012). Mapa estatal de las UTIG (Unidades de "trastorno" de Identidad de Género) [Spanish map of the Gender Disorder Units]. *Diagonal*, December 3.
de Verda y Beamonte, J. R. (1999). La transexualidad en la jurisprudencia del Tribunal Supremo [Transsexuality at the Supreme Court's jurisprudence]. *Revista internáuta de práctica juridical, 2*.
Domínguez Fuentes, J. M., García Leiva, P., & Hombrados, M. I. (2011). *Transexualidad en España. Análisis de la realidad social y factores psicosociales asociados [Transsexuality in Spain. An analysis of the social reality and the associated psycho-social factors]*. Universidad de Málaga y FELGTB.
Espin Alba, I. (2009). *Transexualidad y tutela civil de la persona [Transsexuality and custody]*. Madrid, Spain: Reus.
Feinberg, L. (1992). *Transgender liberation: A movement whose time has come*. New York, NY: World View Forum.
Galofre Molero, P. (2007). La nueva ley ¿es tan buena como nos la venden [The new law, is it as good as they say?]. In M. García Ruiz (Ed.), *Transexualidad: situación actual y retos de futuro [Transgenderism: Current situation and future challenges]* (pp. 147–154). Asturias, Spain: Conseyu de la Mocedá.
Garaizabal, C. (1998). La transgresión del género. Transexualidades, un reto apasionante [The gender transgression. Transgenderism, a passionate challenge]. In J. A. Nieto (Comp.), *Transexualidad, transgenerismo y cultura. Antropología, identidad y género [Transsexuality, transgenderism and culture. Anthropology, identity and gender]* (pp. 39–62). Madrid, Spain: Talasa.
Garaizabal, C. (2006). Evaluación y consideraciones psicológicas [Evaluation and psychological considerations]. In E. Gómez & I. Esteva de Antonio (Eds.), *Ser transexual. Dirigido al paciente, a su familia, y al entorno [Being transgender. For patients, families and their networks]* (pp. 163–174). Barcelona, Spain: Glosa.
García Siso, A. (2003). Conflictos de la identidad sexual en la infancia [Sexual identity conflicts in children]. *Revista de la Asociación Española de Neuropsiquiatría, 86* (April-June). Retrieved from http://dx.doi.org/10.4321/S0211-57352003000200004
Gómez-Gil, E., & Esteva de Antonio, I. (2006). *Ser transexual. Dirigido al paciente, a su familia, y al entorno sanitario, judicial y social [Being transgender. For patients, families and their networks]*. Barcelona, Spain: Glosa.
Gómez-Gil, E., Esteva, I., Cruz Almaraz, M., Pasaro, E., Segovia, S., & Guillamón, A. (2010). Familiality of gender identity disorder in non-twin siblings. *Archives of Sexual Behavior, 39*, 546–552. doi: 10.1007/s10508-009-9524-4

Gómez-Gil, E., Trilla, A., Salamero, M., Godás, T., & Valdés, M. (2009). Sociodemographic, clinical, and psychiatric characteristics of transsexuals from Spain. *Archives of Sexual Behavior, 38*, 378–392. doi: 10.1007/s10508-007-9307-8

Hausman, B. L. (1995). *Changing sex: Transsexualism, technology, and the idea of gender*. Durham, NC: Duke University Press.

Hurtado García, I. (2011). Una propuesta transgresora [A transgressive proposal]. *Cuadernos de Pedagogía, 414*(July), 62–64.

Iglesias Hernández, M. I., Ruiz Peña, M., Guerrero Díaz, M., Macías Sánchez, M., Bergero Miguel, T., Parres Gutiérrez, C., & Asiain Vierge, S. (2010). Transgender sexual behaviors in health care. *European Psychiatry, 25*(1), 499. doi: http://dx.doi.org/10.1016/S0924-9338(10)70494-6

Martín Romero, D. (2004). *La transexualidad, diversidad de una realidad [Transgenderism, a diverse reality]*. Madrid, Spain: Consejería de Familia y Asuntos Sociales.

Martínez, M. (2005). Mi cuerpo no es mío. Transexualidad masculina y presiones sociales de sexo [My body is not my own. Male transgenderism and sexual social pressure]. In C. Romero Bachiller, S. García Dauder, & C. Bargueiras Martínez (GtQ) (Eds.), *El eje del mal es heterosexual. Figuraciones, prácticas y movimientos feministas queer [The axis of evil is heterosexual. Queer feminist inflections, practices and movements]* (pp. 113–129). Madrid, Spain: Traficantes de Sueños.

Mejía, N. (2006). *Transgenerismos [Transgenderisms]*. Barcelona, Spain: Bellaterra.

Martínez Vázquez de Castro, L. (2010). *El principio de libre desarrollo de la personalidad [The principle of free personality development]*. Navarra, Spain: Civitas.

Missé, M. (2012). *Transsexualitat. Altres mirades possibles [Transgenderism: Other possible approaches]*. Barcelona, Spain: Universitat Autònoma de Barcelona.

Missé, M., & Coll-Planas, G. (Eds.). (2010). *El género desordenado: Críticas en torno a la patologización de la transexualidad [Gender in disorder: Critiquing the pathologization of transgenderism]*. Madrid, Spain: Egales.

Moreno, O., & Puche, L. (Coord.). (2012). *Transexualidad, adolescencia y educación. Miradas multidisciplinares [Transgenderism, adolescence and education. Multidisciplinary approaches]*. Madrid, Spain: Egales.

Nieto Piñeroba, J. A. (1998). *Transexualidad, transgenerismo y cultura [Transsexuality, transgenderism and culture]*. Madrid, Spain: Talasa.

Nieto Piñeroba, J. A. (2008). *Transexualidad, intersexualidad y dualidad de género [Transgenderism, intersexuality and gender duality]*. Barcelona, Spain: Bellaterra.

Ortega Arjonilla, E., Romero-Bachiller, & Carmen e Ibáñez Martín, R. (2014). *Discurso activista y estatus médico de lo trans: Hacia una reconfiguración de cuidados y diagnósticos [Trans activist discourse and the medical status: Towards a reconfiguration of care and diagnosis]. Cartografías del cuerpo [Mapping the body], Eulalia Pérez Sedeño & Esther Ortega Arjonilla*. Madrid: Cátedra.

Osborne, R., Longo, V., Monteros, S., Aguirre, V., A. Rojas, L., & Gil, S. (2011). *La situación social de la población migrante TLGB en España, desde un enfoque de género y de derechos humanos [The social situation of migrant TLGB people in Spain, from a gender and human rights perspective]*. Republica Dominicana: ONU Mujeres, Santo Domingo.

Platero, R. (2008). Outstanding challenges in a post-equality era: The same-sex marriage and gender identity laws in Spain. *International Journal of Iberian Studies*, *21*(1), 41–49. doi: 10.1386/ijis.21.1.41/3

Platero, R. (L). (2010). Estrategias de afrontamiento frente al acoso escolar: Una mirada sobre las chicas masculinas [Coping strategies in bullying: Masculine girls at school]. *LES Online*, *2*(2), 35–51.

Platero, R. (L). (2011). The narratives of transgender rights mobilization in Spain. *Sexualities*, *14*(5), 597–614. doi: 10.1177/1363460711415336

Platero, R. (L). (Ed.). (2012). *Intersecciones. Cuerpos y sexualidades en la encrucijada [Intersections. Bodies and sexualities at the crossroad]*. Barcelona, Spain: Bellaterra.

Platero, R., & Gómez, E. (2007). *Herramientas para combatir el bullying homofóbico [Tools to combat homophobic bullying]*. Madrid, Spain: Talasa.

Puche Cabezas, L., Moreno Ortega, E., & Pichardo Galán, J. I. (2012). Adolescentes transexuales en la escuela, aproximación cualitativa y propuestas de intervención desde la perspectiva antropológica (Transgender teenagers at school, a qualitative approach and intervention proposals using an anthropological perspective). In O. Moreno Cabrera & L. Puche Cabezas (eds.), *Transexualidades, adolescencias y educación: Miradas multidisciplinares [Transgenderism, adolescence and education: Multidisciplinary approaches]* (pp. 189–265). Madrid y Barcelona: Egalés.

Ramos, J. (2003). Las asociaciones de transexuales [The transgender associations]. In A. Becerra-Fernández (Ed.)., *Transexualidad. La búsqueda de una identidad [Transsexuality: The search for an identity]* (pp. 125–142). Madrid, Spain: Díaz de Santos.

Soley-Beltran, P. (2007). Transsexualism in Spain: A cultural and legal perspective. *Sociological Research Online*, *12*(1). Retrieved from http://www.socresonline.org.uk/12/1/soley-beltran.html

Soley-Beltran, P., & Coll-Planas, G. (2011). "Having words for everything": Institutionalizing gender migration in Spain (1998–2008). *Sexualities*, *14*(3), 334–353. doi: 10.1177/1363460711400811

Sosa, M., Jódar, E., Arbelo, E., Domínguez, C., Saavedra, P., Torres, A., & Hernández, D. (2004). Serum lipids and estrogen receptor gene polymorphisms in male-to-female transsexuals: Effects of estrogen treatment. *European Journal of Internal Medicine*, *15*, 231–237. doi 10.1016/j.ejim.2004.04.009

Suess, A. (2011). Reflexiones sobre la despatologización [Reflections on depathologization]. Actas del X Congreso Argentino de Antropología Social. La antropología interpelada: Nuevas configuraciones político-culturales en América Latina [Argentina Social Anthropology Conference Publication. The question of anthropology: New political-cultural configurations in Latin America]. Buenos Aires: Universidad de Buenos Aires.

Valentine, D. (2007). *Imagining transgender. An ethnography of a category*. Durham, NC: Duke University Press.

Zaro Rosado, I., Rojas Castro, D., & Navazo Fernández, T. (2009). *Trabajadoras transexuales del sexo: El doble estigma [Transgender sexual workers: The double stigma]*. Madrid, Spain: Fundación Triángulo & Ministerio de Sanidad y Consumo.

Familiarising the Gay, Queering the Family: Coming Out and Resilience in *Mambo italiano*

MICHELA BALDO
University of London, London, United Kingdom

This article explores how two Italian-Canadian families negotiate the coming out of their sons in the film Mambo italiano, *a comedy/drama released in 2003 and set in Montreal, Canada. The Italian-Canadian protagonist, Angelo, after years of living in the closet, decides to tell his parents he is gay, outing at the same time his Italian-Canadian lover, Nino, and provoking initially strong and vexed reactions in their respective families. Although full of stereotypes and clichés on ethnicity and gender identities, and following closely the so-called coming-out films' genre, arguably concerned with positive representations of gay coming-out experiences, the film portrays the ironic, creative, and interesting ways in which these Italian-Canadian families negotiate a coming out despite the homophobic prejudices they are imbued with. Moving from studies of family resilience, this article argues that the major strategies used for integrating gayness into the family are drawn from the resources available to (post)migrant families. These are the use of rituals and the adaptation of ethnic schemata to new realities in order to cope with the unfamiliar, and the ability to envision family as an evolving and changeable reality, as this capability and the hope for a better future is what had sustained the survival of migrants in a hostile land. These considerations are backed up with reference to Italian-Canadian and Italian-North/American gay, lesbian, and bisexual (GLB) writers, whose concerns are similar to those found in* Mambo italiano.

INTRODUCTION

This article explores how two Italian-Canadian families reassess their mutual coming-out stories in the film *Mambo italiano*, a comedy/drama directed by Émile Gaudreault, released in 2003 and set in Montreal, Canada. The protagonist, Angelo, is in his early thirties, and after years of living in the closet, decides to tell his parents he is gay, while simultaneously outing his lover. The film is based on Steve Galluccio's theatrical play, which is inspired by his own coming-out story and is set in an Italian-Canadian family in Montreal. The film is full of stereotypes and clichés regarding ethnicity and gender identities, and follows the "coming-out films" genre, generally preoccupied with positive representations of gays and their coming-out experiences (Bronski, 2000; Dyer, 2003). Despite this, the popular theatrical play on which *Mambo italiano* is based was praised by newspaper and magazine reviews for its realistic portrayal of what being gay means in a close-knit ethnic Italian-Canadian community (D'Haene, 2012).

Given the popularity of both the play and the movie amongst Canadian audiences, this article explores the redefinition of family relations following the disclosure of their sons' coming-out journey. The film's focus on the entire family rather than the individual members is motivated by the role played by family in Italian-Canadian diasporic communities. Following research on the coming-out cinema genre, I noticed that specificities to Italian-Canadian communities were lacking. This article seeks to provide the reader with useful information necessary to understand the analysis of select scenes from the film which are aimed at tackling the role of diasporic families of origins, in specifically Italian-Canadian families, in the coming-out process, and in changing attitudes towards gay, lesbian, and bisexual (GLB) issues and family members.

Mambo italiano and the Comic Coming-Out Film Genre

Both the play and the film are based on Galluccio's own lived experiences. As reported by Leeder (2006), Galluccio describes watching an episode of *Oprah* (http://www.oprah.com/index.html) just after Ellen DeGeneres's coming-out episode, where a Canadian man explains the process of coming out of the closet to his parents. Galluccio also expresses his reservations about such information being conveyed to his Italian family so smoothly, thus producing his own unique, cultural perspective. *Mambo italiano*, as some reviews report, tells the story of Angelo (played by actor Luke Kirby), a nearly 30-year-old man preoccupied with his job, his creative aspirations as a writer, and his longing to permanently move out of his parents' house. He finally decides to take the plunge on his last goal, a decision that upsets parents Gino and Maria (played by actors Paul Sorvino and Ginette Reno), as their son is leaving the house without getting married. What they do not know is that Angelo is gay, a secret he has been keeping from everyone but his older sister Anna (played by Claudia Ferri), who discovers his gay identity by accident. A greater shock to the family occurs when Angelo finally reveals that the guy he shares the flat with, Nino (actor Peter Miller), a local macho policeman whose sexuality is at odds with his profession, is his long-time love and partner. Meanwhile, Nino's Sicilian mother, Lina (played by Mary Walsh), is immediately informed of Angelo's revelation, which in turn provokes resentment in Nino, who confided in Angelo that he was not prepared to tell his mother the truth about their partnership. Eventually, fearing the idea of living a life as an openly gay person in a conservative and traditional Italian-Canadian community, Nino breaks up with Angelo, starts dating a female former Italian schoolmate, and marries her, leaving Angelo heartbroken. Consequently, Angelo starts volunteering at a gay helpline to make new friends and decides to quit his boring job at the travel centre in order to focus on becoming a television writer. Thanks to the help of his quasi-supportive Italian cousin, Angelo achieves stardom by writing a TV sitcom based on his life and family. He finally reconciles with his parents, who now accept his non-Italian new boyfriend within the family. The film's name and soundtrack come from the song, "*Mambo italiano*", written by Bob Merrill in 1954, which became famous in Italy in 1955 thanks to Renato Carosone. The song plays a part in the film plot too. Angelo's aunt Yolanda was a fervid mambo lover who committed suicide because of her Italian family's failure to understand her aspirations to become an actress. The film thus pays homage to Yolanda and stands metaphorically for the vitality, desires, and personal aspirations often unfulfilled of some of the film's characters.

Shot and set in Montreal, *Mambo italiano* premiered at the 2003 New York Gay and Lesbian Film Festival. The reference to Ellen as the genesis of this film and the success achieved by the protagonist, with the adaptation of his family saga for television, hints at the idea of TV as a vehicle for gay liberation and at the crossroads of film and television's sitcoms. Although the outlines of the play (which the film is based on) and the film are the same, the two differ mainly in that the film puts greater emphasis on television and television-like structures. With "its occasional touches of stream of consciousness-type unreality, the film at times falls back on the familiar family-couch cantered aesthetics of the traditional family sitcom" (Leeder, 2006, p. 65). A confirmation of this is the fact that Steve Galluccio followed the film with a sitcom called *Ciao Bella!* (CBC, 2003), which depicts the life of Elena Battista, an Italian-Canadian woman whose desire for a modern lifestyle conflicts with the traditional values of her Italian-Canadian family, similarly to Mambo italiano. Moreover, Mambo italiano possibly owes some of its success to *My Big Fat Greek Wedding* (2002), another ethnic family film that resembles a sitcom (as stated in some of its reviews), and which inspired the brief and unsuccessful 2003 TV series *My Big Fat Greek Life*. Mambo italiano thus closely mirrors a family sitcom television show, which often includes confessional elements to the show, confirmed by the fact that the show's structure was partly inspired by Oprah's talk show, "a format that allows family secrets to be revealed and dirt swept out from under the rug" (Leeder, 2006, p. 72). Family and TV dramatic confessionals are thus two key concepts in Mambo italiano. In reference to the family, a review of Mambo italiano defines it as "more than just a gay love story" but rather "a story about a quintessential Italian family straddling cultures, traditions, and mores of the old and new worlds."[1] In regards to the confessional talk show format, the film is characterised by purging many secrets, not only portrayed in the coming-out segment of the protagonist, Angelo, to his parents, but in his admissions to the anonymous gay helpline volunteer, in the confessions of his sister to the psychiatrist she regularly visits, and in the confessions of Angelo's parents and sister to Angelo in the confessional booth. The closet can perhaps be considered as a metaphor of the confessional. The characters of Mambo italiano are trying to come out of this closet/confessional in various ways, also through the medium of TV through which Angelo exposes himself and reveals the deepest family secrets, which is unavoidably an act of coming out (Dyer, 2003).

Mambo italiano thus inserts itself into the coming-out movie genre that shares some of the features of the confessional talk show. Because of its resemblance to television, we can say, quoting Leeder (2006), that *Mambo italiano* "is designed to be inoffensive and non-provocative" (p. 65). As a confirmation of this, the American distributor of the film was so eager to repeat the huge success of *My Big Fat Greek Wedding* that "they forced the removal of the two on-screen kisses between the protagonist Angelo and his cop lover Nino, interfering considerably with the coherence of the film" (Waugh, 2006, p. 487). Plus, the character of Nino seems less ambiguous in the film than in the play, where he is portrayed at the end as a closeted and troubled man hunting down gay saunas behind his wife's back. However, also in the film, at the very end, there is irony in Angelo's sister's dialogue with her psychiatrist, when she hints at Nino's secret camping romps with other men.

The idea of the coming-out film genre post-Stonewall as a non-offensive movie is found, for example, in the writings of Bronski, who affirms that these films are concerned with positive representations of gay people and that portraying coming out in a positive light is in itself a burden that limits gay characterisation (2000). Similarly, Dyer (2003) affirms that, although the "coming-out" story is one of the first Gay Liberation slogans, a fundamental positive political strategy used to achieve visibility and legitimisation, the coming-out movie genre involving gay male characters tends often to depict a fixed and unquestionable gay identity that is simply awaiting to be revealed, contrary to what happens in the more fluid sexuality depicted in lesbian movies. This, for example, could be seen in the depiction of Nino as a gay man going back to the closet, an understanding of him that ridicules his possible bisexuality and sees it as his impossibility to live as an openly gay person.

Moreover, this is a coming-out Hollywood comedic film, given also the presence of famous Hollywood actors. First, although Hollywood, after the success of the new queer cinema of the 1990s, tried to market some films that explored more open parameters of sexuality, it has been reticent to feature actual queer characters (Benshoff & Griffin, 2004). Second, by being a comedic movie, *Mambo italiano* tends to achieve social change by "putting the audience at ease with humour" (Leeder, 2006, p. 65), a humour which is based, in this specific film, on Italian cultural particularities and familial stereotypes.

Regarding this comic aspect, the film has divided audiences between the "outsiders who found the caricatural humour the most hilarious thing they had ever seen and queers who recognised the moments of truth and the authenticity of the story but found much of the excesses troubling" (Waugh, 2006, p. 487). If humour and laughter find their natural place in a coming-out story format, which plays with the seen and the unseen, the said and the unsaid, as in the popular comedy of errors genre, and if humour and laughter are being heightened with the inclusion of the oddities associated with ethnic communities, coming-out films like this can certainly risk further fixing stereotypes rather than unravelling them.

Notwithstanding the critiques of the film, I would like to praise the movie's ability to authentically portray the creative use of the resources available in ethnic/diasporic families and networks in order to face challenges and produce change by adapting to situations initially perceived as hostile, such as comings out.

MAMBO ITALIANO AND COMING OUT AS GAY IN AN ITALIAN-CANADIAN FAMILY IN MONTREAL

As pointed out by previous reviews, *Mambo italiano*, rather than being simply the story of a coming out, is the story of how two Italian-Canadian families deal with the outness of their sons. In order to understand these family dynamics, we need to draw on migration studies in general (Clifford, 1994; Brah, 1996), studies on Italian-Canadian diaspora, which have analysed the life of Italian migrants and post-migrants in Canada (Jansen, 1988; Perin & Sturino, 1989; Iacovetta, 1992; DeMaria Harney, 1998) and the literature produced mainly by second-generation Italians migrants in Canada (Pivato, 1994; Verdicchio, 1997; Lorriggio, 1996). Even more useful is the reference to essays and anthologies of lesbian, bisexuals, and gay people of Italian descent living in North America and Canada such as *Fuori* (Tamburri, 1996), *Hey Paesan* (Capone, Nico Leto, & Avicolla Mecca, 1999) and *Curraggia* (Ciatu Nzula, DiLeo, & Micallef, 1998), which, although focussing mainly on Italian-North/Americans (with the exception of *Curraggia*, whose editors are Italian-Canadians) share many concerns with Italian-Canadians.[2]

According to these studies, the Italian-Canadian immigrants who arrived in Canada in in the 1950s and 1960s had migrated mainly from rural areas of Southern Italy without the opportunity to pursue a formal education (Verdicchio, 1997). As such, they became the target of many prejudices: they were called "wops" and taunted as rude peasants without manners and little education (Jansen, 1988, p. 167). The men were perceived as violent, sexist, and criminal, while women were seen as submissive and dependent totally on men (Iacovetta, 1992; DeMaria Harney, 1998). Other traits that are described as typical of Italian-Canadians as opposed to the character of Anglo-Canadians include being noisy and fighting constantly over nothing and everything, and being unable to listen, as we find in the description by Angelo of his parents. These bad traits are also described in Lombardi's contribution in *Hey Paesan* (Capone et al., 1999), who is sick of her family noise, and by Cappello (Cappello & Sillanpoa, 1999), who says that in her house there was "a constant inundation of noise and talking" (p. 291). This constant noise is reflected also in the persistent music which accompanies *Mambo italiano*, echoing the lack of silence in the little Italy depicted in it.

In addition to their marginalisation within the Anglo-Saxon Canadian society, the cultural gap between immigrant parents and their children growing up in the new land proved quite severe, due to the traditional family values transmitted to their offspring (Pivato, 1994). Angelo and Nino, for example, are not abiding to the family traditions because they want to leave their home unmarried, as shown in the dramatic and exaggerated reactions of their crying and fainting mothers while their sons leave the family house, scenes that confirm the widespread stereotype of "mamma's boy" (Italian "*mammone*"). Feelings of rejection of their ethnic roots are common among these second-generation immigrants (Pivato, 1994) and can give rise to self-hatred due to the social phenomenon of mirroring (Falicov, 2012). Mirroring is the incorporation by immigrants in the image of themselves and their ethnic identity of social negative reflections of the discrimination and racism experienced (Orozco & Orozco, 2000, quoted in Falicov 2012, p. 304). These feelings are well portrayed in *Mambo italiano*, when Angelo accuses his parents of having never really abandoned the "spit of a village" in Southern Italy from where they came, and is in turn accused by his partner Nino of being "the classic self-hating Italian."

Mambo italiano bases its plot around *la famiglia*, the only structure that Italians have learned to rely on and trust, as some studies discuss (see, for example Iacovetta, 1992, and Pivato, 1994), in centuries characterised by foreign invaders, severe natural disasters, and painful migrations. "Family, dead or alive," as expressed by Carilli (1996), "is all that matters" (p. 87). These considerations are important as they can contribute to a better understanding of the drama and comedy in Angelo's coming out.

Angelo affirms in the film that "there is no fate worse than being gay and Italian," and his sister Anna adds that Angelo's coming out to their parents could even kill them. Coming out is shocking because being gay contrasts with beliefs, often emphasised by the Catholic Church and Italian-Canadians, which uphold the heterosexual family as the only correct institution and only considers specific formulas of masculinity as normative: the macho qualities which gays are not supposed to share. These include being "strong, tough, brutish, uneducated, ignorant, violent, handsome, sexy" and with a big sex drive and desire for the opposite sex (Carosone, 2007, p. 9). Being gay falls out of the very basic foundation of the Italian-Canadian family and is considered, according to some of the Italian-Canadian or Italian-North American writers previously mentioned, a deviance that brings shame to the family, a betrayal of the mores which impose caring for the continuation of the family, and also an illness that must be cured (Carosone, 2007). These views are confirmed in *Mambo italiano* in a number of ways. The parents, for example, try constantly to set their sons up with nice Italian girls. Also, when Angelo comes out to his parents, his father associates his gayness with a lack of interest for hockey, a popular male sport in Canada, and even denies that he, a straight Italian father, could have ever generated a gay boy, while his mother asks him immediately to seek help from a doctor.

In *Mambo italiano* Angelo's sexuality thus problematizes his relations to family members, which are fraught with both submerged and overt hostility. In *Fuori* (Tamburri, 1996), the coming out is seen as the biggest challenge, and the revelation of the failure to fulfil heteronormative and patriarchal ideas of womanhood and manhood runs the risk of "disgracing" the family, inflicting pain on oneself and on family members (Carilli, 1996). Gay sexuality cannot coexist with Italian ethnicity (Carosone, 2007) and one must repress the one or the other, living a split life, as expressed by Capone (1996): "I often feel torn in half.[...] I think my dilemma is one faced by many gay and lesbian people, whose *unpopular* sexual orientation means they end up needing a certain amount of distance from their families," something which is painful "for those of us raised in close knit, ethnic families" (p. 36). Being gay or lesbian marginalises these writers within their heterosexual families. For some of them, coming out is a continual process, as family does not understand and the closet is reexperienced again and again (Bona, 1996). For others, coming out means being asked to leave the parental home, as for Carilli (1996) and for Angelo in *Mambo italiano*.

Coming out for Angelo represents a tremendous problem because he fears rejection from his family, and loss of emotional support. However, coming out is also his compelling desire as, by staying in the closet, he fears losing pieces of himself. Therefore, if being gay/lesbian and being Italian-American or Italian-Canadian constitutes a huge contradiction, the aforementioned authors, nevertheless, speak of their desire and continuous efforts to integrate their sexual identities into their ethnic ones. As the editors of *Hey Paesan* say, while GLB people of Italian descent face intense homophobia, silence, and invisibility within their own ethnic communities, they find only limited solace within the queer community where their ethnicity becomes invisible (Capone et al., 1999). As expressed by Carosone (2007), "the ethnic self is an integral part of the individual" and its denial in the queer community can lead "to low self-esteem and a lack of wholeness in the self-concept" (p. 11). Therefore, faced with a double repression by the ethnic family and the queer community, the authors that appear in *Hey Paesan* and *Fuori* seem to invoke an integration of these two spheres of their life. Avicolla Mecca's dressing in drag and parading down the streets could be connected, for example, with the traditional procession of Madonna or the Sicilian *carnevale* (Bona, 1996). The poet Rose Romano (1994), in her poem "There Is Nothing in This World As Wonderful As an Italian-American Lesbian," stresses the consanguinity among Italian food, desire, and identity. The sexuality of these writers, as they seem to convey, must thus be strictly woven into their relationships to their Italian-American communities and families (Bona, 1996), a link which they believe is central to naming themselves as desiring and loving people, and thus as homosexuals. According to Gambone (1996), for example, a better understanding of his homosexual identity passes through a deeper understanding of his ethnicity and especially of his mother, with whom he shares many concerns, while Lombardi (1999) realises later in life that there are musical patterns in the noise of her parental home which invigorate and comfort her. The metaphorical going home of these writers in order to integrate aspects of their sexuality into their families of origin has also big repercussions for their parents, relatives, and wider community as it makes them negotiate their children's queerness.

Thus, even though being gay and Italian is a supposed contradiction, it is a theme utilised in *Mambo italiano* as a plot device that takes unexpected turns and changes involving Angelo and Nino but more so their family members' and wider community's attitudes towards GLB issues. Rather than focussing on Angelo's and Nino's journeys towards their family, the next sections focus on their families' journeys towards them and the contrasts and subsequent reactions which these produce.

"COMING OUT" AND FAMILY RESILIENCE IN *MAMBO ITALIANO*

As previously stated, coming out is a family matter, a social process that infuses conventional representations of sexual deviance embodied by gay and bisexual people with new meanings. In *Mambo italiano*, Angelo's family reacts initially in a dramatic and confrontational way to his coming out, while

Nino's mother reacts in a more ambiguous way. However, the film stresses the changes which occur over time in this ongoing coming-out process, which culminates with the acceptance of Angelo's sexuality by his family (Nino, on the other hand, chooses to go back into the closet).

The majority of studies on the psychology of coming out which can be helpful here seem to agree that coming out is good for gay and lesbian people's mental health (LaSala, 2000, 2010), as not coming out prevents the family from becoming truly intimate and supportive of one another. However, disclosure to parents can be a very stressful experience, as parents often fall into shock, disappointment, and shame after their children's coming out, or even react with violence (Mallon, 1992, quoted in LaSala, 2000, p. 67). These emotional ranges can lead to tense, disconnected relations with family members, in the same way described in *Mambo italiano* by Angelo, who stops communicating with his parents for a while after disclosure. LaSala (2000) explains that this process is common and parents must spend the initial time after disclosure grieving and obtaining accurate information about gay lifestyles, while lesbians and gay men need support as they struggle to cope with their parents' negative reactions. These studies are thus focused on how to overcome such a crisis. Savin-Williams (2001), on the contrary, deemphasises the notions of crisis and grief, stressing that, if problems occur, they can and are often resolved, as happens in *Mambo italiano*.

Problem solving and family strategies used to face difficult and unexpected situations have been defined as resilience. Family resilience (Walsh, 2006, 2012) involves the capacity for recovery and growth in situations of challenge.[3] Rather than focusing on individual resilience, family resilience emphasises resilience in the family as a functional unit, as a whole. This is a theory that has extended beyond preoccupations with coping mechanisms and adaptation and sees families as having the potential for fostering healing and growth in family members (Walsh, 2012) but also bringing about change within their cultures and communities. This is especially relevant in the present article, which investigates the impact of the family of origins of gay and bisexual people on assumptions and beliefs about them.

Some studies have appeared in the past two decades on resilience across cultures or in ethnic and migrant families (McCubbin, Thompson, Thompson, & Fromer, 1998; Roscoe, 1998; McGoldrick, Giordano, & Garcia-Preto, 2005; McCubbin, 2006; Ungar et al., 2007; Falicov, 2012; McCubbin & McCubbin, 2013). These studies have demonstrated that culture provides meaning to people living through adversity and that resilience is dependent upon individual, community, cultural, and contextual factors (Ungar et al., 2007). Moreover, they have demonstrated that familial ethnic schemas play a big role in family physical, emotional, and social well-being as they might provide "the individual with a context or meaning-making framework in order to feel a sense of control, balance and harmony with both expected and unexpected life events" (McCubbin, 2006, p. 176).

However, studies on resilience in families with gay and lesbian children have been very scarce (Roscoe, 1998; Oswald, 2002). Oswald's (2002) study can be very useful for the discussion of *Mambo italiano*. She discusses resilience in the families of origin of gay and lesbian people, stating that the resources and strategies used by these families might be similar to the practices found in marginalised families, and in immigrant families as well. Within this group she analyses two categories: "intentionality" and "redefinition." Intentionality refers to the strategies that gay and lesbian people and their families use to validate themselves as family members and strengthen their ties to others, and redefinition refers to the development of a system that creates linguistic and symbolic structures to affirm gay and lesbian people (Oswald, 2002). These two elements work together, encompassing both behavioural strategies and ongoing construction of meaning. Intentionality and redefinition are further subdivided into subcategories, among which "ritualising," "integrating gayness," and "envisioning families" are useful concepts which can be used to analyse *Mambo italiano*, and which are addressed in the rest of this article.

With regard to "ritualising," rituals according to Oswald (2002) are symbolic performances that can be used creatively by members of gays' and lesbians' family networks to "affirm identities in the absence of social or legal validation" (p. 369). Rituals have also been considerably analysed in studies on immigrant families. Falicov (2012), for example, describes the emergence of immigrant resilience practices, which she calls spontaneous rituals that "encapsulate in ritualised ways various family, social and cultural restitutive attempts following migration" (p. 298). In *Mambo italiano*, after Angelo's disclosure, his parents Gino and Maria out Nino to his mother, Lina Paventi, in an attempt to gain support from another member of the Italian ethnic community in Montreal. Lina, however, pretends that this revelation is a lie and organises a dinner at Gino and Maria's in order for the families to reconcile with their estranged sons and talk about their lives, but secretly she attempts to match Nino with Angelo's sister and Angelo with her Italian-Canadian female friend. The family dinner is a highly ritualised moment for Italian-Canadians, one in which family matters are discussed and conflict often arises because of the inability of family members to listen to one another (Cappello & Sillanpoa, 1999). Food can become a major topic of discussion and a way to avoid talking about more important matters, as happens when Nino's mother, after learning of her son's homosexuality, lures him into coming home with a bunch of cannelloni she has prepared. The dinner organised by Lina represents the moment of rupture between Nino and Angelo, because the latter will discover that Nino has cheated on him with this female guest, and Nino does not want to continue a closeted relationship with Angelo; it represents a moment of further rupture also for Angelo and his parents, who are scolded by Angelo as backward peasants living meaningless lives and being attached to old-fashioned beliefs.

This dinner shows how Italian-Canadian families use rituals in order to cope with stressful events and reestablish order. However, this familial ritualised reunion, although representing a successful attempt on the part of Nino's mother to reaffirm her son's heterosexuality (as Nino will decide to live a straight life or at least to abide to the Italian rules of public honour, keeping what is shameful private), results in the failure on the part of Angelo's parents to reestablish connection with their son, and instead they will continue to place distance between themselves. As Giordano, McGoldrick, and Guarino Klages (2005) explain, Italian-Americans are often "very engaging and colourful speakers" but "passionate outbursts do not tend to cause permanent ruptures or resentments" (p. 624). Because of this, Angelo's parents, along with his sister, will seek contact with him again, and they will do so at the church, around and inside the same confessional booth that Angelo's mother visits every Saturday after finishing her chores at home. After bribing the priest with a bottle of wine and a packet of cigarettes, Angelo and his sister wait for their mother to enter the confessional booth. Soon the father joins in and the whole family shares sorrows and secrets and apologises to one another for their irrational behaviours. Peace is finally made and connections reestablished.

The Catholic confessional plays a big part in the Italian-Canadian imaginary. As stated by Giordano and colleagues (2005), although talking about everything, Italian-American families do not openly discuss "hot" issues and are hesitant to share family secrets. This is confirmed by Angelo's sister's constant change of psychiatrists because she fears revealing too much information to one single doctor, and by the psychosomatic ulcer attacks of Angelo's father, who is unable to verbalise his sorrow around key issues. The Catholic ritual of confession, rather than the dinner table, is thus the place where secrets are confessed in a way that resembles the act of coming out. The scene shown in the film can be understood as a "ritualising" practice which merges two ritualistic acts involving spheres which are usually separated, since the Catholic Church, along with Angelo's parents, rejects homosexuality. The scene of the confessional booth where the entire family gathers resonates with the psychiatric sessions of Angelo's sister, Anna, who occasionally reproduces this ritual with her brother, pretending to psychoanalyse him in an attempt to help him reconnect with their parents. The film ends with another ritual: Angelo's family parade to the communal garden where many Italian-Canadian families grow their vegetables, which represents a symbol of Italian family traditions. Angelo and his sister are seen for the first time in the film entering this space, which is regularly visited by their parents. Angelo brings to the garden his Anglo-Canadian lover, openly sharing his relationship with the whole Italian community. The garden thus connects family with the broader community: it is the symbol of the outside world as opposed to the more secret world of the dinner table where, as has been previously pointed out, people often cannot talk about hot issues.

The examples of rituals discussed show that, as stated by Oswald (2002), the ability to integrate gay and lesbian loved ones into family-of-origin rituals is key to sustaining resilience. "Ritualising" as a behavioural strategy goes hand in hand with "redefinition" of processes by which Angelo's family affirms the existence of gay people and their relationships. One aspect of these processes is called "integrating gayness" (Oswald, 2002, p. 373).

Although Angelo's father, by continually blaming fate for all his disappointments, gives initially the impression that the family members do not believe in their ability to master the problems they are presented with, ultimately he and Maria are able to use emotional and cultural resources, drawn from the migrant history of the family, to become more resilient. After being scolded by Angelo, for example, they start reassessing their past relationships (which were sometimes troubled) with other family members, in particular with Angelo's aunt Yolanda. The aunt, a mambo lover, had committed suicide, because she was unable to pursue her dreams of becoming an actress in a close-knit ethnic community. Angelo's mother mourns the death of her sister in front of her grave by comparing her failure to prevent her death with her failure to understand her son, who shares similarities with Yolanda (naming the two "one of a kind"). By redefining herself as defective, and rediscovering and renaming rejection and betrayal within her own family, Angelo's mother gets closer to her estranged son, integrating his gayness within their family's lineage.

Despite the differences among groups in adapting to the new country, according to Falicov (2012), the immigrant experience is characterised by loss (of habits, traditions, language), grief, and mourning. The death of her sister triggers in Angelo's mother the memory of other immigrant losses, such as the loss of certainties and the fear of the unknown, which had made her withdrawn and judgemental. By comparing the shame cast on her son to her own shame as a marginalised Italian immigrant to Canada, Angelo's mother starts the process of integrating gayness within the family. Immigrants are able to make positive meanings out of the experiences of migration and, therefore, rekindling a past might bolster rather than prevent the family from adapting to new ways of living (Falicov, 2012).

Angelo's coming out thus triggers the coming out of his parents' buried sorrows. Interestingly, the Italian-North American writer Carilli (1996) believes that her nontraditional sexuality gave her insight into how to recognise and embrace the confusion and ambiguity experienced by her immigrants parents. Cappello as well, suggests that the outsider status of gay, lesbian, and bisexual people within their Italian ethnic families makes them better able to understand and identify with other forms of marginalisation within the very families that marginalise them (Cappello & Sillanpoa, 1999). Cappello thinks it is by virtue of her queerness that she became the reader of the family. A diasporic family, which she labels queer like herself, can be considered, borrowing Fortier's (2001) words, as "always somehow located in a space of betweenness" (p. 418), as living between worlds (Italy and America) and desires. Di Maria (1999), an Italian-American writer featured in *Hey Paesan* (Capone et al., 1999), while sitting at the deathbeds of his emaciated and feverish friends, dying of AIDS, remembers the times in which he was sitting at the deathbed of his grandfather, dying of cancer, unable to tell him that he shared with him the same "sting of being Other," and feeling "the pain of being an alien" in his own land (p. 265). The otherness that links these writers with their families, according to Di Maria (1999), both resembles vinegar and sugar: it is a force "both alienating and enlightening" (p. 267). The metaphorical return to the past by Angelo's parents reminds them of the resources they had previously used in order to survive as migrants. Falicov (2012) says that immigrant families "deal in flexible and creative ways with losses, risks and gains of migration" (p. 319). This is because, contrary to death, losses in migrant contexts (with the exception of refugees escaping from torture, war, violence) are ambiguous, incomplete, partial, and postponed. The lost home is constantly re-created in the new country from the moment of arrival (Brah, 1996), in a way that presence and absence coexist.

The strategy of integrating gayness follows this complex pathway and can, for example, be witnessed in two other scenes of *Mambo italiano*. After the tumultuous family dinner described earlier, Angelo's parents bump into Nino's mother, Mrs. Paventi, who shows false compassion about Angelo's condition, wishing things will improve and also expresses that Angelo could probably find a nice Italian girlfriend. In an attempt to counteract her remarks, imbued by a presumed superiority based on the apparent reestablishment of her son's heterosexuality, Angelo's parents retort by inventing a lie: their son is not alone, and not because he has moved back with them after Nino left him, but because he has found a gorgeous boyfriend who loves him to death. The hilarity of the scene is provoked by a reversal of heteronormative beliefs that the audience had previously encountered and grown accustomed to. This reversal tells us that Angelo's parents are working towards redefining and "integrating gayness" within the family system. More specifically, they are drawing on their family schemas (McCubbin, 2006), understood as their dispositional worldviews, their cultural and ethnic beliefs and values, in order to give meaning to family experiences and facilitate coping and adaptation.

One Italian-Canadian family schema is the importance of "*fare la bella figura*," literally meaning "making a good impression." Italian-American writer Philip Gambone (1996), for example, says that it would be impossible to think about himself as an Italian-American, let alone a gay Italian-American, without considering other experiences in his personal history, such as his grandmother and mother's constant admonishment to make a good impression ("*Sempre fa' 'na bella figura*"). The importance of *fare la bella figura* is shown in the scene in which Angelo's parents out their son to Mrs. Lina Paventi. This outing becomes a list of old macho clichés as a measure of gayness or straightness, in order to preserve a good image of themselves as parents, the *bella figura*, despite their realities. The *bella figura* is also shown in another hilarious scene in which Gino and Maria are trying to portray themselves in the best possible light in front of Lina, to contrast their shame about their son Angelo and their envy of Lina's son, who is about to get married to a woman. An invitation to Nino's wedding arrives by post. Gino and Maria are very disappointed and carefully ponder whether to accept the invitation and how to behave at the wedding (either showing boredom or enjoying the festivity thoroughly to shame Lina), as the wrong gestures risk being interpreted as instances of fare *la brutta figura* (make a wrong impression). In the impossibility of negating their son's homosexuality, and in an attempt to abide to the dictates of *la bella figura*, Angelo's parents in the subsequent encounters with Lina draw on another family schema: the pressure of socialising and participating in the Italian community. It becomes more acceptable to accept Angelo in a healthy, happy gay relationship, rather than imagining him as lonely "like a dog" (the expression used in Italian). The importance of socialising has been remarked by some of the Italian-Canadian writers as an exceptionally significant aspect of their culture. Angelo's sister describes the many events characterised by music, dance, food, and chaos (well re-created by the soundtrack of the film), in which she and her brother were brought up, in the same way that Capone describes her big family dinner rituals (1996), and the way that Cappello (Cappello & Sillanpoa, 1999) emphasises the importance of socialising for her Italian grandfather, who, despite the extreme poverty, had founded a social club and a mandolin/guitar society in the United States. As previously noted, Italians in Canada had to work hard in order to integrate into an often-hostile society, and socialising was a survival strategy.

The final scene of the film hints at another ethnic schema involving the larger extended community, outside Angelo's family. There is a particular scene where Angelo is walking alongside his Anglo-Canadian boyfriend and his family in the communal garden. Two members of the Italian community in Montreal, who happen to be Gino and Maria's friends, comment on the scene with displeasure, not with the fact that Angelo has a boyfriend (as one might expect) but with the fact that the boyfriend is not Italian. The pressure of marrying inside the ethnic community is very high and was also expressed in earlier parts of the film when Angelo and Nino were encouraged by their parents to date nice Italian girls. The scene provokes laughter as it exposes the stereotype of the judgemental gaze and gossip dominating in the close-knit community of little Italy in Montreal but ironically twists the content of the gossip, giving prominence only to one ethnic schema. This is thus another instance of "integrating gayness" within an ethnic schema and shows us the complex strategies used to build up resilience. As expressed by Boscia-Mulè (1999), people's relationship with their ethnic culture is always a strategic compromise, intimately linked to the personal power and resources people have. Despite the hostility against homosexuality, Italian-Canadian families are able to creatively work with ethnic schemas, changing and modifying some on the basis of others.

This redefinition strategy can be fostered by Oswald's (2002) notion of "envisioning family" (p. 379). As Oswald (2002) states, "the ability and willingness to re-imagine family promote resilience" (p. 380). Envisioning family refers to the process of redefining family as an ongoing work in progress that affirms human difference (Oswald, 2002). This ability is certainly strengthened by immigration. Migration disrupts family stability while it struggles to regain continuity in the midst of new challenges. The immigrant family has to constantly negotiate between new and old in order to maintain a sense of identity and coherence. For a family to be flexible, a sense of continuity and identity must be integrated with new evolving patterns of behaviour, according to recent studies on bilingualism and biculturalism (Falicov, 2012) and diaspora and hybridity (Clifford, 1994; Brah, 1996; Gabaccia, 2003). These studies assume that diaspora and hybridity have certain commonalities in their relationships to the notions of disjuncture and subversion of naturalised forms of identities centred on the nation; however, they do not dismiss the power of nationalism and identity construction but rather put emphasis on the concept of diaspora as a process (Clifford, 1994) that mediates the tensions coming from constructed notions of home and abroad, as some scenes of *Mambo italiano* exemplify.

Angelo's parents are able to envision family by reenacting, possibly, some migrant coping strategies, sustained by a sense of hope. Despite the difficulties experienced by immigrants, migration can often "bring a sense of adventure and excitement, hope and new dreams, possibly greater economic stability and prosperity" (Falicov, 2012, p. 302). The experience of immigration also teaches how to put events into perspective as conditions rapidly change and improve with the time spent in the host culture: this is thus hope for change. According to Walsh (2006), hope and optimism have been found vitally important to sustain resilience as they allow family to better cope with stress. Hoping that things will improve is what characterises the resilience of Angelo's parents and their ability to envision a different family in which their gay son can find a place for himself.

To summarise, Gino and Maria deal with the coming out of Angelo by integrating and redefining his gayness through the use of rituals, in order to transform the unfamiliar into the familiar. By doing so, they queer their ethnicity, while Angelo ethnicises his queerness. Ethnicity is a major cause of Angelo's troubles as he cannot be openly gay in his family and community. Yet, the film shows that this very ethnicity is also the major source of the strategies that will lead to Angelo's acceptance within the family. In the battle over *la bella figura* with Nino's mother, Angelo's parents revise their migrant past, giving the spectator the impression that their son's status as an outsider might be comparable to their own condition as first-generation migrants, not yet completely integrated within their host country. Their often-comedic portrayal testifies that being an outsider is a precondition for creating comedy. Laughter is, however, also a strategy used in most Italian-Canadian and Italian-North American families to deal with problems and to deflect pain, as expressed by some of the writers discussed in this article (Tamburri, 1996; Capone et al., 1999). Laughter and irony imbue a sense of possibility to concepts understood as impossible; they create hope for change. By going metaphorically back to the roots of their ethnicity, constructed and reassessed continuously as a consequence of immigration, Angelo's parents are also able to use other ethnic schemas such as socialising and attachment to family in order to de-emphasise the stigma of homosexuality. The impossibility of bearing separation from their son for too long forces them to reinstate communication, which is what facilitates resilience. As expressed by LaSala (2000; 2010), upon disclosure family members should be given necessary space to process the coming out but during this period they should stay connected, as the connection allows families to rework issues, and eventually accept and integrate gayness. Resilience is thus possible because of the emphasis given to the ethnic schema of family unity and community sociability in Italian-Canadian families.

The film therefore shows that familial ethnic identity is in continual evolution as ancestral influences are incorporated "while forging new and emerging group identities, in a complex interplay of members' relationships with each other and with outsiders" (McGoldrick et al., 2005, p. 6). This merging of new and old can be best interpreted following the views on ethnicity expressed by Boscia-Mulè (1999), according to whom ethnicity, rather than an instinctive, integral part of the self, or a free, strategic selection of ethnic traditions, should be perceived as a strategic compromise between choice and constraints, personal power resources, and lack of status, with the consequent creation of possibilities coming from apparent impossibilities.

CONCLUSIONS

This article has shown family members' negotiations of a coming out in the Canadian comedy/drama film *Mambo italiano*, a Hollywood film with a happy ending which reassures rather than troubles (Benshoff & Griffin, 2004). Although these negotiations are inserted into a comedy plot which uses them to create slapstick scenes circulating around the clashes between the "straight" and "non-straight" worlds (where sexual fluidity might be looked upon with suspicion), they also portray the ironic and creative ways in which family members merge what is unfamiliar with what is familiar, in the processing of the coming out of their sons.

In order to understand how the families of the protagonist, Angelo, and his lover, Nino, can overcome the crisis provoked by their coming out, as homosexuality is strongly opposed on cultural and religious grounds, I mainly referred to diaspora studies and Italian-Canadian and Italian-American writers who had narrated their own experiences of coming out to their families, and I used the concept of resilience in immigrant contexts, as understood in family studies. Family resilience, that is, family capacity for taking up challenges and overcoming problems, can be a useful tool to analyse *Mambo italiano*. Using the resources offered by resilience studies, I came to the conclusion that the acceptance of Angelo's gayness is a process of familiarisation: it is the outcome of a journey back to the family's migrant roots in which the use of rituals play a big part. Rituals are catalysts for feeling, thinking, and action and "they validate ties between past and present, gain and loss, ideal and real" (Falicov, 2012, p. 306). Through the use of rituals, Angelo's parents reassess and queer ethnic schemas, integrating gayness within them. Ethnic schemas, that is, values, beliefs, goals, expectations, and priorities, have a huge impact on one's sense of integrity (McCubbin, 2006).

The ability to locate homosexuality within them facilitates resilience since it builds upon existing strengths (Roscoe, 1998). Schemas like attachment to family and *la bella figura*, despite the negative feelings attributed to them in parts of the movie, mean that families may successfully familiarise themselves with the unknown by merging the themes and experiences of dislocated cultures and alienated sexualities. The film *Mambo italiano* seems thus to stress the resources available to ethnic communities when faced with coming-out realities.

NOTES

1. See http://www.metacritic.com/movie/mambo-italiano
2. The big migration to Canada of Italians takes place after the Second World War (Perin & Sturino, 1989; DeMaria Harney, 1998) while the big migration to America preceded this and can be located between 1887 and 1920. Nevertheless, the two migrations share many similarities as confirmed by the declaration of Angelo's father in *Mambo italiano*, whose intention was to go to North America but ended up by mistake in Canada.
3. I use the concept of resilience in this article as opposed to that of resiliency. According to Luthar, Cicchetti, and Becker (2000), the term *resilience* should always be used when referring to the process or phenomenon of competence despite adversity, while the term *resiliency* should be used only when referring to a specific personality trait.

REFERENCES

Reviews of *Mambo italiano*

Dalton, M. *Mambo italiano*. Retrieved from http://gaytoday.com/entertain/062303en.asp

D'Haene, D. (2012). DISHing with *Mambo italiano*. Retrieved from http://www.thebeat.magazine.ca/index.php/dishing-with-donald/1000-dishing-with-mambo-italiano

Hays, M. (2003). His big fat Canadian hit: Montreal writer Steve Galluccio's gay family comedy *Mambo italiano* is a runaway success onstage—and the movie version is due out soon (theater). Retrieved from http://www.advocate.com

Mambo italiano. (2003). Retrieved from http://www.rottentomatoes.com/m/mambo_italiano/

Mambo italiano. (n.d.). Retrieved from http://www.metacritic.com/movie/mambo-italiano

Mambo italiano (film). (n.d.). Retrieved from http://en.wikipedia.org/wiki/Mambo_Italiano_(film)

Mambo italiano (various reviews). (n.d.). Retrieved from http://www.imdb.com/title/tt0330602/reviews

Other References

Avicolla Mecca, T. (1996). Memoirs of a South Philly sissy. In A. J. Tamburri (Ed.), *Fuori. Essays by Italian/American lesbians and gays* (pp. 13–28). West Lafayette, IN: Bordighera.

Benshoff, H., & Griffin, S. (2004). *Queer cinema, The Film Reader*. New York, NY; London, England: Routledge.

Bona, M. J. (1996). Gorgeous identities: Gay and lesbian Italian/American writers. In A. J. Tamburri (Ed.), *Fuori. Essays by Italian/American lesbians and gays* (pp. 1–12). West Lafayette, IN: Bordighera.

Boscia-Mulè, P. (1999). *Authentic ethnicities: The interaction of ideology, gender power, and class in the Italian-American experience*. Westport, CT: Greenwood Press.

Brah, A. (1996). *Cartographies of diaspora: Contesting identities*. New York, NY; London, England: Routledge.

Bronski, M. (2000). Positive images and the coming out film: The art and politics of gay and lesbian cinema. *Cineaste, 26*(1), 20–26.

Capone, G. (J.) (1996). A divided life: Being a lesbian in an Italian American family. In A. J. Tamburri (Ed.), *Fuori. Essays by Italian/American lesbians and gays* (pp. 29–49). West Lafayette, IN: Bordighera.

Capone, G. (J.), Nico Leto, D., & Avicolla Mecca, T. (Eds.). (1999). *Hey Paesan: Writing by lesbians and gay men of Italian descent*. Oakland, CA: Three Guinea Press.

Cappello, M. (1996). Nothing to confess: A lesbian in Italian-America. In A. J. Tamburri (Ed.), *Fuori. Essays by Italian/American lesbians and gays* (pp. 89–108). West Lafayette, IN: Bordighera.

Cappello, M., & Sillanpoa, W. (1999). Compagna/compagno: Excerpts from a conversation. In G. (J.) Capone, D. Nico Leto, & T. Avicolla Mecca (Eds.), *Hey Paesan: Writing by lesbians and gay men of Italian descent* (pp. 290–302). Oakland, CA: Three Guinea Press.

Carilli, T. (1996). Strangled. In A. J. Tamburri (Ed.), *Fuori. Essays by Italian/American lesbians and gays* (pp. 50–59). West Lafayette, IN: Bordighera.

Carosone, M. (2007). *Disgracing the family. The history/non history of Gay-Italian Americans*. Paper presented at the 40th Annual Conference of the American-Italian Historical Association "Italian Passages: Making and Thinking History," November 1–3, Denver, Colorado.

Ciatu Nzula, A., DiLeo, D., & Micallef, G. (Eds.). (1998). *Curraggia. Writing by women of Italian descent.* Toronto, Ontario, Canada: Women's Press.

Clifford, J. (1994). Diasporas. *Current Anthropology, 9*(3), 302–338.

DeMaria Harney, N. (1998). *Being Italian in Toronto.* Toronto, Canada: University of Toronto Press.

Di Maria, T. (1999). More than a comic. An interview with Tom di Maria. In G. (J.) Capone, D. Nico Leto, & T. Avicolla Mecca (Eds.), *Hey Paesan: Writing by lesbians and gay men of Italian descent* (pp. 173–184). Oakland, CA: Three Guinea Press.

Dyer, R. (2003). *Now you see it. Studies on lesbian and gay films* (2nd ed.). London, England: Routledge.

Falicov, C. J. (2012). Immigrant family processes: A multidimensional framework. In F. Walsh (Ed.), *Normal family processes (*4th *ed.)* (pp. 297–323). New York, NY: Guilford Press.

Fortier, A. M. (2001). Coming home: Queer migrations and multiple evocations of home. *European Journal of Cultural Studies, 4*(4), 405–424.

Gabaccia, D. (2003). *Italy's many diasporas: Elites, exiles and workers of the world.* London, England: Routledge.

Gambone, P. (1996). Learning and unlearning and learning again the language of Signori. In A. J. Tamburri (Ed.), *Fuori. Essays by Italian/American lesbians and gays* (pp. 60–80). West Lafayette, IN: Bordighera.

Giordano, J., McGoldrick, M., & Guarino Klages, J. (2005). Italian families. In M. McGoldrick, J. Giordano, & N. Garcia-Preto (Eds.), *Ethnicity and family therapy* (3rd ed.) (pp. 616–628). New York, NY: The Guilford Press.

Iacovetta, F. (1992). *Such hardworking people. Italian immigrants in postwar Toronto.* Montreal, Quebec, Canada: McGill-Queen's University Press.

Jansen, C. (1988). *Italians in a multicultural Canada.* Lewiston, NY: E. Mellen Press.

LaSala, M. (2000). Lesbians, gay men and their parents. Family therapy for the coming-out crisis. *Family Process, 39*(1), 67–81.

LaSala, M. (2010). *Coming out, coming home: Helping families adjust to a gay or lesbian child.* New York, NY: Columbia University Press.

Leeder, M. (2006). Closet and confessional. Television and hybridity in *Mambo italiano. Canadian Journal of Film Studies, 15*(1), 63–74.

Lombardi, C. (1999). The art of noise. In G. (J.) Capone, D. Nico Leto, & T. Avicolla Mecca (Eds.), *Hey Paesan: Writing by lesbians and gay men of Italian descent* (pp. 268–274). Oakland, CA: Three Guinea Press.

Lorriggio, F. (1996). *Social pluralism and literary history: The literature of the Italian emigration.* Toronto, Ontario, Canada: Guernica.

Luthar, S. S., Cicchetti, D., & Becker, B. (2000). The construct of resilience: A critical evaluation and guidelines for future work. *Child Development, 71*(3), 543–562.

McCubbin, D. L. (2006). The role of indigenous family ethnic schema on well-being among Native Hawaiian families. *Contemporary Nurse, 23*(2), 170–180.

McCubbin, D. L., & McCubbin, H. (2013). Resilience in ethnic family systems: A relational theory for research and practice. In D. S. Becvar (Ed.), *Handbook of family resilience* (pp. 175–195). New York, NY: Springer.

McCubbin, H. I., Thompson, E. A., Thompson, A. I., & Fromer, J. E. (Eds.). (1998). *Resiliency in Native American and immigrant families.* Thousand Oaks, CA: Sage.

McGoldrick, M., Giordano, J., & Garcia-Preto, N. (2005). Overview. Ethnicity and family therapy. In M. McGoldrick, J. Giordano, & N. Garcia-Preto (Eds.), *Ethnicity and family therapy* (pp. 1–42). New York, NY: The Guilford Press.

Oswald, F. R. (2002). Resilience within the family network of lesbians and gays: Intentionality and redefinition. *Journal of Marriage and Family, 64*(2), 374–383. doi: 10.1111/j.1741-3737.2002.00374.x

Perin, R., & Sturino, F. (Eds.). (1989). *Arrangiarsi. The Italian immigration experience in Canada*. Montreal, Quebec, Canada: Guernica.

Pivato, J. (1994). *Echo: Essays on other literatures*. Toronto, Ontario, Canada: Guernica.

Romano, R. (1994). There is nothing in this world as wonderful as an Italian-American lesbian. In R. Romano, *The Wop Factor* (pp. 55–56). Brooklyn, NY: Malafemmina Press.

Roscoe, W. (1998). Two Spirit people: Gay American Indians today. In W. Roscoe, *Changing ones: Third and fourth genders in Native North America* (pp. 99–116). New York, NY: St. Martins.

Savin-Williams, R.C. (2001). *Mom, Dad, I'm gay: How families negotiate coming out*. Washington, DC: American Psychological Association.

Tamburri, A. J. (Ed.). (1996). *Fuori. Essays by Italian/American lesbians and gays*. West Lafayette, IN: Bordighera.

Ungar, M., Brown M., Liebenberg, L., Othman, R., Kwong, W., Armstrong, M., & Gilgun, J. (2007). Unique pathways to resilience across cultures. *Adolescence, 42*(166), 287–310.

Verdicchio, P. (1997). *Devils in paradise: Writings on post-emigrant cultures*. Toronto, Ontario, Canada; Buffalo, NY; Lancaster, United Kingdom: Guernica.

Walsh, F. (2006). *Strengthening family resilience* (2nd ed.). New York, NY: The Guilford Press.

Walsh, F. (2012). Family resilience: Strengths forged through adversity. In F. Walsh (Ed.), *Normal family processes* (4th ed., pp. 399–427). New York, NY: The Guilford Press.

Waugh, T. (2006). *Romance of transgression in Canada: Queering sexualities, nations, cinemas*. Montreal and Kingston, Canada; London, UK; Ithaca, NY: McGill-Queen's University Press.

Queer TV Moments and Family Viewing in Italy

LUCA MALICI
University of Birmingham, Birmingham, United Kingdom

Although queer investigations of popular cultures and, in particular, television are both fashionable and flourishing at present, interconnections with audience studies are largely unexplored. The available research on sexuality is yet to provide a more complex interpretation of the multifaceted TV viewing practises and capricious interactions amongst co-present viewers. To date, research in this field remains mostly attached to textuality as well as Anglophone knowledge and contexts. Since the 1990s the increasing representation of sexual dissidence on mainstream TV in Italy has placed families, surfing and zapping through TV channels, in "awkward" situations, being often challenged by alternative and innovative gay, lesbian, bisexual, and transgender (GLBT) narratives, subjects, and lifestyles. What are the reactions of normative people? What does it mean for closeted GLBT viewers to witness representations of sexual nonconformity in the living room with other viewers? Through a triangulation of two qualitative online questionnaires administrated respectively in 2008 and 2009 to a total of 350 participants, I show different approaches, responses, and interactions of both GLBT-identified and heterosexually identified participants (parents but also relatives and friends of GLBT people). Participants provided fascinating stories of coming out, collective negotiations of meaning, and different attitudes towards the limits of what is considered representable on TV. I demonstrate that television has functioned as a core site of debate and struggle between mainstream and minoritised sexualities and, when available and accurate, queer representations have challenged the traditional and heteronormative perception of viewers.

I would like to thank Dr. Charlotte Ross and Ms. Clelia Boscolo as well as the editors of this special issue for their invaluable feedback on this article.

INTRODUCTION

Since mainstream television began to transmit, decisions on if, what, how, and when programmes or films are broadcast have often been influenced by an ideal family audience assumed as exclusively heteronormative. The term *heteronormativity* was coined by Michael Warner (1991), but the concept was firstly introduced as "compulsory heterosexuality" (Rich, 1980) and "heterosexual matrix" (Butler, 1990). They all mean that heterosexuality is pervasively assumed and expected to be the norm throughout, privileging normative forms of heterosexuality over and above other behaviours and practices.

Ellis claims that, especially in the past, television programming choices had to construct, gain, and retain intimacy with nuclear families so that "nothing that was too offensive was to be broadcast" (2000, p. 48). Arthurs expands this further, saying that these concerns are entirely normative and "oriented towards the prevention of 'deviant' behaviour and the promotion of traditional 'family values'" (2004, p. 10). Similar arguments have recently been put forward by Davis and Needham, who reiterate the putative links among domesticity, family, and television as heteronormative configurations (2009, p. 9). However, Aaron reminds us that the family home has not been the exclusive space of TV viewing; there have been other constellations of cohabiting viewers in front of the small screen and, importantly, overall "very little so far has been written on the impact of sexuality on viewing patterns" (2009, p. 73).

In Italy, there has historically been little televised representation of gay, lesbian, bisexual, and transgender (GLBT) individuals. However, since the 1990s, as I explain in the first part of this article, due to an array of concurrent reasons, their televisibility (i.e., their intelligible TV presence) has increased exponentially. Although problematic in terms of both quality and quantity, these representations have entered households, creating what I define as queer TV moments (QTM). These are largely unpredictable instances of confrontation with sexual dissidence, GLBT visibility, and political issues coming from the public sphere. Yet they are usually viewed in the intimate space of the *salotto*—the living room—thus mixing both private and public experiences. Martin, Hutson, Kazyak, and Scherrer (2010, p. 964) cite television amongst the cultural "toolkits" families of origin use in order to make sense of the world and to find strategies to accept, accommodate, or disapprove of their children's homosexuality. To date, there has been no sustained investigation of whether these moments have attempted to challenge heteronormativity in this quintessential bastion or have progressively undermined discourses of compulsory heterosexuality. How have families engaged with the increased visibility of GLBT characters and narratives on Italian TV? Did they decide instead to simply change the channel?

METHOD AND SAMPLE

In this article I intend to address these questions and to assess the possibilities offered by the televisual medium to families of origin as well as scrutinise the limitations posed by the living room setting. My discussion is based on the findings of two online studies I devised and carried out in 2008 and 2010, respectively. The first was a survey administered to 260 Italian GLBT-identified respondents. They commented on the limits of GLBT representation on Italian television and provided a list of titles of what they felt were significant films and programmes (see also Malici, 2012). Short video clips of the titles most frequently named in the survey were subsequently included in the second study: an online questionnaire, disseminated by e-mail using a snowball method of distribution and completed by a non-probability sample of 60 respondents. The questionnaire contained 10 open-ended questions; the participants were invited to give their personal opinions and comments on the visual representations as well as on some of the issues raised by the clips.

The second sample included both females (53%) and males (47%): 70% identified themselves as heterosexuals, 19% as gay males, 8% as lesbians, and 3% as male bisexuals. The majority of respondents came from the centre (45%) and north (40%) of Italy, whereas 15% came from the south. The ages of the sample ranged from 18 to 80 with a mean age of 37 years. This ensured the presence of different generations of viewers. Respondents had a fairly high level of schooling: 72% were pursuing postgraduate and 15% undergraduate studies, and 9% and 4% held secondary and primary education certificates, respectively. Participants' self-identified political party preference was 56% Left, 20% Centre-Left, 11% Centre, and 12% other. In terms of religious beliefs, the majority of participants stated they were Catholic (55%), 28% atheist, 6% agnostic, and 11% of other faiths (e.g., Buddhist, Pagan, New Age). The link to the questionnaire was also sent to specific associations, including the Association of Parents of Gay Men and Lesbians (AGEDO) and to the Italian Parents Movement (MOIGE), which is usually at the forefront of campaigns against GLBT portrayals on TV. Nobody from MOIGE completed the questionnaire and only one member of AGEDO did. Apart from him and the other three cases mentioned in this article, nobody else reported they were part of a family of origin with one or more GLBT members.

Nevertheless, other respondents could potentially have experienced GLBT matters and, after all, viewing TV with other family members was an item discussed in the majority of responses.

FINDINGS

Whereas in my previous study 93% of GLBT respondents perceived Italian mainstream TV as a homophobic space (Malici, 2012, p. 119), an analysis of the data produced by the second questionnaire, on which I focus in this article, shows some rather unexpected results. Almost three-quarters of mainly heterosexually identified participants felt quite comfortable with the challenging representations included in the questionnaire. Respondents acknowledge the transformative value of increasing queer televisibility in offering a platform for information, confrontation, and debate within families of origin and amongst friends around and beyond the TV set. Not only did the media representations encourage discussions about what is televised, but respondents also reflected on the lives and rights of GLBT people in Italy. The issues tackled ranged from the coming-out process within the family of origin to alternative same-sex family formations and the limits posed by more sexualised TV portrayals of queer desire experienced in a family setting.

Crucially, a set of preconceived assumptions by individual respondents about the way GLBT-themed television might be perceived by other co-present viewers appeared to discourage them from watching these programmes in the first place. Even the way respondents answered the open questions and reacted to more confrontational and true-to-life representations of dissident sexuality is significant. Although questions encouraged participants to express their personal opinions, almost 80% of them often speculated on the way in which "others" might react to these representations. The archetypal viewer in their minds is often the heteropatriarchal father or the minor who needs protection. Thus viewing practices seem to be strongly and problematically influenced not so much by the content of the films and programmes, but by a form of third-person perception (TPP): the internalised perception of the views of others, which conditions individuals' consumption of media programmes. This resonates strongly with Michel Foucault's disciplinary theories (1977, 1979, 1980) and the way in which in modern times power is exercised by individuals policing themselves through self-monitoring, self-surveillance, and modern forms of confession. This also reverberates with the very Italian idea of *fare bella figura* (make a good impression), which emphasises external appearance, aesthetics, and appropriate behaviour within families and communities. This "etiquette system" (Mignone, 2008, p. 410) belongs to the realms of the visual and the performative and is governed by the notion of "what would other people think?"; as such, it inherently promotes a set of internalised norms, too.

In this article, I will first discuss the role of TV in an Italian family context while surveying the reasons behind the increasing visibility of GLBT subjects and resistance to this since the 1990s. I then provide the reader with a theoretical framework to queer moments, applied for the first time to television and audience studies. Subsequently, I present some findings from the questionnaire and discuss the transformative potential of these moments in relation to examples of programmes aired on Italian mainstream TV. Finally, by analysing selected representations that faced restrictions on Italian TV, I survey respondents' perceptions of unapologetic and more sexualised portrayals, discussing their TPP. Overall, I demonstrate that qualitative research on an Italian audience helps to shed light on the importance of these QTM as well as reveal the spectators' views on the possibilities and limits of GLBT representations.

Queer Interferences in the *Salotto*: Increasing GLBT Televisibility and the Italian Context

The TV set was the first visual medium to enter households and to be placed at the heart of the family. Initially, it even reorganised the domestic space, soon becoming the new "fireplace" around which a familiar, convivial, and reiterative ritual has, since then, taken place (Spigel, 1992). This continues to be the case in 2012: statistics show that the "Italian television audience coincides with the totality of the population," with 98.3% watching it regularly (CENSIS, 2012b). Although this figure may have altered slightly over time, the supremacy of TV in the previous 20 years has only been slightly dented by the changing mediascape. New media have only altered the *way* in which Italians watch television, not the number of hours spent doing it. Today there are on average 3.02 TV sets per Italian household in different rooms (ISTAT, 2012, p. 7), and the romantic idea of a family gathered around a cathode ray tube has been gradually replaced by more fractured and solitary viewing of flat-screen TVs, computers, and tablets (Nielsen, 2012). Grasso argues that the digital TV has also transformed viewing practices into a more "individualistic, fragmented and personal experience" (Grasso, 2003, p. 233). This notwithstanding, data gathered in 2012 by an Italian statistical body shows that TV viewing is still a collective and familial experience which takes place in the living room for 52.7% of Italians (CENSIS, 2012a).[1] TV remains a platform through which sociocultural cohesion as well as diversity can be negotiated cooperatively.

In Italy, as in most Western countries, the 1990s saw the initial and progressive broadcasting of GLBT-themed programmes and content on mainstream television. These might be described as "queer interferences" in mainstream media discourse; they represented a set of novel and somehow unsettling depictions that interfered with viewers' expectations, altering what they had been used to seeing on television. This does not mean that, in the past, non-normative sexualities were completely absent from mainstream media. Prior to the 1990s, there were sporadic representations of GLBT characters and identities, prevalently in televised foreign cinema. These portrayals were relatively veiled and enigmatic, and, although GLBT audiences could find a space for identification through recuperative readings, they remained obscure to most heterosexual viewers (Malici, 2011, p. 118). In the 1990s we saw the televisual coming out of more clearly intelligible GLBT characters, topics, and narratives.

The initial circulation and development of GLBT televisibility in Italy has been influenced by changing economic, political, and social contexts. In particular, Italian mainstream television programming has been strongly affected by the U.S. televisual market. Becker (2006) explains that the increasing presence of U.S. gay-themed representations in the 1990s resulted from a variety of factors: the development of sexual and multicultural politics, the political situation during the Clinton era, and an increasingly competitive media market threatened by satellite television and the Internet contributed to this growing televisibility. Rather than cater for GLBT consumers, U.S. TV executives aimed at widening the media offering—and concurrent advertising revenue—by introducing provocative subject matters that would appeal to a sizable audience made up of heterosexual, educated viewers. The exploitative nature and economic motives behind GLBT televisibility are fundamental in understanding the points of contact and differences between the U.S. and the Italian contexts. Through broadcasting syndication, Italian networks bought popular U.S. programmes, series, and films in order to increase their advertising revenue. This was considerably cheaper than producing new films and programmes. However, while U.S. television is a largely private and market-oriented system in which programmes are produced and distributed to appeal to specific audiences, the situation is different in Italy. Programmes ended up being broadcast on national mainstream channels directed towards a broad, undifferentiated audience. If on the one hand GBLT representations have opened up opportunities for debate, on the other they have also constantly faced resistance from political and religious institutions.

Italian TV has always been in some way subordinate to politics. Since the 1975 Broadcasting Act (Law 103, April 14) established that a parliament supervisory board should control the national service broadcasting (RAI), Italian television has never been free from political meddling (see, e.g., Hibberd, 2007). This was particularly the case in the 1990s and 2000s, which saw the intermittent presence of media tycoon Silvio Berlusconi as Prime Minister (1994–1996, 2001–2006, and 2008–2011). Berlusconi's indirect ownership, amongst other media outlets, of almost half of the Italian mainstream TV sector, with his three commercial channels (Rete 4, Italia 1, and Canale 5), created a political anomaly and a problematic oligarchy during those years. The impact on GLBT televisibility of the influence of a man who on several occasions has expressed sexist and homophobic views such as "It's better to like pretty girls than to be gay" (BBC, 2013) is undeniable. His centre-right party, *Forza Italia* then *Popolo delle Libertà*, has counted on the support of the Catholic and conservative electorate which historically held traditionalist views on sexuality. Due to conventional assumptions based on the social, moral, and religious value of the nuclear—heterosexual—family, the increasing availability of dissident sexualities, topics, and narratives on TV has inevitably encountered opposition. More than 40% of respondents in both my studies highlighted politics and internalised conservative Catholic morality as two of the main causes of the quantitative and qualitative shortcomings of GLBT representation on Italian TV (Bertone & Franchi, 2014). This has hindered the initial production and distribution of Italian GLBT films and programmes, too.

GLBT topics, narratives, and characters started to progressively emerge on the small screen in the 1990s, yet at a tremendously slow pace and in a problematic manner. GLBT presence on Italian TV in terms of quantity seemed to follow the order of the letters in the acronym. Stereotypical gay characters, in supporting or minor roles, were the most frequently represented group, whereas lesbian and transgender individuals started to appear just before the turn of the millennium. Bisexuals and intersexed individuals have hardly appeared on Italian television. After 2000, Italian film and TV companies started to produce more films and programmes which included GLBT themes and characters, yet continued to relegate them to stereotypical minor roles, rendering them dependent on the rather problematically framed "acceptance" of the main heterosexual protagonists. Although there has been a gradual transformation in the depiction, from the irony of sitcoms to more challenging genres, such as films and documentaries with more sensual and true-to-life representations, these kinds of portrayals hardly ever make primetime: they are usually altered, censored, or scheduled in "graveyard" latenight slots when audience figures are low.

GLBT respondents to my 2008 survey corroborated this interpretation of events (Malici, 2012). They were demanding and critical about the way they have been represented on Italian TV. They confirm that Italian GLBT media offering is scarce and biased, with the majority of representations being U.S. films and series. They ask for more ample, diversified and confrontational portrayals of dissident sexuality able to interrogate Italian viewers and they see mainstream TV as a tool to disrupt heteronormativity on a larger national scale. For them television is an important source of support in that it provides an initial opportunity for discussion and reciprocal understanding within the family of origin, while also easing conflicts and helping with the coming-out process. In this respect, QTM are particularly relevant in Italy as young people live in their parental homes longer and heterosexual marriage—the only form of recognised partnership in Italy—still remains the main reason for leaving the family of origin (see Iacovou, 2010; Saraceno, 2004).

Queer Moments and Audience Research

The increasing yet problematic televisibility of GLBT sexualities in Italy has inevitably had an impact on viewers who have happened to watch a particular queer-themed programme. The significance of and reaction to these unexpected televisual moments do not appear to have been studied in any country. Although this is the first time that the notion of queer moments has been applied to television and audience studies, they have already been analysed by different scholars in other areas.

Drawing on Sedgwick's notion of "homosexual panic" (see Sedgwick, 1990, p. 19) occurring when heterosexual individuals confront the social prohibition of homosexuality, Becker (2006) has developed the concept of "hetero" or "straight panic." He describes it as the heterosexual confrontation with a homosexuality which is represented as "increasingly accepted" (2006, p. 23). While I would like to distance myself from the problematic concept of "acceptance" because it reiterates asymmetries of power and specific imageries of normalised sexuality, I see straight panic as the destabilising moment resulting from a perceived unravelling of compulsory. The concept of "queer moment" finds its roots in studies on queer temporality by Halberstam (2005) and Freeman (2010). For Sedgwick (1994) the 1990s represented "the" queer moment for GLBT visibility but from a historical point of view, Alan Sinfield explored the impact of Oscar Wilde's trial and how this particular temporal and historical instance helped shifting public perceptions towards "same-sex passion" (1994, p. 3). Investigating queerness in popular culture, even Doty calls for an attentive examination of these queer moments which can emerge "whenever anyone produces or responds to culture" saying that "straight-identifying people can experience queer moments" too (1993, p. 3). Sullivan (2003) has added to the debate, saying that these moments are uncanny instances of disruption of the "heteronormative logic" (p. 192), whereas Ahmed (2006) has suggested that ultimately we should embrace such unsettling moments in order to learn from them (p. 4). Finally, Butler (2004) has stressed the importance of tracing the moments during which binary systems are disputed and challenged since they show how the social construction of gender is both "malleable and transformable" (p. 216).

All these theories highlight the challenging and, using Butler's term, "transformative" nature of such moments of confrontation for individuals including families of origin, in understanding, appreciating, and working through discourses about sexual dissidence. With television, viewers can exchange opinions during and after watching, and have opportunities to "elaborate discursively" and debate representations in the short and long term (Thompson, 1998, p. 178). Ellis (2000) has commented that in the Internet age, characterised by an information overload, "mainstream television remains crucial in helping with the constant process of making and remaking sense of the world, and of exploring possibilities" (pp. 75–79). Researching the impact of these queer TV moments on viewers becomes crucial, too.

Although embryonic examples of international studies on G(LBT) fandom and reception of specific programmes and films do exist (e.g., Jenkins, 2004), scholarly and market research has only recently started to show an interest in the ways in which GLBT and heterosexual viewers perceive and react to queer televisibility. The triangulation of TV content with GLBT and heterosexually identified reactions to it can make us reflect critically on viewers' assumptions through more palpable data. Together with recommendations to TV executives and space for improving GLBT TV representations, these investigations serve the important purpose of observing the more general status of GLBT visibility in a given culture, revealing its limitations and potential. I now present some results from the second questionnaire I conducted in Italy, and analyse the potential of QTM, discussing the representative limitations in the last section.

Transformative Instants and Instances of Queerness on TV

As a result of the increasing televisibility of GLBT subjects, many Italian families and individuals have had the chance to confront GLBT issues and representations. More than 70% of participants in the questionnaire are comfortable with and interested in the representations and issues raised by the video clips. Respondents confirmed that, when they engaged with such TV portrayals, in the vast majority of cases they perceived them as important, positive, and transformative moments. Although participants rarely talked in the first person, they say that such portrayals have potentially helped to change viewers' attitudes towards GLBT discourses. Relatively stereotypical and humorous U.S. sitcoms such as *Ellen* (1994) and *Will & Grace* (1998) have been important milestones in the initial televisibility of queerness in Italy; however, respondents engaged in thought-provoking ways with more serious and, particularly, Italian-made representations. In other words, identifying with the Italian context and setting had a greater impact on their viewing activity. I will now analyse the participants' responses to two Italian programmes included in the questionnaire.

Il padre delle spose (*The Father of the Brides*, 2006) was one of the first Italian made-for-TV films to tackle the representation of lesbians in Italy (see also Dines & Rigoletto, 2012; Malici, 2012). The plot follows the story of Riccardo, a stereotypical southern father from Puglia, who goes to Barcelona to see his estranged daughter. Here, after accidentally witnessing a kiss, he discovers that she has married another woman, whose daughter lives with the couple. Participants in the research raised interesting comments in relation to the clip which showed the father's initial vehement reaction and his flight after the involuntary outing of his daughter. One respondent, a 29-year-old female identified as lesbian, said,

> *When it was broadcast, I watched it with my mum who knew about my relationship with a woman but she had always wanted to ignore it. I saw a strange shimmer in her eyes while watching this film and from that moment on, she had a more sensitive and empathic attitude towards my homosexuality even though she has not completely accepted it yet. The power of TV!*

This is an illustrative first-person testimony of the productive impact of queer TV moments on family viewing. Particularly in an environment in which there are some unresolved issues related to an individual's sexuality, GLBT televisibility helps in the working-through process, challenging and potentially transforming the viewers' domestic relations. Apart from this comment, however, rather than giving their personal opinions on the quality and content of the selected programmes, other respondents concentrated their attention predominantly on the extra-textual values and potential effects that this film could have on other, once again presumed heterosexual, viewers and on society at large.

When assessing the TV portrayals of GLBT characters, respondents considered the perspective of the heterosexual parents represented and not that of their GLBT offspring; perhaps because the film itself has an encoded dominant reading that favours a heterosexual point of view. Despite the apparent idea of focusing on lesbian identities, in fact, the film ended up concentrating predominantly on the ways in which the father, the undisputed—male, heterosexual—protagonist, "copes" with and eventually "accepts" his daughter's dissident sexuality. Only seven participants commented on the portrayal of lesbianism in the film. On the contrary, the parents' reactions to coming out and outing proved to be the most popular theme amongst participants. One respondent stated that due to the scarcity of discourses available and the lack of debate in socio-political contexts, finding out about a daughter's or son's homosexuality "is a trauma for a parent, because it is an unforeseen matter." Similarly, a 35-year-old heterosexual female stated, "it is a serious blow probably because parents see their dreams of becoming grandparents disappear or simply because they are not ready yet to face this diversity and understand that love does not have a sex." Another heterosexual female (age 30) said that such discovery "is something that upsets parents, because from the day a son or daughter is born, a parent has some expectation and with such a revelation everything goes up in smoke." These comments are problematic because they reiterate expectations related to biological sex and a fixed understanding of gender and sexuality. Contemporaneously, they also illustrate engagement with these issues and an empathic feeling of being in the father's shoes. This is perceivable in answers such as this one: "I do not envy those parents because I believe that it is emotionally very debilitating and exhausting for many reasons."

This clip helped viewers to challenge and deconstruct other cultural-specific stereotypes, too. The clip prompted some comments on long-held assumptions about people living in the south of Italy (see, e.g., Dickie, 1999). Some participants said that the role of the close-minded southern man runs the risk of "reinforcing pre-existing stereotypes considerably." A 30-year-old heterosexual female from the centre stated that the father's upheaval seems "moderate" compared to the one expected from people she knows living in the south of Italy. Perhaps recalling his personal experience, however, a 30-year-old gay male from the south said that it is "realistic" and, interestingly, "it could have been even worse from a southern father." Whether they challenge or reinforce heteronormativity and stereotypes, these queer TV moments offer important instances for reflection and confrontation, especially when portrayals are discursively elaborated within and outside the family. Yet all these comments are about the heterosexual character. It is important to note, in fact, how not many comments on this clip considered the difficulties that, due to the aforementioned expectations and an often hostile environment, GLBT subjects constantly face in coming out in the family of origin. The implications of the positioning of this sample of viewers show that their viewing practice remains attached to a biased set of assumptions. Heterosexual people tend to identify with heterosexual characters without considering other perspectives.

Many comments also discussed the role of the father performed by a famous heterosexual Italian actor, Lino Banfi. Seventy-five percent of the sample commented positively on Banfi's participation in the film; 49% of respondents commented that, thanks to the popular Italian actor and favourable scheduling time, films like this could appeal to a broad audience made up of "conservative" and "traditional," "non-sophisticated" and "elderly" viewers who had historically considered homosexuality as taboo, and who would not necessarily encounter dissident sexuality anywhere else. Three respondents speculated that his presence might have been linked to ratings mechanisms, which might have impacted on the accessible scheduling time of the film. It was in fact aired on Rai 1 during primetime in 2006, a year of intense debate about GLBT rights in Italy.[2] Despite political and religious protests, the film obtained high ratings, with more than seven million viewers.[3] Respondents felt that the presence of a well-known Italian actor and the primetime showing—and, I would add, the heterosexually encoded narrative—are all important factors for a programme to appeal to a heterogeneous audience made up of parents and grandparents and for them to engage with these queer TV moments, in the first place.

Other programmes featuring more challenging GLBT issues are hardly ever broadcast in primetime; they are often relegated to late-night slots and are less accessible to a large audience. The analysis of the questionnaire shows, however, that such programmes found only apparent resistance on the part of heterosexually identified participants. Instead, they expressed an interest in GLBT-themed TV. This is the case of the second programme used in the questionnaire, *I Viaggi di Nina* (*Nina's Travels*, 2006). This is a series aired in a late-night slot on La7 in 2006. The format of this programme, a documentary-reality, surely has a less heterosexually encoded and apologetic representation of homosexuality than the previous fictional one. The protagonists are in fact different women who happen to love other women in Italy. Their real-life, personal stories cover an array of intertwining topics, such as coming out in the family of origin, same-sex relationships, as well as related broader socio-political issues. The particular clip included in the questionnaire presented the story of Giuseppina and Raffaelle, who live together in Naples and conceived their daughter by in vitro fertilization (IVF) in Belgium. This representation offered some space for reflection and debate on same-sex partnerships and parenting as well as on the absence of fundamental human and legal rights in Italy. This is also a particular example of how television could give visibility to a plurality of alternative family formations as opposed to the assumed traditional heteronormative nuclear family.

While the majority of participants made general comments, three respondents gave more personal and direct impressions about *I Viaggi di Nina*, showing a closer involvement with the text. A 33-year-old heterosexual male from central Italy stated that this programme "helps to sensitise viewers a lot, it has persuaded me completely" whereas a 24-year-old heterosexual male from Naples even said, "It made me cry. We are all people, why are there rights for some, and others with none? It is the reciprocated love between two persons which is important." The transformative significance of such QTM has not only informational but also emotional value as they also provide opportunities for viewers to reflect on broader GLBT rights. For instance, a participant was affirmative towards the good environment same-sex couples could provide for a child, which can be better than in some divorced, heterosexual couples. However, she also questioned what she perceived as selfishness on the part of the two women in having a pregnancy in a country where legislation does not safeguard their union as well as their daughter. Ultimately, she calls for more national debate and rethinking Italian laws.

In their comments on the clip, only very few respondents, less than 8%, were uncomfortable with the clip or found it in some way problematic. One of them expressed a slight concern for the child's well-being: the clip made her question the absence of the father or mother figure in same-sex parenting. Two participants said that a TV programme is not enough to change societal attitude because of institutional, political, and religious barriers. Despite this, 70% of the sample commented positively on the programme, saying it could alter "other" viewers' understanding and perspectives towards GLBT subjects and issues in Italy. Five heterosexual respondents were particularly interested and enthusiastic about this programme. They commented on the quality of the content, and whereas one respondent was positively surprised that such a programme could have been aired in Italy, three of them wished that more programmes like this were available on television.

One participant, a southern heterosexual female (age 26), admitted having watched the whole series and stated "as an uninformed person [about GLBT realities], it allowed me to come into contact and begin to familiarise myself with issues I had never considered before." Nonetheless, the majority of respondents were not previously acquainted with this programme. The whole series in fact did not attract major public debate, and the ratings remained within those expected by the network for that scheduling time and according to the national company for audience measurements. Five respondents, in particular, said that it was a pity it was aired during a late-night slot and that this might be the reason why they had not seen such an interesting programme before. They also said that true-to-life, direct, and quality Italian programmes such as this could have a greater impact on viewers if they were broadcast at a more accessible time.

One-quarter of participants in the questionnaire saw these kinds of representations as targeted to a specific GLBT or "friendly" audience. In other words, initially participants do not perceive that this programme could appeal to them but to viewers who are already interested in, or are themselves, GLBT subjects. On the whole, however, this is discredited by the majority of the comments, which clearly demonstrate that these programmes can be watched by a heterogeneous audience and could have a positive impact on them. Moreover, this shows that when heterosexuals are not represented, viewers engage more effectively and directly with GLBT issues. Importantly, this study can also provide essential network recommendations for future primetime airing of similar programmes in which the protagonists are real, Italian GLBT subjects.

Despite the thought-provoking subject matter, however, *I Viaggi di Nina* does not explicitly portray lesbian sexuality and eroticism at all. More challenging, less stereotyped, and "in your face" representations related to GLBT pleasure and desire are still assumed to be problematic for a heterosexual audience. In this case, the very chance to encounter productive QTM decreases exponentially for a number of reasons. Respondents' main concern is the viewing context and the presence of children and parents.

Coitus Interrupti and Third-Person Perception

Sugar-coated, more accessible, and desexualised Italian representations of GLBT subjects on television do appeal to a heterosexual audience as respondents interpreted portrayals and narratives as productive and potentially transformative QTM. However, two different sets of barriers could prevent audiences from the very possibilities offered by more confrontational portrayals. On the one hand, there are the TV executives' decisions, for example, to broadcast a GLBT-themed film or programme very late at night, when the number of viewers inevitably drop, or to intentionally censor the content partially or even decide not to air the programme at all. On the other hand, there is viewers' TPP. By emphasising the imagined risks, as the title of this subsection suggests, these barriers interrupt the potential pleasures and informative significance offered by sexual GLBT portrayals. Crucially, both barriers are generated by generalisations about others. For the aims of this article, I cannot further analyse the hypothesis that the decision making of Italian networks might be affected by assumptions about the audience. More research in that trajectory is much needed. Here I discuss and analyse some results related to participants' responses to three TV examples of programmes which encountered opposition on Italian TV. Significantly, they are all U.S. productions which have dared to push the boundaries of representation: one was aired very late at night; the second was partially censored even after the *fascia protetta*, the daytime family-friendly time slot; the third programme has never been aired on Italian mainstream TV.

Significantly, two-thirds of the participants in the questionnaire saw these more challenging representation as thought-provoking and felt mostly comfortable with these portrayals on an individual basis. Although they highlight the knotty nature of some depictions, they do not seem to justify television decision making and restrictive regulations. Interestingly, the real problem for one-third of respondents is represented by the viewing context and how the people around them could influence their experience. Unconcerned if they are viewing with friends, they are particularly uncomfortable with the family setting and the possible presence of minors, relatives, and, especially, parents. They have preconceived ideas that these relevant others might not be interested in, or could even be negatively affected by, more sexualised GLBT portrayals. Often they said they felt embarrassed and would change the channel, thinking that other viewers might feel ill at ease. This TPP, which I initially called refractive vision or viewing by proxy, has been investigated in other areas (see in particular Davison, 1983; Perloff, 1999). Some scholars have argued that media messages are elaborated through TPP especially when they are not perceived as normatively and socially acceptable and that this might lead individuals who overestimate media influence on the attitude and behaviours of others to take action; ultimately explaining censorship phenomena (Gunther & Thorson, 1992; Perloff, 1999). Only as recently as in 2012, TPP was applied for the first time to sexuality in a research on the heterosexual perception of same-sex marriages (Winslow & Napier, 2012). Even here, participants thought that, rather than harming their own relationship, same-sex marriage legalisation in the United States could have endangered other people's relationships. A study related to the reception of GLBT TV portrayals, however, has never been conducted before.

The first programme analysed in this section is *The L Word* (Showtime, 2004–2009). It is a U.S. television drama series which portrays the lives of a group of upper-class lesbian friends living in Los Angeles. The clip showed the first few minutes of the pilot episode, in which a lesbian couple finds out that one of the two is ovulating. She says to the other one, "Let's make a baby" and they then start kissing passionately. In the questionnaire, I invited respondents to reflect on the need for age restriction in relation to these more sexualised GLBT portrayals. Fifty-six percent of participants said that an age limit should not exist and half of them believed that identical regulations should be in place for both heterosexual and queer portrayals. For them, it is unjust to deny GLBT representations when heterosexual ones are largely available at all times of the day and night on TV. For the remaining 24% of the sample, the possibility of watching GLBT-themed TV for minors depends on the explicitness of the representation, while 20% said that age limitations depend on the "maturity" of the minor and the possibility to discuss with them. A 30-year-old heterosexual female respondent from Rome explained the importance of this:

> *I have a seven-year-old daughter and in the past she has happened to see a Sapphic kiss. She did ask me some questions and I simply explained that there are women and men that, instead of preferring the opposite sex, prefer their own. Topic closed! No more questions, maybe because my answer was fairly exhaustive. Obviously I avoid more explicit scenes because she is seven! I will have to wait until she is a teenager to let her see more.*

Experiencing television with minors is an important way to educate them on diversity. Also, we should not assume that children are heterosexual until proven otherwise. In a BBC (2012) report, for example, one of the main reasons for viewers' discomfort in front of GLBT TV portrayals was this need and attached ability or incapacity for adult viewers to explain and elaborate images and narratives while watching with minors. Drawing on the work of Jenkins (1992), Buckingham and Bragg (2004) have already discussed how what is considered an explicit representation for minors has changed substantially over time and so have any legally imposed age limits on minors. Similarly to the studies on TPP, they talked of the particular use of constructions of childhood in the "politics of substitution." They stated that "in a climate of growing uncertainty, invoking fears about children provides a powerful means of commanding public attention and support" and that minors are treated "as a vehicle for much broader concerns about the social order" (Buckingham & Bragg, 2004, p. 4). In these cases adults almost unwillingly use the protection of minors as a shield in order to avoid visions and debates adults might perceive as troubling.

For some respondents the presence of minor viewers is perceived indeed as problematic when watching more explicit same-sex intimacy and affection. Only four participants in the questionnaire explicitly declared to be uncomfortable with the same-sex kissing represented. A respondent was particularly concerned that she might happen to watch the kiss while with a minor. However, a solid majority of 85% admitted to being comfortable with it because—I quote respondents—it was "natural," "tender," and "passionate" in an attempt to find analogies with what they consider a "normal" heterosexual kiss. Hence, they do not feel threatened by such imagery. Five participants remarked that it was not the kiss in itself that made them uncomfortable but the very fact that they are not used to seeing them more often on TV as in real life. In relation to this, McKee (1996) suggests that heterosexual kissing is a normal and familiar image on TV, and it is "through repetition that it gains the status of normality" (p. 53). By contrast, same-sex kissing "has been problematic enough to ensure that it does not become common, routine or ordinary" (p. 53). While criticising the limited representation of same-sex kissing on Italian TV, respondents questioned to what extent more visibility would help heterosexual people to better work through their negative or confused reactions to this imagery. These figures alone say that same-sex kissing—at least between women—is not perceived as a limit anymore, and networks should not circumvent them.

As discussed before, the series was produced by a premium and private U.S. cable channel. In Italy, the first series was aired on the national mainstream network La7 in 2005. However, the time of broadcasting was the Italian *terza serata*, a late-night slot starting after 11 p.m. Although the representation is more sexualised, hence presumably confrontational for a heterosexual viewership, it was still shown to Italian audiences without it being censored. In explaining this, heterosexist discourses should not be underestimated. For example, Chambers (2009) says that "lesbian sexuality has long had a role in the structure of heterosexual fantasy being an object of the male gaze in both popular culture and pornography" (p. 94). The fact that representations discussed so far in this article all tackled lesbianism and female same-sex desire might not be an accident, even in Italy. The increasing availability of lesbian portrayals may be used to appeal to and titillate a male heterosexual audience. Inversely, Goldstein argues that due to cultural and economic forces, mainstream television has allowed few images of men that "male, heterosexual viewers may find threatening" (1990, cited in Craig, 1992, p. 203). The archetypal heteropatriarchal male viewer, already identified in the father figure, would suggest the biased assumption that families of origin would feel more comfortable with same-sex images of women rather than men. Crucially, in Italy, even during late-night slots, once minors are in bed after the watershed scheduling, representations of male same-sex desire still found some significant resistance.

An example of this is another clip used in the questionnaire. In 2008, the Oscar-winning film *Brokeback Mountain* (2005) was aired at 22.45 on Rai 2, part of the national service broadcaster, but still underwent partial censorship of scenes with same-sex activity. As a result of the protests that followed, RAI stated that the film received from the distribution house was already unaccountably excised and nobody at RAI realised that before the broadcast. Later on that year, the full-length version of the film was eventually rescreened on Rai 2, this time just before midnight. The sample of viewers who completed the questionnaire stated they had seen the film at the cinema and felt it was "inspiring" and "moving." They did not have problems with the more explicit same-sex scenes, especially because there was no nudity involved whatsoever. None of the 39 respondents (65%) who completed this part of the questionnaire commented on the clip but all made indignant negative comments against RAI. Respondents did not believe it was just a coincidence but once again they blamed the links among politics, religion, and public television discussed previously. These results suggest that similar situations should be avoided in the future and that Italian viewers do not want somebody else to decide what they can or cannot watch.

The last programme discussed in the questionnaire shows, however, that there is another censoring mechanism linked to TPP that takes place in the living room within co-present viewers. *Queer As Folk* (1999) is a British miniseries remade by the U.S. market. Many critics have hailed this programme as a significant advance in the televisual depiction of queer life because it unapologetically ignored debates about "positive images" and portrayed queer characters and communities both empathetically and reprehensibly (Davis, 2007; Keller, 2002; Porfido, 2007).

Such a progressive programme never made it into Italian mainstream TV. Despite being advertised to appear on La7 in 2001, it was substituted with another programme on the day of broadcasting. The reasons behind this decision remain unknown, so I wanted to gather the opinion of the sample of viewers. In order to get more direct responses on the representative limit of this programme and the dynamics around the television set, in this case I used a projective technique to formulate two questions related to the clip. It involves asking individuals to respond to ambiguous test stimuli which minimize the likelihood that individuals would try to respond in a socially desirable manner (Carducci, 2009, pp. 55–56).

The first question asked respondents to watch the clip imagining they were a TV executive and state whether they would agree to broadcast the programme. Sixty-three per-cent of participants said they would because, for example, it was not worse than- many other heterosexual representations usually aired on TV and would help other people to understand the multidimensional and multifaceted lives of GLBT people. Thirty-eight percent said that they would not broadcast it because they believed it to be too transgressive and provocative. Significantly, one-third of them were gay males, who commented on the poor quality and limited representation of this programme. They also said that a number of other existing "romanticised" GLBT-themed films should be televised in preference. In particular, a 23-year-old gay male from the province of Rome says that heterosexual people would find it too difficult to understand, saying for example, "my mum would not like it at all and I would feel embarrassed too. On the contrary, she loves *Will and Grace*." So, even a portion of gay male participants take the idealised perspective of heterosexual parents and almost want to protect them. All these respondents said that "Italian audiences are not ready for these portrayals," and more daring representations "are not suitable for a mass audience," and they argued that in Italy more apologetic programmes such as *Il padre delle spose* would be much more useful than *Queer As Folk*.

The way in which people appear to be looking at a programme through the eyes of other people was further analysed in the last question. I asked respondents to say whether they would change the channel or ask other people to change it while watching this programme in co-presence in the same room. The vast majority—62%—said that they would not, but the reasons given are interesting. They all said that they tend to watch television with friends who, they assume, would be comfortable with such representations. Only two respondents, however, admitted that they would further discuss the issues presented. The remaining 38% of the sample revealed that they would change the channel because they imagine family members sitting with them: parents, relatives, and, once again, children. They assume that they would not be able to understand and they would feel uncomfortable with the subject. A heterosexual female (age 30) from Rome stated, for example, "Personally [the clip] does not bother me. Certainly if I were with my parents I would change channel for their sake." Participants' TPP might also function as an expedient to manage the dilemma to express personal negative attitudes towards sexual dissidence without being condemned. However, this hypothesis is discredited by the fact that the questionnaire was anonymous and a considerable majority of participants had in previous questions made favourable comments on GLBT representations. In these last two questions some patriarchal and gender mechanisms are at play within the viewing context. A 66-year-old heterosexual woman from Rome, for example, admitted the following: "I wouldn't change channel but I would surely be criticised by others, especially my husband." As stated before, this is another example of the idealised heteropatriarchal family viewer who interferes with the very possibility of engaging with GLBT TV texts. Thanks to this and the remote control, QTM could be indeed avoided, silenced, or bypassed and it is essential to confront actual samples of possible viewers to understand who or what affects their viewing experience as well as what the dynamics around the television set are. From this study there seems to be a clear, internalised, archetypal viewer within the family, who functions to maintain the social and nuclear family order, avoid perceived "offensive" material, and preserve an Italian, heteronormative *bella figura*.

CONCLUSIONS

The study on the reception of the increasing GLBT televisibility of the 1990s proves to be a very productive field of investigation in Italy. TV functions as a tool which provides families of origin and viewers with multiplying QTM and working-through strategies that can potentially transform domestic relations. They have a positive impact on the coming-out process and promote reciprocal understanding, easing conflicts within households. QTM have also contributed to deconstructing the very concept of a fixed model of identity, sexuality, and family. They have opened up the array of representations and issues which can be discussed with family members and friends cooperatively. TV, in this case, is a crucial platform to critically consider the broader issues related to GLBT human and legal rights in Italy, too.

In the majority of cases, respondents to the questionnaire felt fairly comfortable with the transformative potential of GLBT portrayals on television. They proved to be "ready" and curious to see even more challenging representations and they were critical about restrictive networks regulations that unreasonably do not apply to heterosexual depictions. More sexualised and unapologetic GLBT representations found, in fact, only apparent resistance from the sample. In this case, respondents' engagement with a text appeared greater when portrayals were Italian, true to life, and with GLBT protagonists. An increasing representation of more challenging affectionate QTM would seem to better challenge viewers with ideas of sexual dissidence and constructed norms.

Although this research shows that attitudes towards dissident sexuality in Italy might be gradually changing—together with discourses of sexual politics and activism—also thanks to the increasing GLBT televisibility, some respondents proved that a heteronormative reading framework still persists. Although more accessible films and programmes with heterosexuality encoded as a dominant reading seem to appeal to traditional and older generations of viewers, respondents to the questionnaire tended to identify solely with heterosexual protagonists, leaving aside GLBT perspectives. A significant minority of participants also avoided commenting in the first person and used third-person perception to present risks and presumed negative effects for a putatively heteronormative ideal of family audience. The assumptions, for example, that exposure to GLBT representation may influence "healthy" minors—always presumed to be heterosexual—and make them queer, might be a way to advance adults' personal anxieties. Usually, in fact, the idealised viewer in the mind of respondents is often framed by hetero-patriarchy and assimilated to the father figure. As a result of this heterosexist postulation, for example, there is an assumption that families of origin would feel more comfortable with same-sex images of women than men. This is a biased approach, because viewers do not take into account the constellation of other viewers—for example, GLBT adolescents trying to come to terms with their desire and sexuality within an often hostile family environment.

The implications of this are that the interests of a good portion of viewers might be often disregarded by the Italian cultural industry and television networks. The hypothesis that production, distribution, and regulation of GLBT televisual products are influenced by this assumed and biased understanding of the audience should be further investigated by future scholarship. Third-person perception leads to avoidance and censorship and it "authorises" what can be represented and who can speak. The role of debate and scholarly research in dissipating these assumptions is paramount. Other future challenges are to reconsider these studies in order to take into account the fast-changing media and technological landscape. Due to the small sample size, this research has limitations. A more sophisticated, expanded version of this study could provide vital recommendations to inform cultural and media policy as well as expand the scope of GLBT and family studies.

NOTES

1. There are, however, generational differences: younger viewers ages 14 to 29 tend to confine themselves in their own spaces; older viewers ages 65 to 80 still prefer to occupy shared places such as the living room or the kitchen.

2. In April 2006, the Left coalition won the national election with Romano Prodi, who promised to give rights to de facto couples. This promise was never kept; debate is still on-going and leaves Italy, even to date, the only Western European country in which any kind of partnership is still unrecognised.

3. See, for example, the press review available at http://www.cinemagay.it/schede-rs.asp?IDFilm=2636 (accessed February 24, 2013).

REFERENCES

Aaron, M. (2009). Towards queer television theory: Bigger pictures sans the sweet queer-after. In G. D. Davis & G. Needham (Eds.), *Queer TV: Theories, histories, politics* (pp. 63–75). London, England: Routledge.

Ahmed, S. (2006). *Queer phenomenology: Orientations, objects, others*. Durham, NC: Duke University Press.

Arthurs, J. (2004). *Television and sexuality: Regulation and the politics of taste*. Maidenhead, UK; New York, NY: Open University Press.

BBC. (2012). Portrayal of lesbian, gay and bisexual people on the BBC – Research update. Retrieved from http://www.bbc.co.uk/diversity/audiences/lgb-consultation.html

BBC. (2013). In quotes: Italy's Silvio Berlusconi in his own words. Retrieved from http://www.bbc.co.uk/news/world-europe-15642201

Becker, R. (2006). *Gay TV and straight America*. New Brunswick, NJ; London, England: Rutgers University Press.

Bertone, C. & Franchi, M. (2014). Suffering as the path to acceptance: Parents of gay and lesbian young people negotiating Catholicism in Italy. *Journal of GLBT Family Studies, 10*(1–2), 58–78.

Buckingham, D., & Bragg, S. (2004). *Young people, sex and the media: The facts of life?* Basingstoke, UK: Palgrave Macmillan.

Butler, J. (1990). *Gender trouble*. New York, NY; London, England: Routledge.

Butler, J. (2004). *Undoing gender*. New York, NY; London, England: Routledge.

Carducci, B. J. (2009). *The psychology of personality: Viewpoints, research, and applications*. Chichester, UK: John Wiley & Sons.

CENSIS. (2012a). *Come cambia l'uso dello spazio domestico: Vince la stanza multiuso [How the use of domestic space changes: Capturing the multipurpose room]*. Retrieved from http://www.censis.it

CENSIS. (2012b). *Comunicazione e Media. 46° Rapporto CENSIS sulla situazione sociale del Paese [Communication and media: 46th CENSIS Report on the social situation of the country]*. Retrieved from http://www.censis.it

Chambers, S. A. (2009). *The queer politics of television*. London, England; New York, NY: I. B. Tauris.

Craig, S. (1992). *Men, masculinity, and the media*. Newbury Park, CA: Sage.

Davis, G. D. (2007). *Queer as folk*. London: BFI.

Davis, G. D., & Needham, G. (2009). *Queer TV: Theories, histories, politics*. London, England; New York, NY: Routledge.

Davison, W. (1983). The third-person effect in communication. *Public Opinion Quarterly, 47*(1), 1–15. doi: 10.1086/268763

Dickie, J. (1999). *Darkest Italy. The nation and stereotypes of the mezzogiorno, 1860–1900*. New York, NY: Palgrave.

Dines, M., & Rigoletto, S. (2012). Country cousins: Europeanness, sexuality and locality in contemporary Italian television. *Modern Italy, 12*(4), 479–491. doi: 10.1080/13532944.2012.706999

Doty, A. (1993). *Making things perfectly queer : Interpreting mass culture [Electronic version]*. Minneapolis, MN: University of Minnesota Press.

Ellis, J. (2000). *Seeing things: Television in the age of uncertainty*. London, England: I. B. Tauris.

Foucault, M. (1977). *Discipline and punish: The birth of the prison*. London, England: Allen Lane.

Foucault, M. (1979). *The history of sexuality*. London, England: Allen Lane.

Foucault, M. (1980). *Power/knowledge: Selected interviews and other writings, 1972–1977* (1st American ed.). New York, NY: Pantheon Books.

Freeman, E. (2010). *Time binds: Queer temporalities, queer histories*. Durham, NC: Duke University Press.

Grasso, A. (2003). Nuovi scenari della TV digitale. [The new scenery of digital TV]. In A. A, VV. (Ed.), *La realtà dell'immaginario: i media tra semiotica e sociologia: studi in ononre di Gianfranco Bettetini. [The reality of the imaginary: the media between semiotics and sociology: study in honor of Gianfranco Bettetini]* (pp. 217–236). Milano, Italy: Vita e Pensiero.

Gunther, A. C., & Thorson, E. (1992). Perceived persuasive effects of commercials and public service announcements: The third-person effect in new domains. *Communication Research, 19*, 574–596. doi: 10.1177/009365092019005002

Halberstam, J. (2005). *In a queer time and place: Transgender bodies, subcultural lives.* New York, NY; London, England: New York University Press.

Hibberd, M. (2007). Conflicts of interest and media pluralism in Italian broadcasting. *West European Politics, 30*(4), 881–902. doi: 10.1080/01402380701500363

Iacovou, M. (2010). Leaving home: Independence, togetherness and income. *Advances in Life Course Research, 15*(4), 147–160. doi: 10.1016/j.alcr.2010.10.004

ISTAT. (2012). Proceedings of the conference "Alla ricerca di statistiche minori e misconosciute" [Looking for minor and unrecognized statistics], 18 April 2012. Retrieved from http://www.istat.it/it/files/2012/04/brochure18maggio.pdf

Jenkins, H. (2004). Out of the closet into the universe. In H. M. Benshoff and S. Griffin (Eds.), *Queer cinema: The Film Reader* (pp. 189–207). London, England: Routledge.

Jenkins, P. (1992). *Intimate enemies: Moral panics in contemporary Great Britain.* New York, NY: Aldine de Gruyter.

Keller, J. R. (2002). *Queer (un)friendly film and television.* Jefferson, NC: McFarland.

Malici, L. (2011). Queer in Italy: Italian televisibility and the "queerable" audience. In L. Downing & R. Gillett (Eds.), *Queer in Europe: Contemporary case studies* (pp. 113–128). Farnham, Surrey, BC; Burlington, VT: Ashgate.

Malici, L. (2012). Italian (s)queer eyes: Surveying and voicing TV representations. In S. Antosa (Ed.), *Queer crossings: Theories, bodies, texts* (pp. 105–122). Milano, Italy: Mimesis.

Martin, K. A., Hutson, D. J., Kazyak, E., & Scherrer, K. S. (2010). Advice when children come out: The cultural "tool kits" of parents *Journal of Family Issues, 31*, 960–991.

McKee, A. (1996). A kiss is just. *Australian Journal of Communication, 23*(2), 51–72. Retrieved from http://eprints.qut.edu.au/42051/

Mignone, M. (2008). *Italy today: Facing the challenges of the new millennium.* New York, NY: Peter Lang

Nielsen. (2012).Double vision—global trends in tablet and smartphone use while watching TV. Retrieved from http://blog.nielsen.com/nielsenwire/online_mobile/double-vision-global-trends-in-tablet-and-smartphone-use-while-watching-tv/

Perloff, R. M. (1999). The third-person effect: A critical review and synthesis. *Media Psychology, 1*, 353–337. doi: 10.1207/s1532785xmep0104_4

Porfido, G. (2007). *Queer As Folk* and the spectacularisation of gay identity. In T. Peele & C. Palgrave (Eds.), *Queer popular culture: Literature, media, film, and television* (pp. 57–70). New York, NY: Palgrave Macmillan.

Rich, A. (1980). Compulsory heterosexuality and lesbian existence. *Signs: Journal of Women in Culture and Society, 5*, 631–660. doi: 10.1177/089124389003002002

Saraceno, C. (2004). The Italian family from the 1960s to the present. *Modern Italy, 9*(1), 47–57. doi: 10.1080/13532940410001677494

Sedgwick, E. K. (1990). *Epistemology of the closet.* Berkeley, CA: University of California Press.

Sedgwick, E. K. (1994). *Tendencies.* London, England: Routledge.

Sinfield, A. (1994). *The Wilde century: Effeminacy, Oscar Wilde and the queer moment.* London, England: Cassell.

Spigel, L. (1992). *Make room for TV: Television and the family ideal in postwar America*. Chicago, IL: University of Chicago Press.

Sullivan, N. (2003). *A critical introduction to queer theory*. New York, NY: New York University Press.

Thompson, J. B. (1998). *Mezzi di comunicazione e modernit: Una teoria sociale dei media [Means of communication and modernity: A social theory of media]*. Bologna: Il Mulino.

Warner, M. (1991). Introduction. Fear of a queer planet. *Social Text, 29*, 3–17. doi: 10.2307/466295

Winslow, M. P., & Napier, R. (2012). Not my marriage: Third-person perception and the effects of legalizing same-sex marriage. *Social Psychology, 43*(2), 92–97. doi: 10.1027/1864-9335/a000087

Sexual Citizenship in Private and Public Space: Parents of Gay Men and Lesbians Discuss Their Experiences of Pride Parades

VALERIA CAPPELLATO
University of Turin, Turin, Italy

TIZIANA MANGARELLA
Meters studi e ricerche, Bari, Italy

This article explores how the boundaries of lesbian and gay citizenship are set by parents in relation to the public/private dimensions of space. We analysed 46 in-depth interviews carried out in Italy in the period 2006–2008 with mothers and fathers who described themselves as accepting their sons' and daughters' gay and lesbian identity.

We show that parents tend to fight for rights confined to the private dimension whereas both the public dimension and the dividing lines between public and private represent problematic areas. Parents do not expect having to deal with the issue of sexual orientation in the public sphere, implicitly supporting its characterisation as a heteronormative space. Pride parades are a case in point. As emerged in the interviews, most of the parents do not see their participation in parades as undermining the heteronormative family model, but rather as a way of legitimising it. Through the mediation of heterosexual parents, there is a process of familisation of citizenship rights for gay and lesbian people, which is reinforced by parents who belong to parents of gay and lesbian associations. Though discourses on normalisation prevail, the Pride parade is a setting of potential tensions allowing debate on sexual citizenship to enter the public arena.

The study reported in this article is the result of a broader research project titled "Family Matters: Supporting Families to Prevent Violence Against Young Gay Men and Lesbians," funded by the European Commission through the international Daphne programme and coordinated by the University of East Piedmont; AGEDO was one of its partners.

INTRODUCTION

In Italy the issues of access to rights linked to sexual practices, the free expression of one's sexual identity, and the legal recognition of same-gender relationships (Richardson, 2000) are still very much open, sparking heated debate and ruptures. In view of this it is interesting to analyse discourses on sexual citizenship including lesbians' and gay males' rights in a setting in which the norms and practices have not yet been codified. The lack of legal references and established cultural frameworks could foster the emergence of more inclusive models for this context of citizenship, which in any case needs to be (re)framed. However, the hypothesis we posit here is that in the current Italian debate significant attempts to subvert traditional heterosexist and gender-normative models coexist with conservative attitudes. Analysing discourses on sexual citizenship can help us gain insight into the difficulties faced by the actors called to establish the boundaries, the tensions that arise when attempting to do so, and also any new arguments that can help shape those confines. To support this hypothesis we decided to explore the discourses formulated by the parents of gay men and lesbians who describe themselves as accepting their sons' and daughters' identities. In this group, following the discovery of their sons' and daughters' sexual orientation, the dominant heteronormative model is no longer a given. This leads these individuals to reflect on the meaning of the terms *equality* and *difference* and their implications in terms of citizenship rights that are still denied to lesbians and gay men (Bilotta, 2008; Bonini Baraldi, 2010; D'Ippoliti & Schuster, 2011).

Access to rights changes over time in relation to the different characteristics that citizens must possess to be considered as such, and the dividing lines erected between the public and private sphere. It is therefore not surprising, in the context of sexual citizenship too, to witness traces of the process of "privatization" of rights—which are thus reframed and relegated to the private arena (Pitch, 1998). In the literature there are many contributions that focus on the construction of gay and lesbian identity starting from the spatial dimension (Binnie & Valentine, 1999), and others, vice versa, focusing on the effects of the presence of gay men and lesbians in terms of redefining urban spaces (Knopp, 1990; Forest, 1995). While some urban spaces are destined to confine and marginalise "sexual dissidents," they can also become a tool for appropriating (territorialising) those very areas, and liberalising sexuality (Bell & Binnie, 2000; Castells, 1983). Pride events—as well as other extremely distinctive initiatives that take place in the traditionally heteronormative public dimension—represent an arena of potential ambiguity and tensions between mechanisms based on normalisation and those seeking to subvert the dominant model. Based on these assumptions, we intend to analyse the parents' discourses on the Pride parade in order to explore how they define the boundaries of sexual citizenship—interpreted here as the right to occupy space (Bell & Binnie, 2000)—for gay men and lesbians.

BEING VISIBLE DURING PRIDE PARADES—UNDER CERTAIN CONDITIONS

Pride marches can stand for diverging claims, being events that connote a space destined for dissidents, who only have the right to occupy it on certain conditions—for example, clothing, sexual expressions, transgressing gender norms—and for a specific period of time (the Parade) and therefore confirming heteronormative assumptions. This reiterates the normalisation of gay men and lesbians who are deemed respectable according to the criteria formulated by heterosexual people who do not impose rules but rather encourage "others" to self-govern (Brannen, 1999), in alignment with heteronormative models. As we will see, the call for social inclusion based on the argument of the "sameness" (Richardson, 2005) of gay men and lesbians was often evoked by the parents interviewed for our study, but does not represent the only argument put forward.

One of the possible responses identified by the interviewees was also the process of acquiring citizenship status for gay men and lesbians—and the right to occupy the street during the Parades—upholding a heteronormative model of citizenship through a process of *familisation of rights*. Coming out to family members occurs within a complex network of family relationships, friendships, and attachments, within which it becomes necessary to find a discourse legitimising the citizenship of gay and lesbian offspring. Besides representing the setting for fulfilment of the individual's desires and expectations (Rose, 1989; Cossman, 2007), the family plays a key role as an institution that "constructs" citizens (Turner, 2008), producing/reproducing normality by pursuing happiness and fulfilment of its members (Rose, 1996). Bertone (2013) argues that sexual citizenship evokes what Cohen (2005) described as an "ill-defined partial membership" that confines children to the private sphere, while it is their parents' responsibility to represent them in the public arena. This also enables family members to support their sons and daughters, even during the marches, on the condition that they adopt lifestyles and models that their parents deem "appropriate" (Bertone, 2013). This trait of sexual citizenship rights therefore resembles what was observed in the case of women's citizenship: its "indirect" nature (Vogel, 1991)—through their husbands for women, through heterosexual parents for lesbians and gay men. The mediation of the parents risks denying gay men and lesbians the status of political actors and relegating their identity to the private sphere once more, hidden within a heteronormative family that thus becomes the subject with the right to access the public arena.

Alternatively, the march can be interpreted as breaking away from heteronormativity, or a process of "contamination" of other (the hetero) people's lives (Enguix, 2009) with both temporary and permanent effects. The carnivalesque spirit of the parades encourages the temporary crossing of boundaries (Bakhtin, 1984), allowing discourses around sexual citizenship to enter the public arena, thus bringing about cultural transformation. Conversely, in our society, carnival and the grotesque can also be used for the purpose of consumption (Evans, 1993). The social aim of the parade could disappear—as we see in some parents' interviews—and the most spectacular trait of it could be seen as a show for the spectator where sexual "deviants" have a short time of visibility under public control, and are then relegated to concealment again (Bakhtin, 1984).

Exploring discourses on citizenship and in particular the meaning attributed to parents taking part or not taking part in Pride events gives us the opportunity to open new channels for interpreting the role of the families of origin in mediating and normalising sexual citizenship or in subverting heterosexist models.

METHOD

This study is the result of a broader research project titled "Family Matters: Supporting Families to Prevent Violence Against Young Gay Men and Lesbians," aimed at exploring the needs expressed by families and the resources available when coping with the issues that can be involved in acknowledging the gay and lesbian identity of a family member (Bertone & Franchi, 2008; see also Bertone & Franchi, 2014).

Participants

The research design was structured around an initial quantitative study with questionnaires compiled for the parents, and a second qualitative stage based on interviews with gay men (25) and lesbians (10) who came out to their families between the ages of 14 and 22, or became visible in that age bracket (excluding bisexual and queer identities), and their close families (parents and siblings). The parents were mainly contacted through AGEDO (*Associazione Genitori di Omosessuali* [Association of parents of gay men and lesbians]) a national organisation, established in 1992, comprising parents, relatives, and friends of lesbians and gay men who fight for gay, lesbian, bisexual, and transgender (GLBT) civil rights. In particular the association strives for the welfare of young gay men and lesbians, by supporting and mentoring their family members during critical stages (coming out or discovering the homosexuality of a son or daughter) and combating all forms of homophobic discrimination.

A minority of parents was also contacted through invitations put out in various media (mainly through Web and GLBT radio) and in other GLBT networks contacted by the researchers. Not all of the parents contacted were willing to take part in the study, meaning that those who participated in the research represent a very distinctive sample of parents with a backstory of acceptance of the homosexuality of their son or daughter (Bertone & Franchi, 2008).

This article is based solely on the in-depth interviews carried out with 46 parents—35 families—between 2006 and 2008. At the time of the interview, 21 parents lived in the centre south of Italy while 25 lived in the north of the country. Out of the 35 families we analyse here, only 6 had at least 1 member playing a militant role in AGEDO, while in most cases the families had been involved in various specific activities (11), or entered into contact with the association on a sporadic or ad hoc basis (3) or, last, were entirely unconnected with any of the activities of the association. Most of the parents define themselves as Catholic (29), 13 (10 of which were mothers) as non-practicing Catholics, and 17 parents define themselves as non-Catholic, either atheist or agnostic.

Interview Method and Data Analysis

The interview's scheme was constructed in order to observe discourses from the perspective of practices—thus bringing forth the normative models that the interviewees referred to when accounting for their practices (Morgan, 1996; Orbuch, 1997). It was decided not to begin with questions regarding the benefit of extending citizenship rights because these would not have evidenced the tensions that the issue of the inclusion of lesbians and gay men actually generates in practice. We focus our attention on Gay Pride march questions contained in the outline of the interview.

The conversations were digitally recorded and transcribed verbatim. We used ATLAS.ti to code the data, writing analytical memos and facilitating the analysis of the themes or categories already devised. In this article we analyse parents' perceptions and experiences of the Pride marches, considering them as a starting point for investigating the mechanisms involved in constructing sexual citizenship.

RESULTS AND DISCUSSION: A REFLECTION ON THE FLUIDITY OF DIVIDING LINES

Before analysing our interviewees' accounts about Pride marches, we intend to reflect more generally on the relevance of the geographical setting in the process of building sexual citizenship.

Family members often return to the idea that "accepting" spaces are those physically distant not only from the place of residence but also from the control of the community one belongs to. "Far from home," lesbian and gay offspring can exercise their right to self-determination and safe sexual practices; the right to define, manifest, and fulfil their identity freely; and therefore also publically take on being lesbian or gay as a lifestyle and identity. One mother, for example, told us the following:

> There's the problem of having to hide it, for these boys . . . . I'd like to see a lot of things changing in Italy . . . . I am happy that my son lives in [a big European city] . . . obviously it wasn't a coincidence, being the biggest gay community. There are all these shops and hotels with signs saying gay friendly and things like that, and I find that reassuring.

Various interviewees mentioned the need to "move away"—abroad—to escape the dynamics of control exerted by the community, with the parents who live in the south of Italy or in small towns describing cities as more hospitable, and Italy as a nation that is still homophobic.

> Before he went away to university my son had gone on study trips to England three times and he always came back revitalized, he had a different kind of life there. (Father)

The idea of emigrating is related to the opportunity of accessing rights regarding practices and identity (Richardson, 2000, 2005), escaping the control of the community, which seems to be more oppressive in small towns than larger cities. Big cities are viewed as a space for social and sexual liberation, offering anonymity, and a chance to escape the claustrophobic relationships that characterise smaller towns (Valentine & Skelton, 2003). Bell and Valentine (1995) have already shown how gay migrations towards cities are motivated by the desire to escape the oppressive mores and prejudice of rural settings. On the contrary, strategies to normalise gay and lesbian identity have to be adopted "near" home. Most of the parents interviewed justify this concealment with the fear that their children might be physically attacked/harassed.

> I was worried that he might become visible in this small town . . . . It is something that still scares me, that he might be attacked by homophobes who could . . . be bothered by certain things . . . and my son was very flamboyant, and I am still sure that he . . . doesn't hide . . . I'm not saying he should, but he could avoid . . . because there can be some situations where in my view you don't actually have to come out. (Mother)

Some parents talk about the extent to which there is still strict moral control in small towns and about how important reputation is when it comes to living in these settings. One mother who lives in a small town had this to say:

> I see it in the station too, there is a load of graffiti by people ... there was a boy who lived near here who people said was bisexual ... and someone had written it on the station wall.

The station, the streets, and public spaces are not asexual but rather "naturally" or "authentically" heterosexual (Bell, Binnie, Cream, & Valentine, 1994; Valentine, 2002). Habit and the repetition of behaviours generate assumptions on the appropriate behaviour to adopt in certain settings that thus acquire a sexual significance, determining what is allowed and what is not. Given that the repetition of habits and behaviours defines and constructs spaces, the difficulty of connoting the street with one's own homosexual presence and lifestyle makes it a place that is highly representative of denied recognition. To subvert this model by enacting transgressive behaviours in public spaces can represent a strategy for destabilizing homophobic processes, and thereby for redefining rights for homosexual people (Duncan, 1996; McDowell, 1999; Johnston, 2005). However, most of the parents who get an image of the Pride event based on indirect experience or selective media representations think that the visibility of the most spectacular aspects of the parade will help to reconfirm the stereotypical idea of gay men and lesbians as deviant people.

Even the choice of which spaces in the city the march can cross can be related to the orientation of the political agenda, based on integrating or marginalising the gay and lesbian community with respect to the heterosexual community. Enguix (2009) observed that in Spain, unlike in the United States, the decision to march through the centre of the city, in view of the fact that these areas have strong heterosexual connotations, does not alter their heteronormative nature. The outcome is that the Pride march merely becomes a spectacle for consumption, losing its political meaning (Bakhtin, 1984). Although it is not possible here to analyse the routes of the Pride marches in the various cities in Italy in relation to the political strategies of inclusion/exclusion of the gay and lesbian community, it should be noted that the possibility to occupy well-known areas during Pride marches did not escape the notice of some parents.

> I've seen certain things that you just shouldn't see, private things, in the squares, one of the most important places in Rome and they'd hired vans, small trucks I think, that kind of thing and these boys were kissing each other and the girls and women too. My son says it's because it's a provocation, it's a protest ... but I'm like no way, that's not right. (Mother)

The media attention devoted to the most carnivalesque aspects of the Pride parades seems to reinforce the process of spectacularization of the event. Furthermore, those who take part in the march are exposed not only to the people who are attending the event, but also to spectators who feel distant from it. The concepts of near and far thus become detached from physical locations and traverse their confines, complicating the framework of analysis.

PRIDE MARCHES AND PARENTS' PERSPECTIVES

The first Pride parade in Italy took place in Turin in 1978; it was organized by FUORI (Fronte Unitario Omosessuale Rivoluzionario Italiano–Italian Revolutionary Homosexual United Front), a gay association, and witnessed a limited participation. In the 1980s, the gay movement adopted a somewhat more institutional approach which was coordinated by nationwide organisations covering a whole range of subjects, from more mainstream to radical associations (Rossi Barilli, 1999). Despite the emergence of several gay and lesbian associations throughout the country, we have to wait until 1994 for the National Pride Parade in Rome to attract mass participation from all over the country. In 2000 the World Pride Parade in Rome took place. Since then, the number of events has steadily increased all around Italy (Ross, 2008, 2009) and the media have increasingly given resonance to the parades, although showing almost exclusively their most carnivalesque traits (Trappolin, 2004).

People's reflections on taking part in Pride marches took various forms and revealed different dimensions and nuances. For the purposes of this study we identified two groups with different stances: those who took part in the event and those who did not.

Among parents who did not take part in the parades, the main discourses are over visibility (public/private and publicisation of "private" bodies) and the means of representation (what to show, why to show, how to show).

The group of parents who participated in marches were almost all people with a backstory of acceptance of homosexuality that developed within AGEDO. In recent decades the voluntary sector in Italy has shifted from being purely voluntary to gradually becoming more specialised and more structured. As some authors have noted, by the early 1990s this led to a potential work overload for the sector, as well as dependency on public funding (Ranci, De Ambrogio, & Pasquinelli, 1991). At the end of the 1980s and the beginning of the 1990s the voluntary sector gained new impetus, focussing on redressing the inefficiency of public social policies, the lack of material resources and support structures, and the vacuum of representation and recognition of rights in relation to the emergence of new needs and new subjectivities (Balbo, 1985). In that period the voluntary sector began to produce its own services, rather than restricting its work to supporting social demand for intervention and monitoring the consolidation of a public system of universalistic services. In this process of transformation, some have detected the risk that the state and public administration end up delegating the very functions that concern safeguarding rights, and upholding the familisation of those rights, permitting the public sphere to play a "subsidiary role" in respect to responsibilities of the family (Saraceno, 2003). Voluntary sector support for families in Italy, in terms of rights for gay and lesbians, has followed the pattern described earlier despite being a fairly recent phenomenon. AGEDO, as we already said, was established at the beginning of the 1990s and took part in a national march for the first time in 2000 in Rome. Since then it has been steadily present and warmly welcomed in national and local parades. The association interacts with public policies and civil society with the aim of guaranteeing citizenship rights to lesbians and gay men. The notion of a system of family rights and responsibilities prevailing over a system of subjective rights thus intersects with the issue of representation. Those elements influence the discourses of some of the parents involved in AGEDO's activities who claim the rights to sexual citizenship as a demand for family rights. It must also be said that some elements of change can be detected in the discourses formulated.

Moreover, both parents who do not take part in the parade and those who do are involved in a process of "contamination" (Enguix, 2009) and of reflexivity on the boundaries of sexual citizenship in terms of right to occupy space.

In the following section we will examine those who formed opinions of Pride marches without having direct experience of them, before analysing the discourses of those who have taken part in the event.

Between Spectators and Television Viewers

One preliminary observation regarding the composition of the group of parents who did not take part in the march: they all share the characteristic of not being members of AGEDO. It should also be noted that the media images played a key role in shaping this group's opinions of the event: their responses are linked to how the Pride parade is presented on television and the resulting image of homosexuality.

> There's just one thing that upsets me ... that the message ... gets twisted ... interpreted in a different way ... because what you hear people saying ... after an event like that ... is that they're all perverts ... depraved ... smooching ... exhibitionists ... lecherers .... (Father)

These accounts highlight the quest for alternative forms of expression that avoid emphasising gay and lesbian diversity. Thus, in many cases the desire for gay sons and daughters to be accepted as "normal" leads parents to distance themselves from more transgressive representations (Fields, 2001; Bertone, 2013). On the other hand, discourses on the "sameness" of their offspring are evoked as successful strategies that should help prevent potential problems. While the "old model" of gay and lesbian identity had to be controlled from the outside, the new one, which has interiorised the norms, exerts self-control, from the inside, thus becoming respectable and responsible (Hubbard, 2001).

The normalising tactics and strategies that the parents put forward possess a range of different nuances. Words like "exhibitionism," "exaggeration," "limits," and "decency" are frequently used, shaping discourses that define the boundaries within which rights can be claimed:

> We are many ... respect us ... love us ... okay, but within the boundaries of common decency. (Father)

The serious struggle for rights appears irreconcilable with the more creative representations of gay and lesbian identity that make the participants look like "clowns," "buffoons," without authority.

> I didn't like it because they were almost clowning around for people ... if they want to do something ... it has to be something serious ... not making a show of their diversity ... but getting their problems out there and getting their voice heard ... not all that fooling around on floats and all the things they get up to ... at least that's how I see it. (Mother)

These transgressions also define the identities of those engaging in them, rendering them unsuitable to entering the political arena. The idea of being respectable is linked to the way people represent themselves in public and their ability to conform to the dominant models.

> Gay pride with all those half naked men ... is something I can't accept and I reckon that it might well be a rebellion but that makes no difference. If you're impeccable then the government, and people in general, will listen to you, but if you're going to be like that then no way. (Mother)

Some of the discourses thus attempt to make a distinction between those who conform to the traditional gender model and adopt behaviours deemed appropriate for the public space they are occupying and those who violate the gender-normative or heteronormative model, thus losing consensus for their right to occupy the streets.

> Fooling around that some of them do, that detracts from the value of those who are serious about it. It should be done more often, but in a more serious way. (Mother)

It is above all the parents who describe themselves as practising or non-practising Catholics who manifest their disapproval of the visibility engendered by Pride events, in some cases explicitly referring to the disputes between the gay and lesbian movement and the Catholic Church.

> [What] I find quite hard to deal with is all the exhibitionism and mockery. They make fun of themselves and they also make fun of the church, the bishops, and on one hand fair enough but what I mean is that in the public eye they are seen as fooling around, putting on a show in public or making fun of each other and others. I don't like that image. (Father)

The idea of display can be intimidating because it subverts the customary heteronormative model that connotes streets and public places. There is the fear that this transgressive image can consolidate the stereotypes around the perceived inherent perversion of homosexuality.

> I don't want people to say ... "See those homosexuals ... see what perverts they are ... what they're like ...." They are just normal couples .... (Mother)

Many parents express their concern over what "others" might think of Pride, in the belief that displays and behaviours that do not conform to the heterosexual/heterosexist norm can contribute to homophobic reactions.

> You want to have a parade? You want to protest? Do it, but with dignity ... simplicity ... quietly .... That might even have more effect ... no? They should try and do a silent gay pride ... mute ... just a silent protest. (Father)

Going visible and acting in public in a way that violates gendernormativity, for example with transvestism or transgenderism, or goes against the heteronorm, like public displays of affection between people of the same sex, risks turning Pride into a show for "consumers" (Enguix, 2009). Some parents see this as abasing the spirit of the march, which should have an explicitly political meaning and thus be carried out "seriously." Fooling around and carnival antics are viewed in a negative light, despite the fact that the event's carnivalesque atmosphere—with the focus on transgression and subverting norms—has an intrinsic political meaning, evoking the transformation of social regulation. According to Bakhtin (1984), carnival and popular/folk events offer a different, nonofficial aspect of the world and of human relations. Even the "grotesque" could undergo certain changes and may be used to interrogate and ultimately subvert the dominant model. A small minority of parents saw transgression as a strategy to highlight the rigidity of traditional models and to elicit a more complex reflection on sexual citizenship rights, as one mother relates:

> It's not that being homosexual is cool now, everything is cool, it depends on how you experience it, there are some things that might be a bit over the top, but when you see them on the march it's fun too, because they make fun of themselves, maybe they flaunt certain things in a very obvious way, but when it comes down to it, it gets people talking.

Thus, a minority of parents mention the fact that a queer presence in public spaces can help destabilise heteronorms (Bell & Valentine, 1995) or, at least, it can be said to have led parents to a more reflexive stance. This stance was only manifested by a small number of interviewees, with calls for normalisation being more common. Yet as can be seen in the excerpts included here, these calls can take different forms. A range of different strategies can therefore be identified, promoting the following in turn: concealment or exclusion from the public arena; a controlled form of visibility that represents the normality of being gay or lesbian; or, as we will see in the following section, a vision of lesbians and gay men as embedded in heteronormative relationships.

Parents and Associations at Pride Events: Their Role in Constructing a Citizenship Embedded in the Family of Origin

We will now take a look at AGEDO and the accounts of parents involved in the association, in terms of how they enter into the debate on social and antidiscrimination policies in the public arena, and their role in the construction of inclusive citizenship. In particular this analysis considers the accounts of both militant members of AGEDO and family members who enter into contact with the association for a limited period of time.

Our analysis of the empirical material shows that only a small minority of those interviewed got to the point of mentioning social policies and equal opportunities policies, referring to legal regulation and a system of ad hoc interventions.

These interviewees underlined both the inability to frame the question of safeguarding rights correctly, in the absence of specific anti-homophobia norms, and the institutional vacuum that is also reflected in the lack of dedicated services, albeit with the due distinctions between different geographical areas.

Militant activism therefore enters the public sphere, representing an element of discontinuity in the heteronormative model. This process involves experiences of active citizenship—producing claims for rights and policies—and at times also absorbing autonomous responses in terms of awareness-raising, information, and services: there is criticism of the fragmented nature of measures aimed at preventing homophobia—in terms of the lack of integration between different sectors (social, health services, education, active policies in the world of work, equal opportunities, etc.)

and the absence of both specific training for health workers, trainers, and teachers, and specialised local services (helplines, counselling and psychological support, including for parents, etc.).

> I think that families also need a lot of help from social services and the health services .... Schools have to change .... Social services and the health service have to adapt ... to get up to speed and train their workers .... (Mother)

This kind of social action, however, was undertaken by very few people who decided to raise awareness of the issue by working in an organised structure and being willing to stand up and be counted, in a sort of collective coming out. In most of the accounts, the family association was seen exclusively as somewhere to meet others, learn something, offer mutual support, grow, and redefine—in the private arena—what is initially perceived as a "problem," something that upsets the status quo.

> She's a mother like I am ... she found it hard like I did at the start, then she managed to move on ... so she got where I was coming from ... she wasn't pushy about explaining things to me ... just very gradual and gentle ... she helped me see that there's nothing bad about it ... that it's just the way things are .... (Mother)

With a net presence of mothers, the association functions as much as protection for parents as it does for young lesbians and gay men, implementing (primary and secondary) prevention of homophobic violence in the family.

> I think it's very important to have some kind of support when you find things hard going, like in the initial period of disorientation, because if you've never really thought about it before you have no way of knowing ... it's not a case of throwing your child out, it's not some kind of dishonour .... (Father)

Belonging to an organisation of this kind does not in any case necessarily entail full support for the struggles for civil and social rights, or imply becoming an expert on the issue: this appears to be the case for a smaller group of parents who also took on roles of responsibility, going from being service users to taking on a more advanced, more structured role of advocacy.

Those who play a more active role in AGEDO interpret their role in a more structured way and find the self-help aspect a reductive one, placing the emphasis on advocacy instead (Broad, Crawley, & Foley, 2004; Broad, 2011). Parents are encouraged to undertake a journey that starts with the coming-out process, learning to accept their child's homosexuality with the help of the association and then appealing to their love of their children, leading to active support for gay and lesbian community and its battles, including by formulating critical stances and statements, as in the case of their opposition to reparative therapies.

> My wife experienced a gradual process of acceptance and then from acceptance she moved onto the fight for rights .... (Father)

Many parents, however, come to the association in order to meet other parents who have had similar experiences, and in some cases when they feel they are being urged to actively support advocacy initiatives they cease to be involved.

> So I realised that AGEDO was based on that concept [the commitment to advocacy] and not about parents needing help ... so I stopped going .... (Mother)

Other parents continue to attend the association but state that they had not developed the competencies to intervene in public debate. Different levels of legitimation to participate in public debate thus appear to emerge, based on one's ability to formulate the "correct" discourses and assert them effectively. One account seems to attest to the existence of a script to follow:

> We were very close to an activist in the association ... who also opened our eyes to a whole series of things both with regards to the issues facing homosexuals and the pitfalls of the homosexual world, attitudes, prejudices, etc., that say that you are either in, inside the debate or outside of it, so I don't feel qualified to talk about homosexuality, I've got my own experience ... but apart from that I'm no expert .... (Father)

The family association therefore appears to have a dual function, on one hand claiming and guaranteeing rights and on the other acting to normalise gay and lesbian lifestyle, providing a lexicon of "acceptance" and redefining the boundaries between what is legitimate and what is not (Bertone, 2009).

Even the calls to guarantee rights would appear to be dictated by very different motivations: for some parents it is a question of guaranteeing equal opportunities and dignity, while others are motivated by the aim of providing more protection for their children. Indeed, children appear to be a greater cause for concern, with the perception of a higher level of social and personal vulnerability.

The minority of parents who express willingness to support the gay men's and lesbians' cause are, however, ambivalent towards what are perceived as more spectacular manifestations and reflect on the significance and consequences that a strategy of visibility taken to extremes can have in terms of subverting the dominant model.

> Gay pride is different from everyday life. You have to be there. There are those who are bolder and then obviously those who like being on show ... perhaps that's the right setting. It's a way to provoke people. Because if no one makes a stand no one is going to benefit. (Mother)

Those Catholics that are involved with AGEDO are attentive to provocations directed at the Church, but unlike the Catholic non-activist in AGEDO, they frame the more transgressive aspect of the parade through a discourse of acceptance. One mother says the following:

> You have to see it yourself to judge whether it's just carnival high jinks or not .... And we heterosexuals get up to those often enough ourselves... but for those who don't accept homosexuality the first thing they talk about is that .... They say that they can live their lives without mocking nuns, priests, etc. But when we take part in a carnival what are we doing?

To combat the fear that the event can be stripped of its political meaning and judged by heterosexuals as mere high jinks, the parents' accounts reflect mechanisms similar to those detected in the GLBT associations. There is an attempt to construct boundaries within the Pride event, defining those who are "out," namely not acceptable and not in line with a certain definition of the gay and lesbian identities (Snow & Benford, 1988).

It is interesting to note that family members who have taken part in the event can be placed along a sliding scale of various stances: from those who marched in the parade, as part of a specific group, to those who took part on the margins. The few who remained on the margins are those who talk about the aspect of rules being subverted, highlighting the fact that at that moment in time public space is no longer governed by heteronorms and the effects that can arise as a result. One father relates the following:

> I would be a little wary of taking part in an event of this kind, a bit intimidated .... I think that at an event like that a heterosexual would feel different.

These words could be read as an example of the process of "contamination" of the other (heterosexual) (Enguix, 2009) that could be generated by the event. Those who take part in the parade, on the other hand, in some cases frame themselves as having the right to occupy public space in view of being heterosexual citizens. In these discourses families thus act as the intermediary that legitimates society to accept and accommodate the requests of gay men and lesbians and acknowledge their right to occupy these spaces, framing them in the context of heteronormative relationships, namely as the children of heterosexual couples.

> The first time I went on a Pride march I found it very liberating, a great experience. My daughter was playing the samba, all dressed in pink, my son was on the march, us too, and I said, this is great, we are all here on this march because we want rights, for ourselves too. (Mother)

In the words of this mother we can trace the process of *familisation of rights* mentioned earlier. She frames the event as an opportunity to fight for rights for "ourselves"— parents and children—outlining a model of citizenship based on the relationships that individuals have with the family of origin.

> While the fact of talking about it, the fact of showing that there are [normal] people, that ... and the families bearing witness to this issue and wanting society to take it on board in the right way, that's the point, the right way to tackle the problem, the right approach to help these youngsters to have fewer problems and get on with their lives in our society. (Father)

These discourses construct a citizenship linked to the role inside the family—as sons or daughters—and are mainly produced in the interactions between members who attend AGEDO, within which a shared vocabulary forms that becomes a tool used to familise gay and lesbian rights.

The added element in the case of most of the parents connected to these associations is the relational dimension that they implicitly refer to. Sexual citizenship rights are claimed starting from the need to protect the heterosexual families of origin and their children. This seems to confirm the idea that to be a citizen it is necessary to "exist within a particular frame" (Plummer, 2003, p. 53), in this specific case within an institution, namely the heterosexual family, that cannot be called into question. In some cases these narrations thus seem to represent a script that the interviewees rely on to justify their love as parents, and their positions and demands, by virtue of being "normal" heterosexual citizens.

CONCLUSION

The discourses of family members, albeit varied, construct sexual citizenship rights in relation to the distinction between the public and private spheres. While private spaces are defined as those where the individual must be guaranteed the right to make his or her own decisions and at the same time enjoy the privacy of the domestic sphere, public spaces, physically and symbolically, strongly influence the definition of context-appropriate gay and lesbian behaviour. Despite the range of different nuances described, most of the discourses of the parents interviewed appear to contribute to the construction of heteronormative spaces characterised by mechanisms that aim to normalise gay men and lesbian behaviour by adhering to traditional gender models.

However, it must also be said that some elements of innovation can be detected in the discourses formulated. One example of this is the already mentioned process of *familisation of rights*. Adopting this perspective, claims for gay and lesbian access to sexual citizenship rights become a demand for family rights by parents who desire equal recognition for themselves and their sons.

A Pride parade is the lens through which these processes can be observed in all their complexity, as well as in terms of the disruptive nature of the event as an inversion ritual (Turner, 1977; Bakhtin, 1984), not only rendering gay men and lesbians visible in traditional heteronormative spaces, but also legitimising them to occupy these spaces, at least temporarily. On the other hand, the parade could be just another way by which social control is exerted over deviants (Bakhtin, 1984). From this perspective, the folkloric traits of the parade reinforce the heteronormative foundations of citizenship rather than challenging their stability.

The dividing line between the private and public spheres, and the attitudes and behaviours that can be assigned to these spheres, are thus called into question. The context the interviewees were asked to comment on generated inevitable tensions between the urge to demand inclusive citizenship, although often relegated to the domestic sphere, and the impulse to normalisation in public spaces. These tensions produce unexpected effects, including a process of "contamination of others" (heterosexual people) (Enguix, 2009) also involving those who did not attend the parade but who are called to think over the meaning of the march.

This need for conformity can be seen in interviewees who ask their children to be more "composed" while taking part in Pride events, setting aside any transgression that might jeopardize the political significance of the event and turn it into a "mere carnival." The parents who have never taken part in a Pride march are also those most critical of the transgressive, exhibitionist aspects of the event, but the image they have of it is strongly conditioned by media representation and reporting, which construct their—mediated—experience of the initiative. Another element that tends to exacerbate critical stances on the event and public displays of non-heteronormative behaviours is religious belief.

The group of parents that took part in the event can in turn be divided into those who marched in the parade and those who watched from the margins. The former are almost all people with a backstory of acceptance of gay and lesbian identity that developed within AGEDO. The association tends to foster a shared lexicon pertaining to sexual citizenship, and also to the role that parents can play in the process of accessing rights for gay men and lesbians. These parents do not talk about justice and equal opportunities; it is their love that prompts them to fight for inclusion for their children (Broad, 2011), and their participation in Pride events should be interpreted in these terms. Fields (2001) and Broad (Broad et al., 2004) had already highlighted the fact that the way in which heterosexual parents talk about their gay and lesbian children reproduces the values of the traditional family. These parents feel that their heterosexuality places them in a position of authority, and that the fact of being parents legitimises them to fight for rights for their children. The unconditional love that these parents declare for their children was the central argument in some of the discourses analysed, in particular those of AGEDO members, lending legitimacy to their stances. Albeit in conflicting ways and in different directions, while these parents on one hand stated that they were in favour of the free expression of lesbian and gay identity in the private sphere—supporting, for example, the recognition of same-sex relationships—in the public dimension these tensions became more pronounced and hegemonic messages emerged, with the traditionalist components of the heteronormative family resurfacing.

Though discourses on normalisation and privatisation prevail, the Pride march is a setting for privileged interactions between sexual dissidents and heterosexuals that takes place in a public, visible place (Enguix, 2009). As Bakhtin suggests, carnival "is not a spectacle seen by the people; they live in it, and everyone participates because its very idea embraces all the people" (Bakhtin, 1984, p. 7). From this perspective, parades' subversive potential is acknowledged, as also emerges from the words of the parents who take part in the event, who describe the suspension of the heterosexist rules that traditionally characterize that space and those streets.

REFERENCES

Bakhtin, M. (1984). *Rabelais and his world*. Bloomington, IN: Indiana University Press.
Balbo, L. (1985). Le potenzialità inespresse delle nuove soggettività e dei diritti quotidiani [The unexpressed potential of new subjectivities and everyday rights]. *Democrazia e diritto*, *5*, 75–88.
Bell, D., & Binnie, J. (2000). *The sexual citizen: Queer politics and beyond*. Cambridge, UK: Polity Press.
Bell, D., Binnie, J., Cream, J., & Valentine, G. (1994). All hyped up and no place to go. *Gender, Place and Culture*, *1*, 31–47. doi: 10.1080/09663699408721199
Bell, D., & Valentine, G. (1995). *Mapping desire*. New York, NY: Routledge.
Bertone, C. (2009). *Le omosessualità [Homosexualities]*. Roma, Italy: Carocci.
Bertone, C. (2013). Citizenship across generations: Struggles around heteronormativities. *Citizenship Studies*, *17*(8), 985–999. doi: 10.1080/13621025.2013.851147
Bertone, C., & Franchi, M. (2008). *Family matters: Le esperienze dei familiari di giovani lesbiche e gay in Italia [Family matters: The experiences of family members of gay and lesbian in Italy]*. Retrieved from www.euroflag.net

Bertone, C., & Franchi, M. (2014). Suffering as the path to acceptance: Parents of gay and lesbian young people negotiating Catholicism in Italy. *Journal of GLBT Family Studies*, *10*(1–2), 58–78.

Bilotta, F. (Ed.). (2008). *Le unioni tra persone dello stesso sesso. Profili di diritto civile, comunitario e comparato [Unions between persons of the same sex. Listings of civil law, common and comparative]*. Udine, Italy: Mimesis.

Binnie, J., & Valentine, G. (1999). Geographies of sexuality: A review of progress. *Progress in Human Geography*, *23*(2), 175–187. doi: 10.1177/030913259902300202

Bonini Baraldi, M. (2010). *La famiglia de-genere. Matrimonio, omosessualità e costituzione [De-gendered family. Marriage, homosexuality and constitution]*. Udine, Italy: Mimesis.

Brannen, J. (1999). Discourses of adolescence: Young people's independence and autonomy within families. In M. Woodhead, D. Faulkner, & K. Littleton (Eds.), *Making sense of social development* (pp. 114–129). London, England: Routledge.

Broad, K. L. (2011). Coming out for parents, families and friends of lesbians and gays: From support group grieving to love advocacy. *Sexualities*, *14*(4), 399–415. doi: 10.1177/1363460711406792

Broad, K. L., Crawley S. L., & Foley L. (2004). Doing "real family values": The interpretive practice of families in the GLBT movement. *The Sociological Quarterly*, *45*(3), 509–527. doi: 10.1111/j.1533-8525.2004.tb02301.x

Castells, M. (1983). *The city and the grassroots: A cross-cultural theory of urban social movements*. Berkeley and Los Angeles, CA: The University of California Press.

Cohen, E. F. (2005). Neither seen nor heard: Children's citizenship in contemporary democracies. *Citizenship Studies*, *9*(2), 221–240. doi: 10.1080/13621020500069687

Cossman, B. (2007). *Sexual citizens*. Stanford, CA: Stanford University Press.

D'Ippoliti, C., & Schuster, A. (Eds.). (2011). *DisOrientamenti. Discriminazione ed esclusione sociale delle persone LGBT in Italia [Dis-orientation. Discrimination and social exclusion of LGBT people in Italy]*. Rome, Italy: Armando.

Duncan, N. (1996). Renegotiating gender and sexuality in public and private spaces. In N. Duncan (Ed.), *Body space: Destabilising geographies of gender and sexuality* (pp. 127–189). London, England: Routledge.

Enguix, B. (2009). Identities, sexualities and commemorations: Pride parades, public space and sexual dissidence. *Anthropological Notebooks*, *15*(2), 15–33.

Evans, D. (1993). *Sexual citizenship: The material construction of sexualities*. London, England: Routledge.

Fields, J. (2001). Normal queers: Straight parents respond to their children's "coming out." *Symbolic Interaction*, *24*(2), 165–187. doi: 10.1525/si.2001.24.2.165

Forest, B. (1995). West Hollywood as symbol: The significance of place in the construction of a gay identity. *Environment and Planning D: Society and Space*, *13*(2), 133–157. doi: 10.1068/d130133

Hubbard, P. (2001). Sex zones: Intimacy, citizenship and public space. *Sexualities*, *4*(1), 51–71. doi: 10.1177/136346001004001003.

Johnston, L. (2005). *Queering tourism: Paradoxical performances at gay pride parades*. New York, NY; London, England: Routledge.

Knopp, L. (1990). Some theoretical implications of gay involvement in an urban land market. *Political Geography Quarterly, 9*(4), 337–352. doi: 10.1016/0 260-9827(90)90033-7

McDowell, L. (1999). City life and difference. In J. Allen, D. Massey, & M. Pryke (Eds.), *Unsettling cities* (pp. 143–160). London, England: Routledge.

Morgan, D. H. J. (1996). *Family connections: An introduction to family studies*. Cambridge, UK: Polity Press.

Orbuch, T. L. (1997). People's accounts count: The sociology of accounts. *Annual Review of Sociology, 23,* 455–478. doi: 10.1146/annurev.soc.23.1.455

Pitch, T. (1998). *Un diritto per due [A right for two]*. Milano, Italy: Il saggiatore.

Plummer, K. (2003). *Intimate citizenship*. Seattle, WA: University of Washington Press.

Ranci, C., De Ambrogio, U., & Pasquinelli, S. (1991). *Identità e servizio: il volontariato nella crisi del Welfare [Identity and service: Volunteering in the context of the welfare crisis]*. Bologna, Italy: Il Mulino.

Richardson, D. (2000). *Rethinking sexuality*. London, England: Sage.

Richardson, D. (2005). Desiring sameness? The rise of a neoliberal politics of normalisation. *Antipode, 37*(3), 515–535. doi: 10.1111/j.0066-4812.2005.00 509.x

Rose, N. (1989). *Governing the soul*. London, England: Routledge.

Rose, N. (1996). *Inventing our selves*. Cambridge, UK: Cambridge University Press.

Ross, C. (2008). Visions of visibility: LGBT communities in Turin. *Modern Italy, 13*(3), 241–260. doi: 10.1080/13532940802069531

Ross, C. (2009). Collective association in the LGBT movement. In D. Albertazzi, C. Brook, C. Ross, & N. Rothenberg (Eds.), *Resisting the tide* (pp. 204–216). New York, NY; London, England: Continuum International Pub. Group Inc.

Rossi Barilli, G. (1999). *Il movimento gay in Italia [The gay movment in Italy]*. Milan, Italy: Feltrinelli.

Saraceno, C. (2003). *Mutamenti della famiglia e politiche sociali in Italia [Family changes and social policies]*. Bologna, Italy: Il Mulino.

Snow, D. A., & Benford, R. D. (1988). Ideology, frame resonance, and participant mobilization. *International Social Movement Research, 1,* 197–217.

Trappolin, L. (2004). *Identità in azione. Mobilitazione omosessuale e sfera pubblica [Identities in action. Homosexual mobilisation and public sphere]*. Roma, Italy: Carocci.

Turner, B. S. (2008). Citizenship, reproduction and the state: International marriage and human rights. *Citizenship Studies, 12*(1), 45–54.

Turner, V. (1977). *The ritual process*. Ithaca, NY: Cornell University Press.

Valentine, G. (2002). Queer bodies and the production of space. In D. Richardson & S. Seidman (Eds.), *Handbook of lesbian and gay studies* (pp. 145–160). London, England: Sage.

Valentine, G., & Skelton, T. (2003). Finding oneself, losing oneself: The lesbian and gay "scene" as a paradoxical space. *International Journal of Urban and Regional Research, 27,* 849–466.

Vogel, U. (1991). Is citizenship gender-specific? In U. Vogel & M. Moran (Eds.), *The frontiers of citizenship* (pp. 58–85). London, England: Macmillan.

Mars to Venus or Earth to Earth? How Do Families of Origin Fit into GLBTQ Lives?

ESTHER D. ROTHBLUM
San Diego State University, San Diego, California, USA

This article examines some of the themes in the special issue about the families of origin of people who are gay, lesbian, bisexual, transgender, or queer (GLBTQ). Coming out to families of origin is a pivotal event that changes the family system. Race, ethnicity, and immigration intersect with a family member's disclosure of sexuality and gender identity. Families are both private and public institutions, and are influenced by, and influence, the media. Families may take advantage of professional advice about GLBTQ issues but may also need to educate professionals about these issues. This article concludes with suggestions for further research.

INTRODUCTION

Gay, lesbian, bisexual, transgender, and queer (GLBTQ) individuals and families of origin were oil and water in past decades; the two terms didn't mix. When GLBTQ people discussed the families they were born into, it was with negative emotions—fear, anxiety, anger, disappointment, or rage. Research on GLBTQ youths focused on the risks of running away from home, with concomitant substance abuse and suicide, as the result of physical violence or lack of support from family members (see D'Augelli & Patterson, 2001, for an overview). Gender nonconformity in childhood was associated with violence by family members as well (Factor & Rothblum, 2008a). GLBTQ people of all ages who came out to family members braced themselves for negative reactions and often moved far away from their hometown (Rothblum,

Balsam & Mickey, 2004). In turn, parents and relatives kept the knowledge of a GLBTQ family member secret not only from friends and neighbors, but even in conversations with one another. It was as if GLBTQ people and heterosexual families of origin were living on different planets.

Lukes and Land (1990) have pointed out how members of religious, ethnic, or immigrant minority groups often grow up in minority families and neighborhoods, so that they first become acculturated into the dominant culture by the media or when they enter school. In contrast, GLBTQ individuals grow up in heterosexual families and need to find their community. In the decades before the Internet, this meant knowing where to look for GLBT communities, knowing what GLBT people looked like, and needing to "queer" oneself in order to be identifiable to these communities.

Unable to rely on their immediate or extended family, GLBTQ people looked for a supportive community. Sometimes they used the term *family of friends* for this endeavor. Kurdek and Schmidt (1987) found same-sex couples to report more support from friends than from family of origin compared with heterosexual couples. The book *Families We Choose: Lesbians, Gays, Kinship* (Weston, 1991) has a chapter titled "Is Straight to Gay As Family Is to No Family?"

There has been little research focusing on families of origin of GLBTQ individuals, and so the current journal issue is a welcome addition to GLBTQ family scholarship. The articles are both interdisciplinary and international, focusing on case studies, qualitative interviews, and media analysis in Australia, Canada, Italy, Slovenia, Spain, and the United States. Participants in the research studies include lesbians, gay men, bisexual women and men, transgender and gender-nonconforming individuals, and those who are intersex. In this article I discuss some of the themes that transcend these articles, and provide suggestions for future research.

Coming Out to the Family Is Pivotal

By the time GLBTQ people come out to their family of origin, they have usually come out to a number of friends. Alenka Švab and Roman Kuhar describe how, regardless of the number of friends to whom GLBTQ individuals have disclosed their sexual or gender identity, coming out to family members is a pivotal stage for lesbians and gay men because it "importantly shapes family reality and relationships between family members" (p. 16). In their study of the daily life of lesbians and gay men in Slovenia, some of their respondents perceived the coming-out process to family as "the only real coming out since no other instance of coming out is as demanding in terms of the emotional strain involved" (p. 21). Not surprisingly, younger respondents came out to their families at an earlier age than did older respondents, who had lived through a time when homosexuality was still a crime in Slovenia.

Parents too describe the experience as very important. Erika L. Grafsky interviewed eight parents in the United States whose son or daughter came out to them in adolescence. Parents described that coming-out experience as stressful, emotional, tearful, surprising, and shocking. Some parents felt "as if the picture they had envisioned of their child's life was shattered" (p. 47). Chiara Bertone and Marina Franchi state how the discovery of their child's non-heterosexual identity "requires parents to address unexpected problems of action since a taken-for-granted element of their scenario, heterosexuality, has been disrupted" (p. 59). Just as Švab and Kuhar found younger respondents to come out to their families at an earlier age, Grafsky reports that younger parents were more comfortable with a child coming out than were older parents.

Similarly, Michela Baldo compares the closet to the "confessional." She describes scenes from the Canadian film *Mambo italiano*: the gay main character, Angelo, calls an anonymous gay helpline, his sister confesses his sexuality to her psychiatrist, and the entire family enters the Catholic Church confessional booth.

Coming Out Changes the Family System

Švab and Kuhar emphasize how the coming-out-to-family process is relational in that everyone is affected by the disclosure, whether the reaction is positive or negative. Some parents rationalize homosexuality as the "lesser evil" (p. 24) when compared with substance abuse or academic problems. Others look for cures. Some respondents told their mother and asked her to serve as the mediator to their father; others interpreted a neutral reaction or silence as positive since they had feared worse reactions. But whatever the reaction to coming out, new relationships with family members needed to be forged after the disclosure.

Echoing Švab and Kuhar, Baldo states, "coming out is a family matter" (p. 175). Angelo, the main character in the film *Mambo italiano*, "fears losing pieces of himself" (p. 174) if his family reacts negatively to him after he comes out. The family is a large piece of his identity. Furthermore, Angelo's family is in "continual evolution (. . .) creation of possibilities coming from apparent impossibilities" (p. 183). Grafsky states, "Becoming the parent of a queer son or daughter is a complex process that emphasizes the relational nature of the experience of disclosure to family (. . . .) It is an active, ongoing process" (p. 49).

Susan L. Johnson and Kristen E. Benson offer an extensive case study. When Sarah, the mother of Lee, a six-year-old transgender child in the United States, was willing to raise her child as female, the mother received "accusations from her family suggesting child abuse or neglect" (p. 132). Consequently, the mother and child were not invited to some family gatherings. Sarah states, "I went from patting myself on the back for being such a progressive parent ... to being really concerned that I must be doing something terribly wrong to cause this gender 'confusion.' EVERYONE, mostly my mother and ex-husband told me I was being too permissive ... " (p. 133). In this case study, it was the child's mother who "came out" about her child's gender nonconformity and had to deal with negative repercussions from the family. Surprisingly, it was Sarah's conservative Christian grandmother who was the most supportive.

Janet B. Watson portrays bisexual individuals as having "nomadic trajectories" (p. 107) in relation to their families of origin, given the fluidity of their identities. How does the family adapt to a daughter who had been heterosexually married, monogamous, and planning to have children later coming out as bisexual, in a relationship with a woman, and polyamorous? Or what does it mean if a man living in rural Australia sees himself as a bit gay? Further complicating notions of identity are individuals whose gender identity changes along with their sexual orientation.

I want to focus specifically on Švab and Kuhar's use of the term *gatekeeping* for the phenomenon where one family member begs or demands that no one else be told, or that the information be kept from a specific family member. The consequence of this is that sexual orientation cannot freely be discussed at family gatherings, and so the conversation stays in the closet, so to speak. For example, in the film *Mambo italiano* it is the main character's sister, Anna, who warns her gay brother not to come out to his parents because his disclosure could kill them.

Sexuality and Gender Identity Intersect with Race, Ethnicity, Immigration, and Religion

Valerie Q. Glass interviewed black lesbian couples in the United States about their interactions with extended families of origin, focusing on family rituals. She explains how family rituals create a sense of belonging in an oppressive society; these events can be major holiday or life cycle celebrations as well as daily routines. Baldo also describes family rituals, such as the large family dinner, as a ritual in ethnic immigrant families. Yet for lesbian couples, feeling part of an extended family means making decisions about how to integrate sexuality, outness, and identity of their partner into extended family gatherings and rituals. Lesbians might attend a family celebration without their partner, or be asked not to express physical affection to their partner. In other words, lesbians found extended family events crucially important yet could not present their real selves at these events.

Racquel (Lucas) Platero interviewed a Roma couple in Spain who had a gender-nonconforming child. The parents had to deal not only with strict gender roles in the Roma community, but with negative stereotypes about Romas in their child's school.

Baldo draws on theories of migration to understand how the two Italian immigrant families in the film *Mambo italiano* come to terms with gay sons. She emphasizes both the importance of family among immigrants and the generational differences between the parents who came from "the old country" and their children who grew up familiar with gay sexuality. Yet immigrant families are themselves stereotyped and marginalized. This means that heterosexual immigrant parents, like their GLBTQ offspring, have been targeted by the mainstream culture as deviant—a shared experience.

In Watson's narratives of bisexual women and men in Australia, those from Asian immigrant families had to juggle progressive language and attitudes about sexuality and gender with the more covert ways in which gender and sexual nonconformity are expressed when visiting family of origin in Asia. GLBTQ individuals of color thus led different lives when working in Australia or visiting families of origin in India or Sri Lanka.

Glass describes how white GLBTQ individuals often leave families of origin when they or their partner are not accepted. When I teach about race and ethnicity in my Lesbian Lives and Cultures course, I ask students why white lesbians are so estranged from their families. Immigrant families and families of color can serve as a model for white GLBTQ people about how to work on staying connected with extended family members. GLBTQ individuals of color are also more likely to have children, and in that sense may feel more connected with, and want their children to be aware of, their family heritage and rituals.

Bertone and Franchi interviewed 46 parents of lesbian or gay children in Italy in order to examine the role of Catholicism in the coming-out process. They describe the intersection of religion and sexuality, particularly the role of organized religion in "framing sexual orientations outside the heterosexual norm as a social problem and in upholding social hostility" (p. 59). Consequently, parents need to integrate their child's experience with the dominant heterosexual discourse of the Catholic Church. Some parents frame love, regardless of gender, as a fundamental tenet of Christianity. Some search for open-minded priests as well as friends and family members. Parents may cope by "claiming a direct connection with God bypassing institutional mediation" (p. 72) in order to separate religion from the bigotry of their individual church.

Families Are Both Private and Public Institutions

Watson collected narratives of bisexual women and men in Australia about coming out to families of origin. She emphasizes that the "social space of family is (...) uniquely located at the interface of private and public domains of engagement. Consequently, the 'family closet' is drawn in complex ways that sees it as a source of both sanctuary and censorship depending upon family dynamics" (p. 107).

Valeria Cappellato and Tiziana Mangarella interviewed parents of lesbians and gay men in Italy who described themselves as accepting of homosexuality. Defining citizen rights as "the right to occupy space" (p. 213), the authors explain how parents with a lesbian, gay, or bisexual son or daughter negotiate this identity in public settings. Parents described the need for their adult child to move away from home in order to escape public homophobia in small towns and find a supportive community. Some parents had joined the Association of Parents and Friends of Homosexuals (AGEDO), in order to meet parents with similar issues and concerns. Parents were asked specifically how they felt about gay pride marches; some felt that the public expressions of sexuality were unacceptable whereas others had participated in the marches. In this way parents of GLB children similarly make decisions about coming out to the public. Ethnic and migrant families in particular may have thin boundaries between the family and their ethnic/immigrant community, so that having a child come out also affects the family's standing in the community.

Negotiating private and public spaces is even more salient for parents of transgender children. Platero describes the various strategies that parents of young, gender-nonconforming children use when the children want to "pass" as the other gender in public parks or playgrounds. Similarly, a single mother of a six-year-old transgender child in the United States, in Johnson and Benson's extensive case study, had not informed the community that her daughter's birth sex was male.

The Media Educate Families about GLBTQ Issues

Luca Malici describes how television broadcast companies portray families in TV programs, thus influencing millions of viewers about what is "normative" in family relationships. Consequently when what Malici terms "queer TV moments" appear in situation comedies, these are viewed by families at home and influence their opinions about what is normative sexuality. Heterosexual family members may view the TV characters as people who would not be accepted in their own rural town, for example, but they find the characters, played by popular film stars, interesting, important, and positive. In this regard, television is transformative in changing family attitudes about GLBTQ topics.

According to Malici, the television set has replaced the fireplace as the site where families gather. Despite the advent of the Internet and multiple-TV households, the majority of Italians still watch television in the living room. Malici quotes a lesbian daughter who watched television with her mother and noticed her mother becoming more accepting of lesbianism while watching a sitcom about a conservative father coming to terms with his lesbian daughter. Television network executives are nervous about programming that may shock or offend their audiences, yet Malici's research indicates that

Italian audiences are ready for this programming and don't in general believe that GLBTQ themes should be limited to late-night time slots when young children aren't watching.

Baldo examines how the film *Mambo italiano*, about an Italian-Canadian family living in Montreal, portrays a young adult son, Angelo, coming out to his parents, in the process outing his lover, who works as a policeman. Baldo describes how the "coming out movie genre" faces the pressure of depicting coming out as a positive process, which "... is in itself a burden that limits gay characterization" (p. 171).

Families Often Educate Professionals about Sexual Orientation and Gender Identity

Several authors describe how family members, rather than finding supportive and informed professionals, instead had to educate these professionals about GLBTQ issues. As a mother stated in Cappellato and Mangarella's study: "Social services and the health services have to adapt... to get up to speed and train their workers" (p. 223).

Platero interviewed parents in Spain who had gender-nonconforming children aged 4 to 19 years old. A major theme was the lack of information among public service organizations and professionals, so that parents had to educate their children's teachers, social workers, and health care workers. Parents had to search the Internet and often travel a considerable distance to find a professional who was knowledgeable about transgender issues. Sarah, the mother of a transgender child in Johnson and Benson's case study, referred to the mental health services as "crappy" (p. 134) and professionals as poorly educated about transgender issues. Some of the parents in Bertone and Franchi's study not only obtained professional help but told the Catholic priests to get more informed about sexuality issues.

Yet when families need to take the lead in educating professionals about sexuality and gender identity issues, they often feel a sense of agency and pride in their support of their child, according to Platero. Johnson and Benson similarly describe how Sarah and her child, Lee, feel like pioneers.

Legal Status May Not Parallel Social Change

No country had legalized same-sex marriage at the national level until the twenty-first century when same-sex marriage began in the Netherlands in 2001. As of this writing, Argentina, Belgium, Brazil, Canada, Denmark, France, Iceland, the Netherlands, New Zealand, Norway, Portugal, South Africa, Spain, Sweden, the United Kingdom, and Uruguay have same-sex marriage. A number of other countries have same-sex legislation at the national level that is legally equivalent to marriage but is called something else, such as civil pacts or registered domestic partnerships. These include Andorra, Austria, Colombia, Czech Republic, Ecuador, Finland, Germany, Greenland, Hungary, Ireland, Isle of Man, Jersey, Lichtenstein, Luxembourg, Slovenia, and Switzerland.

Yet legal status of same-sex marriage or other nondiscrimination legislation may be different from social acceptance. Despite the fact that Spain was one of the first nations to legalize same-sex marriage, Platero describes how transgender rights and even basic information about transgender issues lag far behind. Conversely, even though Italy is strongly influenced by the Catholic Church and has no anti-homophobia legislation, Malici's television audience research indicates that the Italian public has "come to terms" with queer TV moments.

Need for Continuing Research

In sum, families of GLBTQ individuals as well as families in general are becoming more open to discussions of sexuality and gender identity. They are often ahead of media executives, health and mental health professionals, schoolteachers, and policymakers when it comes to knowledge about GLBTQ issues, particularly on gender nonconformity and transgender activism.

This collection has significantly added to the scholarship on GLBTQ families of origin. It is striking how heavily the focus is on parents in the preceding articles; parents are obviously the most important figures in the family constellation for most people. It would be interesting to have a follow-up issue in a few years that "extends out" to other relatives, including siblings, grandparents, aunts, and uncles.

In the film *Mambo italiano*, Angelo was close to his aunt, who modeled a nontraditional path for him when he was young (the film seems to imply that she died soon after she was pressured into marriage). In what ways does the "maiden aunt" or "bachelor uncle" serve as a mentor for young GLBTQ individuals, modeling alternative lifestyles without marriage or children?

Research by Patterson, Hurt, and Mason (1998) about grandparents' contact with children of lesbians in the United States demonstrates that children had regular contact with the parents of both the biological and nonbiological mother, contrary to stereotypes that these children would be isolated from the extended family of origin. Furthermore, children with more contact with grandparents had fewer behavioral problems.

Brothers and sisters are demographically very similar, but take many of these similarities for granted. They usually have the same race and ethnicity, and are often similar in age. Being raised in the same family, they shared the same religion in childhood, and grew up in a particular socioeconomic class. They went to the same schools, and may even have shared a bedroom. Such shared environments should result in high sibling similarity. Yet some researchers have questioned the influence of shared environments of siblings, demonstrating that each sibling may experience the family environment quite differently. Developmental psychologists such as Feinberg and Hetherington (2001) argue that parenting should be viewed as a within-family variable, given that parents treat children differently on such variables as warmth and negativity. Research in child development (e.g., Whiteman & Christiansen, 2008) and clinical settings (e.g., Schachter, 1985) indicates that siblings de-identify with one another so as to emphasize their own uniqueness. Indeed, research has suggested that siblings are actually quite different from one another (Dunn & Plomin, 1992).

When I began my research comparing U.S. lesbian, bisexual, and heterosexual sisters (Rothblum & Factor, 2001), I had assumed that lesbians and bisexual women would come from liberal families so that the sisters too would be nontraditional. I was wrong. Heterosexual sisters of lesbians were married with children, still practicing the same religion as their parents, lived closer to their parents, and had moved to their current location for their husband's job or children's education. Lesbians, in contrast, had attended a college that was farther from home, were more highly educated, less religious, more politically liberal, less likely to have children, and perceived less support from and had less contact with their families of origin. Bisexual women, like lesbians, were more highly educated, less likely to have ever been married, less likely to have children, and less religious than the heterosexual women. Gay men too had less contact with and perceived less support from families of origin than did heterosexual men (Rothblum et al., 2004). Gay men were less religious, less likely to have children, and had often moved to large urban areas. Gay men who became fathers reported more social support from friends than from family of origin (Crosbie-Burnett & Helmbrecht, 1993). In contrast, bisexual men were more like heterosexual men—they tended to be married, have children, live in smaller towns or rural areas, and have lower levels of education than gay men (Rothblum et al., 2004).

Later research comparing transgender and non-transgender siblings in the United States (Factor & Rothblum, 2008a,b) found that transmen, transwomen, and those who identified as genderqueer were more highly educated, less religious, less likely to be married or have children, and less likely to perceive social support from their families than non-transgender brothers and sisters. In addition, transmen lived farther from their parents than non-transgender siblings, and transwomen were less likely to be out about their gender identity to their parents than transmen or genderqueers.

As the articles in this journal demonstrate, greater awareness of GLBTQ issues has allowed increasingly complex research into families of origin. Bertone and Franchi state that "parents' strategies show us the possibilities of combining contradictory elements of different cultural repertoires, while helping us to identity the common frames underlying seemingly divergent understandings" (p. 60). As families become more comfortable with the spectrum of sexuality and gender identity, it is becoming easier to conduct research on GLBTQ issues. In that regard, the twenty-first century is a promising time to learn more about GLBTQ families of origin.

REFERENCES

Baldo, M. (2014). Familiarising the gay, queering the family. Coming out and resilience in *Mambo italiano*. *Journal of GLBT Family Studies*, *10*(1–2), 168–187.

Bertone, C., & Franchi, M. (2014). Suffering as the path to acceptance: Parents of gay and lesbian young people dealing with Catholicism in Italy. *Journal of GLBT Family Studies*, *10*(1–2), 58–78.

Cappellato, V., & Mangarella, T. (2014). Sexual citizenship in private and public space: Parents of gay men and lesbians discuss their experiences of Pride parades. *Journal of GLBT Family Studies*, *10*(1–2), 211–230.

Crosbie-Burnett, M., & Helmbrecht, L. (1993). A descriptive empirical study of gay male stepfamilies. *Family Relations*, *42*(3), 256–262.

D'Augelli, A. R., & Patterson, C. J. (2001). *Lesbian, gay, and bisexual identities and youth: Psychological perspectives*. New York, NY: Oxford University Press.

Dunn, J., & Plomin, R. (1992). *Separate lives: Why siblings are so different*. New York, NY: Basic Books.

Factor, R. J., & Rothblum, E. D. (2008a). A study of transgender adults and their non-transgender siblings on demographic characteristics, social support, and experiences of violence. *Journal of LGBT Health Research*, *3*(3), 11–30. doi: 10.1080/15574090802092879

Factor, R. J. & Rothblum, E. D. (2008b). Exploring gender identity and community among three groups of transgender individuals in the United States: MTFs, FTMs, and genderqueers. *Health Sociology Review*, *17*, 241–259. doi: 10.5172/hesr.451.17.3.235

Feinberg, M., & Hetherington, E. M. (2001). Differential parenting as a within-family variable. *Journal of Family Psychology*, *15*, 22–37. doi: 10.1037/0893-3200.15.1.22

Glass, V. Q. (2014). "We are with family": Black lesbian couples negotiate rituals with extended families. *Journal of GLBT Family Studies*, *10*(1–2), 79–100.

Grafsky, E. (2014). Becoming the parent of a GLB son or daughter. *Journal of GLBT Family Studies*, *10*(1–2), 36–57.

Johnson, S. L., & Benson, K. E. (2014). "It's always the mother's fault": Secondary stigma of mothering a transgender child. *Journal of GLBT Family Studies*, *10*(1–2), 124–144.

Kurdek, L. A., & Schmidt, J. P. (1987). Perceived emotional support from family and friends in members of homosexual, married, and heterosexual cohabiting couples. *Journal of Homosexuality*, *14*(3–4), 57–68. doi: 10.1300/J082v14n03_04

Lukes, C. A., & Land, H. (1990). Biculturality and homosexuality. *Social Work*, *35*, 155–161. doi: 10.1093/sw/35.2.155

Malici, L. (2014). Queer TV moments and family viewing in Italy. *Journal of GLBT Family Studies*, *10*(1–2), 188–210.

Patterson, C. J., Hurt, S., & Mason, C. D. (1998). Families of the lesbian baby boom: Children's contact with grandparents and other adults. *American Journal of Orthopsychiatry, 68*(3), 390–399. doi: 10.1037/h0080348

Platero, R. L. (2014). The influence of psychiatric and legal discourses on parents of gender-non-conforming children and trans youths in Spain. *Journal of GLBT Family Studies, 10*(1–2), 145–167.

Rothblum, E. D., Balsam, K. F., & Mickey, R. M. (2004). Brothers and sisters of lesbians, gay men, and bisexuals as a demographic comparison group: An innovative research methodology to examine social change. *Journal of Applied Behavioral Science, 40*, 283–301. doi: 10.1177/0021886304266877200420

Rothblum, E. D., & Factor, R. J. (2001). Lesbians and their sisters as a control group: Demographic and mental health factors. *Psychological Science, 12*, 63–69. doi: 10.1111/1467-9280.00311

Schachter, F. F. (1985). Sibling deidentification in the clinic: Devil versus angel. *Family Process, 24*, 415–427. doi: 10.1111/j.1545-5300.1985.00415.x

Švab, A., & Kuhar, R. (2014). The transparent and family closets: Gay men and lesbians and their families of origin. *Journal of GLBT Family Studies, 10*(1–2), 15–35.

Watson, J. B. (2014). Bisexuality and family: Narratives of silence, solace, and strength. *Journal of GLBT Family Studies, 10*(1–2), 101–123.

Weston, K. (1997). *Families we choose*. New York, NY: Columbia University Press.

Whiteman, S. D., & Christiansen, A. (2008). Processes of sibling influence in adolescence: Individual and family correlates. *Family Relations, 57*, 24–34. doi: 10.1111/j.1741-3729.2007.00480.x

Index

Aaron, M. 189
acceptance 3; gender-nonconforming children 157-9; and love 67-70; narratives 29-31; parental 72-4; trans youths 157-9; unconditional 30
age: parents 50-1
Ahmed, S. 195
Ancis, J.R.: and Phillips, M.J. 39
anthropology 5
Arthurs, J. 189
Asia: East 108-9
Association of Families of Transgender Minors 150
Association for Lesbian, Gay, Bisexual and Transgender Issues in Counseling (ALGBTIC) 140
Association of Mothers and Fathers of Gays and Lesbians (AMPGIL) 150
Associazione Genitori di Omosessuali (AGEDO) 9, 10, 66-7, 69, 190, 236; pride parades and parents 214, 215, 218-19, 222-6, 227, 228
Australia 3; bisexuality 7-8, 101-23, 234, 235

Bakhtin, M. 221, 228
Baldo, M. 9, 168-87, 233, 235
Banfi, L. 198
Basque Country: transgenderism 150
Bauer, R. 119
BBC (British Broadcasting Corporation) 202
Becker, R. 193, 195
Bell, D.: and Valentine, G. 216
bella figura 180-1, 182, 184
belonging: religious 70-2
Ben-Ari, A. 39
Benedict XVI, Pope 75
Benson, K.E.: and Johnson, S.L. 8, 124-44, 233-4, 236, 237
Berlusconi, S. 193-4

Bertone, C.: and Franchi, M. 4, 7, 58-78, 213, 233, 235, 237
bisexuality 66, 73, 239; Australia 7-8, 101-23, 234, 235; becoming concept 105, 106, 109, 112, 116, 120; Catholicism 114; conservative upbringing 112; cultural hybridity 107-12; dualism navigation 106-7; East Asia 108-9; elephant in room syndrome 114-16; and family 101-23; and gender 109-10; and geographic distance 107, 108; heteronormativity 107-8, 112, 114, 117; homonormativity 107-8, 117; negative elimination 116-18; nomadism 105, 106-7, 110; parents 112-13; positive accentuation 118-19; secret lives 112-14; Sri Lanka 110; strength and resilience 116; study participants *103-4*; swinging 119
black feminist theory 83-4
black lesbian identity 7, 79-100, 234-5; community rituals 81-2, 87-8, 94-5, 96, 98, 99; daily family rituals 90-2; extended family rituals 88-90, 97, 98; family of origin rituals 88-90; study participants 84-6; wedding rituals 82-3, 92-4, 96-7
black pride festivals 94-5
blame 25
Boscia-Mule, P. 181-2, 183
Bourdieu, P. 109
Bragg, S.: and Buckingham, D. 202
Broad, K.L. 228; Crawley, S.L. and Foley, L. 64; et al. 139
broadcasts: late night 201, 202
Brokeback Mountain (2005) 204
Bronski, M. 171
Buckingham, D.: and Bragg, S. 202
Butler, J. 195

Canadian families *see* Italian-Canadian families

INDEX

Cappellato, V.: and Mangarella, T. 9, 211–30, 236, 237
Cappello, M. 179, 181
Carilli, T. 173, 179
Carosone, M. 175
Catholicism 7, 235; bisexuality 114; confession 178; love and acceptance 67–70; pride parades and parents 220–1, 225; religious belonging and Christian love 70–2; and sexuality 64–6, *see also* Italian Catholicism
censorship 201
Chambers, S.A. 203
Charmaz, K. 42
childhood: protective 26
children: transgender 131–2, *see also* gender-nonconforming children
Christmas 91
Chrysallis 150
cities: migration 216
citizenship rights: sexual 211–30
cognitive dissonance 60–1
Cohen, E.F. 213
Colucci, P.: and Johnson, T.W. 50
comic coming-out genre 169–72
coming out: age 20; comic genre 169–72; family system change 233–4; fear 21; narrative 19–20; pivotal nature 232–3
Communication Privacy Management (CPM) 3–4
community rituals 81–2, 87–8, 94–5, 96, 98, 99
Connell, R.W. 111, 152
Connolly, C.M. 5
constructivist grounded theory 40, 42, 47, 52
coping strategies 31–2
Costello, C.Y. 8
countertransitions 3
Crawley, S.L.: Broad, K.L. and Foley, L. 64
Cultivation Theory 8
cultural hybridity 107–12
cultural toolkits 58, 62, 68, 189
Curraggia (Ciatu et al.) 173

daily family rituals: black lesbian identity 90–2
Darby-Mullins, P.: and Murdock, T.B. 51
D'Augelli, A.R.: et al. 37, 49
Davis, G.: and Needham, G. 189
decolonization 10
DeGeneres, E. 169, 170
Deleuze, G.: and Guattari, F. 105, 106, 109, 115–16, 117
denial strategy 156–7
Di Maria, T. 180

Diagnostic and Statistical Manual of Mental Disorders 147, 149–50
disclosure: event and parents 45–6, 49; sexual minority youth (SMY) 36–57
disease: *International Classification* 147, 149–50
Doty, A. 195
Dowsett, G.W. 106
dualism 106–7
Dyer, R. 171

East Asia: bisexuality 108–9
education levels 239
Eeden-Moorefield, B. van: Proulx, C.M.; and Pasley, K. 127
Ehrensaft, D. 140
elephant in room syndrome 114–16
Ellen 196
Ellis, J. 189, 196
emigration 216
Enguix, B. 217
Europe: Southern 2
European Union (EU) 17
evangelical groups: and gay identity 60–1
extended family rituals: black lesbian identity 88–90, 97, 98

Falicov, C.J. 177, 179
Families and Friends of Lesbians and Gays (PFLAG) 10, 50, 63
Families We Choose (Weston) 232
familization of rights 213, 217, 226
family: acceptance 3; and bisexuality 101–23
Family Adaptability and Cohesion Evaluation Scale 52
family closet 18, 19–20, 27–9, 60, 105, 107, 109, 111–14, 120; gatekeeping 28–9; keeping information to oneself 28
family dynamics: and parents 45
family of friends 232
family resilience: and *Mambo italiano* (2003) 175–83
family rituals: black lesbians 7
family silences 4
Father of the Brides, The (2006) 196–8
fathers 22–4, 25, 38
fear 21–2
Feinberg, M.E.: and Hetherington, E.M. 239
Fields, J. 31, 39, 50, 228
Focus on the Family 132
Foley, L.: Broad, K.L. and Crawley, S.L. 64
Fortier, A.M. 179–80
Foucault, M. 191
Franchi, M.: and Bertone, C. 58–78, 233, 235, 237
Freeman, E. 195

INDEX

friends: family of 232
fundamentalism: religious 10
Fuori (Tamburri) 173, 174, 175

Galluccio, S. 168, 169, 170
Gambone, P. 175, 180
Garelli, F. 65
Gaudreault, E. 168-87
gay identity: and evangelical groups 60-1
gay men 15-35
gender: and bisexuality 109-10
gender identity: transgender children and mothering 131-2
Gender Identity Disorder Units: Spain 150-1, 152, 162, 163
Gender Spectrum 141
gender-nonconforming children 145-67, 236; acceptance 157-9; denial strategy 156-7; Gender Identity Disorder Units (Spain) 150-1, 152, 162, 163; Internet 156; Law 41/2002 150; parent-professional relationship 153-9; professionals 159-62; psychiatrists 161; psychologists 154-6; Roma community 158-9; Spain 152-67; Spanish transgender rights 147-50; teachers 159-61; and trans youths 145-67
geographic distance: and bisexuality 107, 108
Giordano, J.: McGoldrick, M. and Guarino Klages, J. 178
Glass, V.Q. 4, 7, 79-100, 234, 235
Gonzalez, K.A.: et al. 39, 126-7, 139
Goodrich, K.M. 39
Grafsky, E.L. 7, 36-57, 233
grandparents: and lesbians' children 238
grieving process 64
Guarino Klages, J.: Giordano, J. and McGoldrick, M. 178
Guattari, F.: and Deleuze, G. 105, 106, 109, 115-16, 117

Halberstam, J. 195
health: mental 3, 8
hegemonic masculinity 111, 152
Hemmings, C. 116
heteronormativity 107-8, 112, 114, 117, 189, 190, 194
Hetherington, E.M.: and Feinberg, M.E. 239
Hey Paesan (Capone et al.) 173, 175, 180
HIV/AIDS 24
homonormativity 107-8, 108, 117
homophobic space 191
Horne, S.G.: et al. 6
Hurt, S.: Patterson, C.J. and Mason, C.D. 238
hybridity: cultural 107-12

identity: formation and developmental models 17-18; gay 60-1; gender, transgender children and mothering 131-2; trans 8, *see also* black lesbian identity
identity card 149
Illouz, E. 63, 68
Institutional Review Board (IRB) 39
intentionality 177
International Classification of Disease 147, 149-50
Internet 156; and peer support 136-7, 138
Ireland 3
Italian Catholicism 58-78; individualized 72; love and acceptance 67-70; parental acceptance conditions 72-4; public role criticism 70-1; religious attendance 67; religious belonging and Christian love redefinition 70-2; religious pluralism 72; and secularization 65; sexuality and Catholicism 64-6
Italian family: and Italian television 192-5
Italian Parents Movement (MOIGE) 190
Italian Revolutionary Homosexual United Front 218
Italian television 188-210, 236-7; audience research and queer TV moments 195-6; Broadcasting Act (1975) 193; *Brokeback Mountain* (2005) 204; censorship 201; *Father of the Brides* (2006) 196-8; gay-themed content growth 192-4; heteronormativity 189, 190, 194; homophobic space 191; and Italian family context 192-5; *The L Word* 202; late night broadcasts 201, 202; and minors 202-3; *Nina's Travels* (2006) 199-200; *Queer as Folk* (1999) 204-5; same-sex kissing 203; southern Italian stereotypes 198; third person perspective 191, 201-6; transformative moments 196-200; transformative queer TV moments 196-200; US programming 193, 194, 196, 201-6
Italian-Canadian families: *bella figura* 180-1, 182, 184; family resilience 175-83; and *Mambo italiano* (2003) 172-5
Italy 2, 7; National Pride Parade 218; parents and pride parades 211-30

Jenkins, H. 202
Johnson, S.L.: and Benson, K.E. 8, 124-44, 233-4, 236, 237
Johnson, T.W.: and Colucci, P. 50
Journal of GLBT Family Studies 1

kissing: same-sex 203
Kübler-Ross, E. 64

INDEX

Kuhar, R.: and Svab, A. 4, 7, 15-35, 232, 233, 234
Kurdek, L.A.: and Schmidt, J.P. 232

L Word, The 202
Land, H.: and Lukes, C.A. 232
Lannutti, P.J. 3
LaSala, M. 176, 183
late night broadcasts 201, 202
Leeder, M. 169, 171
legal status: and social change 237-8
lesbians: children and grandparents 238, *see also* black lesbian identity
liberal families 239
Lombardi, C. 175
love: and acceptance 67-70; Christian 70-2
Lukes, C.A.: and Land, H. 232

McGoldrick, M.: Giordano, J. and Guarino Klages, J. 178
McKee, A. 203
McQueeney, K. 62, 69
Madrid Service for Homosexuals and Transgender People 157
Malici, L. 9, 188-210, 236, 238
Mambo italiano (2003) 9, 168-87, 233, 234, 235, 237, 238; and comic coming-out genre 169-72; and family resilience 175-83; and Italian-Canadian coming-out 172-5
Mangarella, T.: and Cappellato, V. 9, 211-30, 236, 237
Markowe, A.L. 16
marriage: same-sex 3-4
Martin, K.A.: et al. 64, 189
Mary Magdalene 72-3
Masciadrelli, B.P.: and Oswald, R.F. 98
masculinity 23; hegemonic 111, 152
Mason, C.D.: Patterson, C.J. and Hurt, S. 238
Mayock, P.: et al. 2, 3
media: consumption 9-10; pride parades and parents 219-20
men: gay 15-35
mental health 3, 8
migration 216
minors: and Italian television 202-3
Moon, D. 63, 72
moralizing strategy 62, 69
mothering *see* transgender children and mothering
mothers 22, 23, 24, 26, 28-9, 31, 38
Murdock, T.B.: and Darby-Mullins, P. 51
My Big Fat Greek Wedding (2002) 170-1

narratives: acceptance 29-31; coming out 19-20; of pain 63; rejection 31-2
Navarra: transgenderism 150

Needham, G.: and Davis, G. 189
Nina's Travels (2006) 199-200
nomadism 105, 106-7, 110
norm subversion: and transgression 221-2, 225, 228
normalization 64, 220, 222, 224, 228
Norwood, K. 8

online surveys 10
Oprah 169, 171
organizations 10
Oswald, R.F. 82, 177, 179, 182; and Masciadrelli, B.P. 98; and Suter, E.A. 82, 96

pain 72; narratives 63
Pallotta-Chiarolli, M. 3, 106
parent-child closeness 41, 45, 49
parent-professional relationship 153-9
parents 7, 8, 9, 10, 16, 18; acceptance narratives 29-31; age 50-1; bisexuality 112-13; blame 25; and disclosure event 45-6, 49; emotional context and initial reaction 46-7; Families and Friends of Lesbians and Gays (PFLAG) 10, 50, 63; family dynamics 45; fear 21-2; first reactions 24-7; Italian Catholicism 58-78; love and acceptance 67-70; rejection narratives 31-2; religious belonging and Christian love redefinition 70-2; sexual minority youth and disclosure-to-family process 36-57; sexual minority youth and parent perspective 38-57; Slovenia 22-7; Spanish gender-nonconforming children 152-67; study demographics 43-4; study findings 42-57, *see also* family closet; pride parades and parents
Pasley, K.: Proulx, C.M. and van Eeden-Moorefield, B. 127
Patterson, C.J.: Hurt, S. and Mason, C.D. 238
perversion: domino effect 119
Petronio, S. 3
Phillips, M.J.: and Ancis, J.R. 39
Pichardo Galán, J.I. 58
Platero, R.L. 8, 145-67, 234, 236, 238
Plummer, K. 15
pluralism: religious 72
polyamorous families 5
Poulos, C.N. 4
pride parades and parents 211-30; AGEDO role 222-6, 227, 228; Catholic Church 220-1, 225; Italian origins 218; media images and discourses 219-20; normalizing tactics 220, 222, 224, 228; perspectives 218-22; television coverage 219; transgression and norm subversion

INDEX

221-2, 225, 228; visibility 213-14, 220-1, 224; voluntary sector 218-19
private and public space 211-30
professional help: transgender children and mothering 127, 134-6, 139-41
professionals: gender-nonconforming children 159-62
protective childhood 26
Proulx, C.M.: Pasley, K. and van Eeden-Moorefield, B. 127
psychiatrists 161
psychologists 154-6
psychology 5, 154-6
public space 211-30

Queer as Folk (1999) 203
queer theory 127
queer TV moments: audience research 195-6; *Brokeback Mountain* (2005) 204; censorship 201; and Italian television 188-210, 236; *The L Word* 202; late night broadcasts 201; *Queer as Folk* 204-5; third person perspective 201-6; transformative nature 196-200

RAI 203
Ream, G.L.: and Savin-Williams, R.C. 37
redefinition 177
rejection narratives 31-2
relational coming out process 18, 19, 27, 33
religion: gay and lesbian identity negotiation 60-2; narratives of pain 63; and sexuality 60-4; stigma management 61-2, 71, *see also* Italian Catholicism
religious belonging: and Christian love 70-2
religious fundamentalism 10
religious pluralism 72
resilience: family 175-83
rights: familization 213, 217, 226; sexual citizenship 211-30, *see also* Spanish transgender rights
rituals 177-9, 184; and black lesbian identity 79-100; community 81-2, 87-8, 94-5, 96, 98, 99; daily family 90-2; extended family 88-90, 97; family of origin 88-90; wedding 82-3, 92-4, 96-7
Roma community 234; gender-nonconforming children 158-9
Romano, R. 175
Rosario, M.: et al. 37
Rothblum, E.D. 6, 231-41
Rust, P.C.R. 102
Ryan, C.: et al. 38

Saltzburg, S. 39
same-sex kissing: television 203

same-sex marriage (SSM) 3-4
San Francisco 4
Savin-Williams, R.C. 176; and Ream, G.L. 37
Scherrer, K.S. 16
Schmidt, J.P.: and Kurdek, L.A. 232
secondary stigmatization 124-44
secret lives 112-14
secret-keeping 4
secularization 65
Sedgwick, E.K. 19, 31, 195
self-esteem 38
sexual citizenship rights: private and public space 211-30
sexual minority youth (SMY): disclosure benefits 38-9, 51; disclosure-to-family process 36-57; parent perspective 38-57
sexuality: and Catholicism 64-6
silence: family 4; navigating 112-16; transparent closet 27
Sinfield, A. 195
Slovenia 7, 15-35, 232; coming out age 20; fear 21-2; first parental reactions 24-7; focus groups 20; parents 22-7; political and social context 17; protective childhood 26; survey 20
Smith, B. 83
social change: and legal status 237-8
Social Cognitive Theory 9
sociology 5
Southern Europe 2
space: private and public 211-30
Spain: Basque Country 150; Gender Identity Disorder Units 150-1, 152, 162, 163; gender-nonconforming children 152-67; Madrid Service for Homosexuals and Transgender People 157; trans youths and gender-nonconforming children 145-67
Spanish transgender rights 147-50; Constitutional Act 3/2007 149-50; Gender Identity Law (2007) 149; identity card 149; Penal Code 148
Sri Lanka 110, 235; bisexuality 110
stereotypes: southern Italian 198
stigma management 61-2, 71
stigmatization: secondary 124-44
straight panic concept 195
suicide 38
Sullivan, N. 195
Suter, E.A.: et al. 81-2; and Oswald, R.F. 82, 96
Svab, A.: and Kuhar, R. 4, 7, 15-35, 232, 233, 234
Swidler, A. 58, 62, 68, 69
symbolic interaction theory 50, 53
symbolic interactionism 83

Tamburri, A.J. 173, 174
teachers 159-61

INDEX

television *see* Italian television; queer TV moments
therapy: transgender children and mothering 127, 134-6, 139-41
Thumma, S. 60
trans identities 8
trans youths: acceptance 157-9; denial strategy 156-7; Family Allies 141; Gender Identity Disorder Units 150-1, 152; and gender-nonconforming children 145-67; Internet 156; Law 41/2002 150; parent-professional relationship 153-9; professionals 159-62; psychiatrists 161; psychologists 154-6; Roma community 158-9; Spain 145-67; Spanish transgender rights 147-50; teachers 159-61
transgender children and mothering: and adversity 132-4; case description 131; education and advocacy 137; father role 134; gender identity 131-2, 139; Internet and peer support 136-7, 138; literature review 125-8; professional help 127, 134-6, 139-41; rejection 126; secondary stigmatization 124-44; self-esteem 126; therapy 127, 134-6, 139-41
transgender issues 146-7
Transgender Network 141
transgender rights *see* Spanish transgender rights
transgenderism 150
transgression: and norm subversion 221-2, 225, 228
transparent closet 18, 19, 27-9; silence 27
transparent families of origin: and family closets 15-35
TransYouth Family Allies 141

unconditional acceptance 30
United Kingdom (UK) 5
United Methodist Church 62-3
United States of America (USA) 4, 5
upbringing: conservative 112

Valentine, G.: and Bell, D. 216
Viere, G.M. 81
visibility 216
voluntary sector 218-19

Walsh, F. 182
Warner, M. 189
Watson, J.B. 7-8, 101-23, 234, 235
wedding rituals: black lesbian identity 82-3, 92-4, 96-7
Weston, K. 4-5, 7, 97
Wilde, O. 195
Will & Grace 196, 205
World Pride Parade 218
World Professional Association for Transgender Health (WPATH) 150

Yip, A.K.T. 61, 62, 71
youth *see* sexual minority youth (SMY); trans youths